DD Sherman Tank Warriors

DD Sherman Tank Warriors

The 13th/18th Royal Hussars through Dunkirk,
D-Day and the Liberation of Europe

Andrew May

Pen & Sword
MILITARY

First published in Great Britain in 2024 and reprinted in 2025 by
Pen & Sword Military
An imprint of Pen & Sword Books Limited
Yorkshire – Philadelphia

Copyright © Andrew May 2024, 2025

ISBN 978 1 03610 458 0

The right of Andrew May to be identified as
Author of this Work has been asserted by him in accordance
with the Copyright, Designs and Patents Act 1988.

A CIP catalogue record for this book is available from the British Library

All rights reserved. No part of this book may be reproduced, transmitted, downloaded, decompiled or reverse engineered in any form or by any means, electronic or mechanical including photocopying, recording or by any information storage and retrieval system, without permission from the Publisher in writing. NO AI TRAINING: Without in any way limiting the Author's and Publisher's exclusive rights under copyright, any use of this publication to "train" generative artificial intelligence (AI) technologies to generate text is expressly prohibited. The Author and Publisher reserve all rights to license uses of this work for generative AI training and development of machine learning language models.

Typeset by Mac Style
Printed in the UK by CPI Group (UK) Ltd, Croydon, CR0 4YY.

The Publisher's authorised representative in the EU for product safety is Authorised Rep Compliance Ltd., Ground Floor, 71 Lower Baggot Street, Dublin D02 P593, Ireland | www.arccompliance.com

For a complete list of Pen & Sword titles please contact
PEN & SWORD BOOKS LIMITED
47 Church Street, Barnsley, South Yorkshire, S70 2AS, England
E-mail: enquiries@pen-and-sword.co.uk
Website: www.pen-and-sword.co.uk
or
PEN AND SWORD BOOKS
1950 Lawrence Rd, Havertown, PA 19083, USA
E-mail: uspen-and-sword@casematepublishers.com
Website: www.penandswordbooks.com

This book is dedicated to William Henry Hollands, his sister Barbara Mortley (née Hollands) and to all the brave men who fought with the 13th/18th Royal Hussars (QMO) during the Second World War.

> Cannon to right of them,
> Cannon to left of them,
> Cannon in front of them
> Volley'd and thunder'd;
> Storm'd at with shot and shell,
> Boldly they rode and well,
> Into the jaws of Death,
> Into the mouth of Hell
> Rode the six hundred.
> From 'The Charge of the Light Brigade',
> by Alfred, Lord Tennyson

Contents

Foreword ix
Preface x
The Light Dragoons Charitable Trust, Colonel's Appeal Fund xiii

Chapter 1	Mechanisation, the British Expeditionary Force and Dunkirk	1
Chapter 2	Back on the Home Front	7
Chapter 3	An Entirely Novel Manner	18
Chapter 4	Prelude to Invasion	33
Chapter 5	Preparations for the Assault	39
Chapter 6	Operation Overlord	48
Chapter 7	Battle for Normandy	66
Chapter 8	The Breakout from Normandy and Operation Market Garden	110
Chapter 9	Into the Fatherland	128
Chapter 10	Advance to Bremen	162
Chapter 11	British Army on the Rhine	180

The Last Post 189
We'll Meet Again 190
Fury 201
Notes 206
Acknowledgements 209
Bibliography 211
Index 213

Foreword

As an experienced TV and military historian, it gives me great pleasure to write the foreword for this book written by Andrew May. My regular TV programmes, *Combat Dealers*, and podcasts, *Amazing War Stories*, are always extensively researched but in the case of this publication, I am staggered by the amount of exceptional detail captured by Andrew, depicting some of the most ferocious fighting endured by the soldiers during WWII.

This detailed study of the 13th/18th Royal Hussars is precisely recounted in Andrew's book and explains the sacrifices made by the brave men who fought in this unit.

Unfortunately, many of these men are no longer with us, though Andrew's publication gives those fine men a voice so we can remember both them and their heroic actions.

Like Andrew, for many years, I have been meeting and interviewing veterans from WWII and here Andrew pays tribute to them, helping to keep their memories alive for future generations. This book is truly an exceptional exercise in the recording and the telling of those events, and of the brave men who fought and so gave us the freedom that we all enjoy today. I can personally guarantee that this is a must-read for any serious military enthusiast.

Bruce Crompton

Preface

I must begin by confessing that neither am I a professional military historian nor have I attempted to write a book before. What follows will be my best attempt to pay tribute to the brave men of the 13th/18th Royal Hussars (QMO) who served during the Second World War, and their families. My intention is not to offer a comprehensive historical record of all that the regiment did in the war, but to describe what I hope will be representative actions and personal stories, to provide an insight into their collective accomplishments and experiences. I have drawn inspiration from several publications and diaries covering this period of the regiment's history and some of those titles can be found at the end of this book. Although details of a particular event or operation may vary between sources, every attempt has been made to try to provide an accurate portrayal of the actions in which the regiment played a part. However, it should be noted that some of my information has come from veterans, many decades after these events took place, and armed with this knowledge, I hope that the reader will allow me a little latitude. What is clear, though, is that all of these soldiers sacrificed some of the best years of their young lives to defend freedom, many sacrificed their health, and sadly, too many sacrificed their lives.

The catalyst that initiated my interest in the regiment was my wife Fiona's Uncle Henry – Trooper William Henry Hollands. I was told how my mother-in-law, Barbara, had lost her dear elder brother when she was still in her teens. It transpired that no one in the family had ever had the means to travel over to Normandy to visit his final resting place, so we decided to put that right in 1996, when my wife and I took the ferry over to Ouistreham with her parents, Barbara and Don. At that stage, we knew little of the regiment's exploits but fifty-two years after the loss of her only sibling, Barbara was finally able to stand at her brother's grave in the peaceful Commonwealth War Graves cemetery at Douvres-la-Délivrande.

That occasion was emotionally charged enough, but as we gave Barbara a few quiet moments alone at the graveside, I wandered amongst the neat ranks of white headstones. I was 26 at the time and I became quite overcome with sadness as I walked along an entire row of Paras killed on 6 June 1944 (D-Day) and not a single one of them had reached my age; all had been killed in their prime. That was quite humbling!

Preface xi

Trooper William Henry Hollands.

Henry had originally held aspirations of joining the RAF and becoming a fighter pilot but his medical examination identified that his eyesight did not meet the required standards. Consequently, he found himself joining the Army and was posted to the Royal Armoured Corps before his final posting to A Squadron, 13th/18th Royal Hussars. He joined his regiment in 1943, when it was stationed at Wickham Market in Suffolk.

After landing with A Squadron on D-Day, when they spearheaded the whole assault onto Sword Beach at Lion-sur-Mer, Henry was to become the only member of his regiment killed on 27 June 1944 – an incident that we shall revisit more fully further into the story. The family had been told, in a letter sent from Henry's tank commander, that he had been outside of his vehicle and was killed by an explosion. That was all the information provided and, as was typical at the time, the official telegram from the War Office announcing his death did not provide any further details.

Several years after that first visit to Normandy, I was again discussing Henry with my mother-in-law and she was clearly troubled that she had never discovered what had transpired on that fateful day. That led me to begin my quest to try to find out what events had led Henry to his death, although back then I could have had no idea of the remarkable journey of discovery I was about to embark upon. A chain of events followed that would bring new friends into my life, both in terms of D-Day veterans and family members of other wartime '3&8s' – an abbreviation and nickname of the 13th/18th.

It has been a genuine privilege to get to know these brave men. They played such an important role in world history, and through this research I have been fortunate to learn about other members of the regiment, most of whom I sadly never had the opportunity to meet in person. Amongst the spouses, sons, daughters, nephews and nieces of the 3&8s that I've met there is a genuine sense of family and all have been unwaveringly friendly and generous with information they have shared with me. Most importantly of all, I would like to acknowledge that the compiling of this book has only been possible with their help and collective blessing, along with that of my wife's family.

The Light Dragoons Charitable Trust, Colonel's Appeal Fund

Please note that 100 per cent of the author's royalties from the sale of this book will be donated to The Light Dragoons Charitable Trust, Colonel's Appeal Fund.

The Light Dragoons Charitable Trust, Colonel's Appeal Fund provides support and benevolence to veterans of all ages who fall on hard times, including many 3&8s.

If you would like to make a donation in memory of those who fought for our liberty and freedom during the Second World War, please send your donation to:

The Light Dragoons Regimental Association Charitable Trust
Sort code: 30–11–75
Account number: 00747329

Chapter 1

Mechanisation, the British Expeditionary Force and Dunkirk

A makeshift cross was placed on the tank and they were left at the scene.

Following the First World War, as the British Army's strength was naturally reduced, it was apparent that the nature of warfare had shifted. With the introduction of armoured vehicles came a new type of land warfare and, in turn, combined arms warfare. It was already clear from the First World War that there would be less of a role for traditional cavalry in any future conflicts. However, rather than disband regiments, it was decided to amalgamate them and convert to tracked vehicles, thus preserving regimental honours and traditions. Through this process the number of line cavalry regiments shrank to half their original number and an amalgamation of the 13th Hussars and the 18th Hussars was to form a new regiment, the 13th/18th Hussars, with Her Majesty Queen Mary as their colonel-in-chief.

The two original regiments, both formed in the eighteenth century, had served with distinction, both at home and abroad, and had fine reputations. For a short period in the 1790s, the Duke of Wellington held a commission in the 18th Light Dragoons. Both regiments fought at Waterloo on 18 June 1815. In Crimea, as part of the Siege of Sevastopol, on 25 October 1854 the 13th Light Dragoons formed the right flank in the first line of cavalry at Balaclava. This remarkable action was of course immortalised in Alfred, Lord Tennyson's poem 'The Charge of the Light Brigade'.

The newly formed 13th/18th Hussars boasted three sabre squadrons and a headquarters squadron, when posted to North-West India in October 1931. Initially, the regiment was posted to Sialkot, but later moved to Risalpur in 1936 (both cities are now part of modern-day Pakistan, following the Partition of India in 1947). While they were abroad, an Army Order was published on 31 December 1935 to approve changing the designation of the 13th/18th Hussars to 13th/18th Royal Hussars (Queen Mary's Own).

In 1938, after their long voyage home from India, the regiment landed at Southampton on 31 October, ready for mechanisation. Centuries of soldiering on horseback were about to end, to be replaced with armoured vehicles. It is said that 'Good grooms make bad chauffeurs'. However, once established at Risborough Barracks, at Shorncliffe in Kent, the troopers took to mechanisation well and training got under way in January 1939. Willingness and enthusiasm were certainly there, but not so much the means to get the job done. The men of the regiment were left having to source tools, parts and equipment for themselves, where these had not been issued by the Army. When the first few Vickers Mk VI light tanks were supplied, they were generally in poor repair and required much attention, but hard work, dedication and regimental pride ensured that they were soon up to the required standard.

Unfortunately, the 3&8s did not have time on their side, because at dawn on 1 September 1939, Germany's forces invaded Poland. The British Government's ultimatum, issued by Prime Minister Neville Chamberlain, expired at 11 am on 3 September and once again, the British Empire found itself at war with Germany.

The conscription of service personnel began, bolstered by soldiers from the reserve Territorial Army and old soldiers recalled to the Colours. Fortunately, the regiment was provided with thirty reservists from the Royal Tank Corps who would act as an invaluable core of experienced drivers and tank gunners.

In ten short months, the 3&8s had been transformed from a mounted regiment operating on the North-West Frontier of India to a fully mechanised cavalry regiment, mobilised for war in Europe, when, on 15 September 1939, it left Shorncliffe bound for Southampton. The 13th/18th Royal Hussars (QMO) were to join the BEF (British Expeditionary Force) in France as a Reconnaissance Regiment of the 1st Armoured Reconnaissance Brigade.[1] The BEF would stand alongside the French Army, in an attempt to halt Hitler's intentions of expanding his empire into Western Europe.

The regiment was still coming to grips with its new role and still deficient in equipment and vehicles. On the last afternoon before sailing from Southampton, additional vehicles were supplied. To the troopers' horror, these consisted of grocery lorries, bakers' vans and the like, still bearing their former owners' names and all in their peacetime bright colours. Without any orders being issued, the men immediately set to work and spent their final night in England repainting the vehicles khaki. This example of 'mend and make do' was typical of the rush to prepare the British Army for service on the Continent at that time.

With their light tanks, scout carriers and an assortment of other vehicles, the regiment embarked at Southampton Docks on 18 September, arriving at Brest in Brittany the following morning, where they would remain for ten days. The next journey was by train to Arras in northern France, during which, thankfully, the BEF's movements through France received no interference from the enemy. In fact, with German forces fully engaged in crushing Poland, the British troops massing on the Western Front were left almost entirely unmolested.

Mechanisation, the British Expeditionary Force and Dunkirk

Vickers Mk VI tanks of the 13th/18th with the BEF in the Vimy Ridge area of northern France. (*Courtesy of Imperial War Museums – Image O 681*)

What was to become known as the 'Phoney War' would then extend to eight months, as both British and French troops awaited the arrival of German forces. This lull in activity did at least afford the 3&8s and the rest of the BEF an opportunity for further preparation and training, which at that stage was badly needed.

This quiet period ended abruptly on 10 May 1940, when the Wehrmacht (German Armed Forces) entered Holland and Belgium. The regiment advanced north-east to meet this oncoming threat, moving through Arras, into Belgium and through Tournai and Brussels. The column would move through Brussels to scenes of jubilation as well-wishing crowds gathered around the vehicles, showering the occupants with flowers. Unfortunately, it would not be long before the German advance forced a tactical withdrawal of the BEF. Through their tactics of blitzkrieg ('lightning war') and exploiting ruthlessly the use of mobile, manoeuvrable forces, the Wehrmacht were able to advance at speed. The devastating impact of modern combined arms tactics had moved from concept to reality in very practical terms. The German use of armour, mobile infantry, artillery, close air support and efficient radio communications enabled a flexible, co-ordinated strategy, which had just been used to devastating effect in Poland. Despite the overwhelming odds, the regiment was at least successful in giving the forward enemy forces a bloody nose as they withdrew.

The chaos the regiment would witness included roads soon to be obstructed with military vehicles, refugees clutching their few possessions, smouldering ammunition trucks shot up by the Luftwaffe (German Air Force), and scenes of general devastation.

It was not long before the regiment would find itself called upon to support what for the Allies was now becoming a fighting withdrawal across Belgium and northern France. On 19 May, before all the 3&8s could retire to the south-west away from Brussels, Lieutenant Wormald of A Squadron was approached by a staff officer of the 1st Infantry Division who told him to report to the general officer commanding, Major General Alexander. The general explained that the right flank of his infantry was exposed and that he required the lieutenant to provide a right flank guard, to enable the infantry to retire from the area. Four troops of A Squadron of the 3&8s moved out to provide protection, as requested; Lieutenant Wormald devised a plan that would enable them to retire through Tournai in three defensive bounds, intended to delay the arrival of German forces. 1st Troop found themselves encircled by German troops near the village of Ogy and were instructed to get themselves out of it by any means they could and retire from that area. Through the presence of mind of their troop sergeant, the tanks burst out of their predicament without loss, but taking orders a little too literally, withdrew all the way back to Tournai. Having retreated to the second bound, 4th Troop spotted the forward elements of the German advance 600 yards up the road and were able to inflict a few casualties upon them. At 1700 hrs, the 17th Field Regiment Royal Artillery commenced firing onto Flobecq, which helped to delay the German advance still further. By 1930 hrs, no situation updates had been reported nor any further orders received, so Lieutenant Wormald then sent the squadron despatch rider, Trooper Cheal, to Brigade Headquarters. He returned to confirm that the building that had housed the HQ was now ablaze, he had seen no other British soldiers, and had been strafed by German aircraft. Lieutenant Wormald discussed the situation with Lieutenant Stancomb, commanding the 3rd (Carrier) Troop, and they agreed that they could assume that the infantry had now vacated the area and they should retire themselves. Therefore, the remaining three troops headed for Tournai, only to discover that someone had been a little premature in assuming that all British troops had already retired through the town. A Royal Engineers officer on the far bank confirmed that the bridges over the river had been blown prior to their arrival, and they were unable to drive their tanks to the other side. Therefore, Lieutenant Wormald gave the order to ditch their tanks and carriers in the river, still enabling the crews to cross the river on foot, via a damaged bridge.

When the whole regiment finally managed to reassemble at La Verderie, they discovered that they had lost a total of sixteen tanks and twenty-four scout carriers; most had been destroyed, then abandoned. Eight junior ranks were missing, with one officer and one trooper wounded.

On 25 May, the regiment suffered its first combat deaths of the war south of Dunkirk, near Forêt de Nieppe, when two tanks were knocked out by enemy fire. Lieutenant Akers-Douglas examined Sergeant James Hubbard's tank, after it had been set alight by an anti-tank gun. It was discovered that all the crew had been killed, but it was impossible to recover the bodies from the burning tank. A makeshift cross was placed on the tank and they were left at the scene.

During this fighting withdrawal, the regiment did participate in a counterattack on 27 May, the objective being the Ypres–Comines Canal. Although the Germans were forced to retire back across the canal, after his tank had been struck by an anti-tank round, Major James Hawker (commanding B Squadron) was badly wounded in the leg and would subsequently die of his injuries. The following day, Belgium capitulated, and since the BEF was becoming hemmed in to a pocket around the coastal town of Dunkirk, the decision was taken that it must evacuate France.[2] Although kept secret until quite recently, 'Ultra' intercepts at Bletchley Park had enabled the British to listen in on the forward forces of the Wehrmacht approaching the British Army at Dunkirk, providing them with a clear appreciation of the situation. This intelligence was delivered directly to the Admiralty and gave them additional time in which to organise the naval assets, assisted by the flotilla of little ships, required to evacuate what was left of the British Army from northern France.

Before the regiment could be evacuated, heavy and accurate shelling around Poperinge was to claim the life of Lance Sergeant Russell Coward, with Major Davies being seriously wounded and taken to a casualty clearing station. Congestion on the road beyond Ghyvelde, East of Dunkirk, made further progress by vehicle impossible, so orders were given for the destruction of the regiment's vehicles to deny them to the enemy. On 30 May, the regiment was then formed up and moved on foot to Bray-Dunes to the east of Dunkirk, where the headquarters of 1st Infantry Division had been established. General Alexander then gave Lieutenant Colonel Stirling, commanding the 13th/18th, the option to embark his regiment directly from the beach, or march the 7 miles to the large stone breakwater in Dunkirk, known as The Mole. The colonel opted for the latter, drier method and the regiment set off in groups of fifty, arriving in Dunkirk at 2100 hrs. They were forced to cover the final 200 yards to The Mole at the double, owing to spasmodic enemy fire. They were fortunate indeed that a cross-channel steamer was about to cast off, when the regiment was packed on board, disembarking in Folkestone at 0900 hrs the following morning. The regiment had spent just one day in the dunes at Dunkirk and had suffered no casualties there!

Chapter 2

Back on the Home Front

Within five minutes my precious tank beret had disappeared.

Under the command of Lieutenant Colonel D.A. Stirling, on 31 May 1940, the regiment disembarked from its overnight dash from northern France at Folkestone. The weary men were immediately moved by train to Gloucestershire and billeted at Wotton-under-Edge. Their colonel-in-chief, Queen Mary, visited and inspected the regiment on 2 June and she was told of the men's experiences in France.

Ten days later, the regiment moved to Bovington, where it would be tasked with coastal defence around Poole Harbour and Corfe. However, having sabotaged and left all their vehicles back in France, they did not represent a particularly potent defence force, armed only with Lee Enfield rifles and a little ammunition. They were issued with Standard Beaverette motor cars, which although had a little armour around front and sides, had no roof!

Following the evacuation of most of the BEF from Dunkirk, Britain now faced the spectre of a full-scale invasion by German forces. The plan for Hitler's forces to invade Britain was known as Operation Sealion, but even if the British Government would not accept Hitler's terms to end the war, he still required tactical superiority over the English Channel and the skies above Britain in order to launch an invasion. However, the valiant efforts of the Royal Air Force and Commonwealth Air Forces during the Battle of Britain from July to October 1940 denied this to Hitler and Operation Sealion was cancelled, with the Germans turning their attentions to the east and Russia.

In November of that year, the regiment moved to the outskirts of Towcester in Northamptonshire; its headquarters and officers' mess were at Cornhill, just outside the village of Bugbrooke. It was during this period that the 1st Armoured Brigade was re-established as the 27th Armoured Brigade, forming part of the new 9th Armoured Division.

The regiment began to receive drafts of young soldiers, fresh from the Royal Armoured Corps training regiments dotted around the country. One such product of the 58th Training Regiment (RAC) at Bovington was a young Bill Mawson, from Croydon.

From April 1941 through to June, the regiment was slowly issued with Covenanter Cruiser Mk V tanks, which proved to be quite unreliable mechanically, were lightly armoured and only carried a 2-pounder gun. Worse still, the commander's turret lid had an unpleasant habit of working loose when driving over rough terrain, giving many tank commanders a forceful blow to the back of the head.

With no idea yet of the important role that awaited the regiment in the years to come, the men of the 3&8s settled down to life in their sleepy corner of Northamptonshire. It was certainly an important period for Corporal James Downie Bell of A Squadron, a professional solider who had served with the regiment in India, the BEF, and had returned from Dunkirk. Corporal Bell, known as Jerry, was originally from Paisley in Renfrewshire and was a keen sportsman, excelling in boxing. He was to win the heart of a local girl from Bugbrooke, Enid Nightingale, and they married on 14 June 1941 at Bugbrooke Church.

Bill Mawson, wearing the first pattern RAC cap badge, worn from 1939 to 1941, before the more familiar 'mailed fist' cap badge was introduced.

A Covenanter Tank of the 13th/18th. (*Courtesy of The Tank Museum, Bovington – Image 11422–001*)

Enid's bridesmaid was her cousin, Freda Bannard. Freda's young brother, Stan Bannard, keen to serve his country and wanting to join the same regiment as Jerry, was ultimately successful in joining the 13th/18th too and would join B Squadron.

In August, Lieutenant Colonel Stirling (bound for the Middle East) handed over command of the regiment to Lieutenant Colonel R.A. Moulton-Barrett. Soon after, in September, the regiment moved temporarily to Thetford in Norfolk for Exercise Bumper. This period served to highlight shortcomings in equipment, communications and control. Having learned these lessons, the regiment returned to its billets at Towcester.

Stan Bannard.

As the regiment trained on the home front, spirits were kept high by various sporting activities and even the occasional theatrical performance. In January 1942, the regiment staged a pantomime, *Trooper Aladdin*, in aid of The Regimental Prisoners of War Fund. The pantomime was produced by Captain

Peter 'Cosy' Comfort.

Peter Lyon, second-in-command of A Squadron, who also performed the role of Trooper Aladdin's mother, Widow Twankey!

March 1942 brought the unwelcome news that the regiment was to be placed on a non-mobilised footing, making it a low priority for stores and equipment. This was followed in May by a wholesale move from Towcester to Chippenham Camp, near Newmarket in Suffolk.

It was at Chippenham Camp that a young Peter Comfort from Deal in Kent, known as 'Cosy' to his friends, was to join his new family in HQ Squadron, then B Squadron. Keen to serve like his elder brother Ron, who was overseas with the Royal Army Service Corps, Peter had attempted to sign up during a recruitment drive in Canterbury but had been rumbled by the recruiting sergeant as being underage. His second attempt was more successful, then aged just 17 years and 10 months and fresh from basic training. He recounted his introduction to the regiment thus:

> I escaped at last from Perham Down, Tidworth, somewhat battered and bewildered. The 54th Training Regiment, Royal Armoured Corps, had that effect. With seven other child soldiers, arrived at Chippenham Park, Suffolk. Lambs to the slaughter amongst old sweats! Within five minutes my precious tank beret had disappeared. That evening I sewed on my Panda – the 9th Armoured Division – and looked at my first 13th/18th Cap Badge and Collar Dogs.

Cosy Comfort was trained as a loader/operator, which was a busy role because not only was he responsible for all aspects of communications within his tank, but he was also required to load the main armament, as well as assist with keeping the tank's machine guns operational. Back at the Royal Armoured Corps (RAC) training establishments dotted around the country, the young troopers were trained in the use of the Phonetic Alphabet (which would have to be relearned with the later involvement of American forces), plus Morse code. Cosy remembered: 'The sudden click of the brain after weeks or was it months? The Morse Code flowed, never to be forgotten. Sergeant Vickery smiled quietly – success after so much patience.'

The Panda shoulder patch of the 9th Armoured Division.

At that time the radio setup required recruits to familiarise themselves on three systems. Firstly, the 'A' Set was used for communication over long distances, encompassing the squadron or regimental nets. Next was the '3' Set, used for receiving and passing messages within a troop of four tanks. Lastly, the 'IC' or Intercom, provided a means of communication between members of an individual tank crew.

Another fresh-faced 17-year-old, straight from his RAC training establishment, was Doug Kay. Doug was born in Richmond, North Yorkshire, in August 1924 and grew up in Darlington. His Service and Pay Book states: 'Trade on Enlistment: Salesman (Boot & Shoe Trade)'. Now far from home, he would be trained as a tank gunner and was posted to C Squadron.

Since the real purpose of a tank is for its main armament to be used to good effect, arguably the gunner has the most important role within a tank crew. However, gunnery training was

John Douglas Kipling Kay (Doug).

conducted on the 2-pounder gun, which although literally useless against the German armour that the regiment would face, was all that was available to train with at this stage of the war. Fire control orders were kept simple. In his book *Young Man in a Tank*, Patrick Hennessey describes these as follows:

> For example, only three types of tree were ever mentioned: Bushy Topped, Fir and Poplar. All trees conform to one of these basic shapes, so there was no need to resort to long-winded botanical titles. Similarly, only seven basic colours were ever used – White, Red, Yellow, Green, Brown, Blue and Black. In other words, the Snooker set, less pink!
>
> We were also taught the duties of every member of a tank crew. This would pay dividends, as there is no room for demarcation disputes in the heat of battle.

June 1942 gave the regiment's gunners an opportunity to test out their skills, as ten days were spent shooting at the tank ranges at Linney Head in Pembrokeshire.

Driving was, of course, another key skill that both the RAC training establishments and the regiment attempted to teach the young soldiers. Patrick Hennessey remembered being taught to drive a Guy 15-hundredweight (15cwt) truck at Bovington, followed by a Valentine Tank, using two levers instead of a steering wheel. He was taught about the three compartments of the Valentine: driving compartment, fighting compartment and engine compartment. However, mastering large vehicles came to some more easily than it did to others. From his early days with the regiment, Cosy Comfort recalled:

> I was temporarily posted to Transport Troop to fill a gap, of which there were many at that time. Driving with six hours previous instruction was not my forte. My first encounter was with a Fordson fifteen hundred weight truck. A somewhat light vehicle with a fearsome large engine, a nightmare clutch and gearbox which soon showed me who was the master; indeed it, the truck, purposefully failed to negotiate the wide entrance to Chippenham Park, graciously marked by two brick pillars, surmounted on top by two-foot, or perhaps larger, concrete balls – rather stately, rather grand – or was, for with a crash, it, the ball, toppled not slowly embedding itself into the bonnet before my horrified eyes. A crowd gathered – no wrath, no words, just grins. The silence was broken, one word… 'Corrr!!' I thought fourteen days Cookhouse fatigues was quite reasonable.

While the regiment was busy absorbing more numbers into its ranks in Suffolk, an operation was about to take place that would have a significant impact on the

(*Artwork by Andrew May*)

role of the 13th/18th Royal Hussars. The Russian Red Army on the Eastern Front was suffering heavy losses and there was political pressure for Britain and the Commonwealth to try to relieve some of that strain. Also, for two years a large number of Canadian troops had been training for war in Britain, but were yet to be tested in battle. In order to raise their morale, plus demonstrate to the public back in Canada that their troops were making a tangible contribution to the war, they were selected for a raid on the French port of Dieppe in the summer of 1942. What was termed a 'reconnaissance in force' would enable Allied commanders to assess how successfully different arms of the armed forces could co-operate in a combined operation. It would also enable a thorough appreciation to be made of the strength and depth of Wehrmacht defences around an occupied port. An added hope was that such an operation would draw out the Luftwaffe, so that the RAF could inflict significant losses upon it, in terms of both aircraft and pilots.

However, secrecy was key to such a raid. The initial attempt to launch the Dieppe raid, Operation Rutter, was set for the first week of July 1942, but was cancelled owing to poor weather. Unfortunately, a convoy of ships was spotted and attacked by Luftwaffe aircraft, thus alerting the German High Command to the likelihood of an amphibious operation. In addition, everyone involved in the operation knew that the target was Dieppe, so security was slack. Despite the government's 'Careless Talk Costs Lives' posters, word of the planned raid was sure to leak out, but it was optimistically hoped that the Germans would never believe that the same troops would attempt to attack the same port a month later.

When 'Operation Jubilee' finally went ahead on 19 August 1942, the landings were rather chaotic and benefitted from only a comparatively light naval bombardment, and no significant softening up of the target by heavy bombers. Some of the Canadian Infantry missed their beach and were landed further along the coast, whilst those who landed on the correct section of the beach were met with fierce resistance from the German defenders. The planned armoured support, largely in the form of the new Churchill tanks, arrived late, leaving the infantry exposed. Of those tanks that did reach the beach, many floundered and became bogged down in the soft shingle, making them sitting ducks. Any tank that did manage to make it onto the promenade was able to accomplish little. Many infantry units were pinned down where they landed on the beach and could advance nowhere. Without effective armoured support, the Canadian Infantry suffered significant casualties, in terms of dead, wounded and those ultimately taken prisoner, losing 3,367 from a force of nearly 5,000. The Canadians were not able to advance far into the town and any moderate achievements made were at tremendous loss. Commando raids were taking place on both flanks to support the main landings, but the only unit to accomplish its task for the day was No. 4 Commando, led by Lieutenant Colonel, The Lord Lovat. They were successfully able to knock out a gun battery overlooking the port on the right flank of the assault, but of around 1,000 commandos taking part in the raid, 247 of them would be lost. However, The Lord Lovat would reappear in a prominent role at another operation in two years' time.

The debacle at Dieppe became a propaganda coup for the Germans. The German High Command viewed this success as a full vindication of its approach to having strong, fixed fortifications to repel any amphibious invasion force. This approach centred on strong coastal defences preventing any significant lodgement to be established, and then armoured reserve units would be brought forward to drive the Allies back into the sea. A handful of commando raids on the Channel Islands had prompted Hitler to order in 1941 that they be made into a veritable fortress. Then, in March 1942, this directive was to extend to the entire coastline from the north of Norway right down Continental Europe as far as the Bay of Biscay. Work on Hitler's 'Atlantic Wall' began in earnest, with strong fortresses at ports such as Calais and Cherbourg, linked by smaller outposts and routine patrols along more than 2,400 miles of coastline. However, Hitler's inflexible, defensive mentality completely overlooked the words of Frederick the Great of Prussia, who had said, 'He who defends everything, defends nothing.'

On the other side of the English Channel, the Allies drew very different conclusions from the Dieppe raid. Firstly, that an attempt to storm a strongly defended port from the sea would be enormously costly, if it could be achieved at all. Co-operation between the three services was found wanting and it was clear that any large-scale amphibious operation would require them to be much more closely integrated. Both heavy naval and air bombardment would be necessary to soften up the chosen landing grounds, with airborne forces dropped inland to seize and hold vital positions ahead of any landing, to prevent or at least slow enemy reinforcements reaching the coast. It was imperative that armour could successfully get ashore to support the infantry and new techniques and specialist armour would need to be developed to combat the beach defences being constructed all along the coast. A much larger fleet of landing craft would also be required, in order to land large numbers of troops as quickly as possible. More than anything, operational security would need to be absolutely watertight in order to keep the German High Command guessing as to where and when the Allies might attempt to land their decisive blow.

Back in England, the 13th/18th were given orders to relocate from Newmarket to Skipton in North Yorkshire, which took place on 8 September 1942. The men were warmly welcomed by the local residents into their new environment of textile mills and cobbled streets and were billeted in requisitioned buildings around the town. Indeed, many of the curbs in Skipton today still bear the scars of the regiment's tank tracks. In his diary, the adjutant, Captain Julius Neave, wrote of Skipton:

Off-duty hours in Skipton, for those who had any, were less attractive for the officers than for other ranks. This rather drab West Riding town had a number of textile factories employing many girls, which in itself was sufficient to give it blessing in the eyes of the men. The local W.V.S. [Women's Voluntary Service] ran an excellent canteen and there were cinemas and dance halls. It was immensely popular with the men. Many married local girls, and of those that brought their wives to stay there, many settled down.

Aside of the unwelcome guard duties on a Saturday night, Cosy Comfort's time at Skipton would prove to be a difficult period. Here he would learn that his mother had passed away, aged 48. Following that came news of his elder brother, Ron, who at age 22 had been serving in North Africa with the Royal Army Service Corps. When his troopship had sailed after calling in at Malta, it was dive-bombed by the Luftwaffe and Cosy lost his brother to this action. If that were not enough, his father's ironmongery shop in Deal was bombed by the Luftwaffe and Cosy's younger brother was left with a bad laceration across his face. (He too would later join the Royal Armoured Corps and would serve for two years after the war as a 3&8).[1]

At the time, the regiment had been sending large drafts out to the Middle East as reinforcements for the campaign against Rommel's forces in the North African desert. Subsequently, the regiment was below strength, but started to receive intakes of new men from the RAC training establishments to bring it back up towards full strength by the end of 1942.

The move to Skipton also heralded a departure from the 9th Armoured Division, over to the newly formed 79th Armoured Division, which had been created at a time when the armoured divisions were reorganised to comprise one armoured brigade, instead of two, and one infantry brigade. 79th Armoured Division was commanded by Major General Sir Percy Hobart, otherwise known as 'Hobo'. Hobo was a Royal Engineers officer who had served in the First World War. Although he had retired with the rank of major general, he was serving as a lance corporal in the Chipping Campden Defence Volunteers unit in October 1940, when his skills were personally requested by Winston Churchill. The role of the 79th Armoured Division was 'to devise and procure specialised armour to overcome the natural and man-made hazards likely to be encountered on the beaches'; the result of one of the key lessons learned from the Dieppe raid. This would lead to the development of a wide range of unusual armoured vehicles, which would become known as 'Hobart's Funnies'. More of those later.

The Bull shoulder patch of the 79th Armoured Division.

Cosy recalled one parade at Skipton where General Hobart inspected the regiment and their Covenanter tanks. 'Start 'em up!' he ordered, and several tanks failed to start. Then he inspected the tanks and found the doors at the back of one were held shut by some wire; it should have been an inch-thick bolt. Hobart went mad, according to Cosy Comfort!

At that time the regiment was commanded by Lieutenant Colonel R.A. Moulton-Barrett, who had come across from the 4th/7th Dragoon Guards. Julius Neave described him as 'not a terribly popular CO and quite a taskmaster. However, he was fair with integrity.' His second-in-command was Major R.T.G. Harrap. With Captain Julius Neave as adjutant, the squadron commanders were:

A Squadron – Major D.B. Wormald
B Squadron – Major A.A.K. Rugge-Price
C Squadron – Major Sir D.J.A. Cotter
HQ Squadron – Major J.R. Cordy-Simpson.

The regiment's officers in 1943. (*Courtesy of Charge!, the museum of the Light Dragoons*)

Other key positions within the regiment were the quartermaster, Captain F. Sweeting, the technical adjutant, Captain A.W.P. Lyon-Clark, and the regimental sergeant major (RSM), WO1 A.L. Hind, known as 'Duffy' Hind.

The winter of 1942/3 at Skipton was spent in intensive training, which Julius Neave described as:

> tedious and exhausting in the extreme. Few who took part in this high-pressure training will forget the life of charts and coloured chalks, of classrooms and blackboards, instructors and syllabi. Our noses were kept to the grindstone, and it was an exhausting process. No one escaped the tolls of the chart. But no one will deny that all this paid a dividend and by the spring the number of our tradesmen was very creditable. Hardly a man could plead ignorance of tank maintenance, gunnery or the intricacies of wireless operating.

Time out of the classroom was spent at Midhope tank gunnery ranges, on the moors close to Sheffield. Its exposed location through the winter delivered an uncomfortable cocktail of unceasing wind, rain and mud to the Hussars training there. Training on road convoys also took place, along with moving cross-country on the moors with live firing at Warcop in Cumbria, and Holmfirth, north-west of Sheffield.

In April 1943, General Hobart revealed the role for which the regiment was to train. They were to be 'put ashore in an entirely novel manner'.

Chapter 3

An Entirely Novel Manner

Did you put that bloody candle out?

The 'entirely novel manner' that General Hobart had alluded to, proved to be that the regiment would spearhead the invasion of Europe in amphibious DD (Duplex Drive) tanks, which would swim ashore under their own power.

Hungarian-born engineer Nicholas Straussler is credited with the development of the Duplex Drive tank. From the lessons learned from Dieppe, it was clear that if the tanks could propel themselves to shore, it would reduce the risk to both the tanks and their LCTs (Landing Craft Tank).

This new and important development now elevated the regiment from its non-mobilised footing and made it a priority for equipment. The news also heralded a move from their Skipton home to a camp at Glevering Hall, near Wickham Market in Suffolk, to enable training to commence on amphibious tanks. The move took place on 28 April 1943.

After training on the bleak moorland throughout the winter, Cosy Comfort recalled his new, pleasant environment of Suffolk in the spring: 'Evening walks with Sid Beesley. Friendly, wonderful country perfumes. Dawn mist, a cuckoo. The drone of returning bombers to Mildenhall filled the air. God speed to safety!'

The 3&8s were the first regiment to be sent to Fritton Lake, south of Great Yarmouth, for DD freshwater training by Instructional Wing 'A' of 79th Armoured Division, which comprised Canadian instructors. Since the DD tank was so secret and was planned to play a key role in the future invasion, security was tight at Fritton Lake. Even local farmers could not tend their land overlooking the lake without first seeking permission from the Army. The whole area was fenced off and no unauthorised personnel admitted access. Everyone in the regiment had to sign the Official Secrets Act and lectures were given to the men at frequent intervals about security. Captain Julius Neave stated: 'They (the men) reacted extremely well and in the whole of our training, we had nothing worth calling trouble on the security side.'

A and B Squadrons would be introduced to the DD Valentine tank and learn beach launches during the first two weeks, followed by C Squadron and

The Duplex Drive (DD) Valentine. (*Courtesy of The Tank Museum, Bovington – Image 11422–002*)

Regimental HQ. It was initially planned that all three sabre squadrons would be landed in DD tanks, but later this would change to just A and B Squadrons, with C Squadron and RHQ landing 'dry-shod' behind. The regiment had received its first Valentine tanks in April and they were not sad to see the Covenanters go.

The Duplex Drive tank was fitted with a canvas screen, which was attached to reinforced track guards. Each section of the screen was supported by horizontal rails, locked in position by vertical struts. The screen was raised by inflating rubber tubes attached to the inside of the screen with compressed air, and these supported the weight of the screen. To propel the tank in water, the Duplex Drive Valentine had just one propeller, which was driven off the tank's gearbox. This propeller could be locked in the 'up' position when the tank was driven on land and was lowered and engaged once the tank was afloat. The limited freeboard offered by the canvas screen did not make the DD tank appear to be the most seaworthy vessel. One drawback of the DD Valentine variant was that the turret had to be traversed so that the gun was facing the rear before the canvas screen could be raised, owing to the forward placement of the Valentine's turret. The main armament could only be used in anger once the canvas screen was collapsed and the turret was traversed back around, leaving the vehicle somewhat vulnerable for a short while. The DD Sherman variant did not suffer this problem and its crew could commence firing its main armament the moment the screen was collapsed.

20   DD Sherman Tank Warriors

The Duplex Drive (DD) Sherman, with canvas screen collapsed. (*Courtesy of The Tank Museum, Bovington – Image 0143-C3*)

View of the DD Sherman tank with canvas screen raised. (*Courtesy of Imperial War Museums – Image MH 3661*)

On the DD Sherman, which the regiment would later take to war, the canvas screen was thickest at the bottom, comprising three sheets of canvas, then two sheets for the middle section and just one sheet at the top. The Sherman also had twin 26-inch propellers, which could be used for steering and could generate a forward speed of 4 knots. For navigation purposes, a Kelvin sphere magnetic compass was used, plus later, the driver's compartment would house a gyrocompass, as it was difficult for the driver to see much from behind the canvas screen, with only a narrow periscope to help him. The commander could assist with steering the tank, standing on a platform to the rear of the turret to allow him to see over the raised screen. Once ashore, the joints on the metal struts

The DD Sherman tank's twin 26-inch propellers. (*Courtesy of Imperial War Museums – Image MH 2214*)

would be broken and a switch thrown which expelled the air from the rubber tubes, allowing the screen to collapse, which enabled the tank to operate as a normal fighting vehicle. Now ready to fight, the crew positions were as follows: the commander sat in the turret, the gunner to the right of the gun, the loader/radio operator to the left of the gun. As a US vehicle, the driver sat on the left to the front and the co-driver alongside him on the front right.

The men were taught how to launch the tanks into the water, how to manoeuvre them once afloat, and then how to bring them back onto dry land, ready to engage an enemy. Nautical commands of 'Port' and 'Starboard' now became familiar to the crews as they entered their new world on the water. On one occasion on Fritton Lake, Lieutenant Eric Smith was given the honour of taking Brigadier Prior-Palmer out onto the water during a night exercise, and then was to suffer the immense embarrassment of his tank running out of fuel and coming to a halt in the middle of the lake.

In the event of a capsize, the crews were issued with breathing apparatus, known as the Amphibious Tank Escape Apparatus (ATEA). This was based on the Davis Submarine Escape Apparatus (DSEA). Adjacent to Fritton Lake was a deep pit containing a tank chassis, which would be filled with thousands of gallons of water. Each crew would climb down a ladder and take up their regular positions wearing their ATEA equipment. Once the pit was full and the tank was fully submerged, the crew would leave the tank using the ATEA, in a predetermined order. This was all good in theory but did rely on the tank sinking the right way up.

Each day at Wickham Market began with Trooper 'Kip' Kippax sounding his bugle at 0600 hrs, sometimes standing by his hut wearing nothing but his underpants, according to Cosy Comfort!

An amusing incident took place when Cosy was chatting with his friend 'Fairy' Fairbanks. Fairy was the son of a vicar; he was an accomplished organist, but very absent-minded. He was shaving in a Nissen hut by the light of a candle balanced on a table knife, stuck in some woodwork. They were both meant to be on fire piquet duty that night, keeping a watch around camp for any fires. Duties were based on a rota and they were currently 'off duty' although both were meant to remain on the camp, in case they needed to tackle a fire.

'Fancy a pint in Wickham Market?' Fairy suggested. 'They'll never miss us, Cosy.'

Returning rather later than planned, they spied a glow in the sky, accompanied by a lot of shouting. Fairy's Nissen hut was well ablaze.

'Did you put that bloody candle out?' Cosy asked. A slow shake of the head. They silently joined the fire fighters, and then stole away into the darkness with their secret.

The regiment was able to train at the Orford Battle area at Orford Ness, near Ipswich. Squadron training followed troop training and gunners were able to fire at the Orford AFV (Armoured Fighting Vehicle) ranges. All of this was then practised at Exercise Thet in early August, which was on a full brigade level and enabled the regiment to deploy complete and obtain much confidence in their new vehicles.

The regiment continued to receive further intakes of men from the RAC training depots throughout the summer of 1943 and it was during this period that another young man was to swap his RAC training beret for a new 13th/18th one. Trooper William Henry Hollands,

Henry 'Dutch' Hollands in his RAC training beret.

2nd Troop, B Squadron in the summer of 1943 at Wickham Market proudly show off their new Shermans. Sitting on the turret top left (Tank 47) is the troop commander, Lieutenant Aldam, with Trooper Bill Mawson to his left.

originally from Kensington, was posted to A Squadron. Owing to his surname, he was quickly rechristened by his new, adoptive family as 'Dutch' Hollands!

It was at Wickham Market that the regiment received its first Shermans, which were clearly far superior to the previous Covenanters or Valentines. After getting over that pleasant surprise, some of the men discovered that stuffed down the barrels of the guns were scarves, balaclavas and watches, with notes wishing 'the Tommies in England the best of luck and good wishes from your good buddies in the U.S of A'. Once this was discovered, the supplies of goodies dried up very quickly. In July, personnel from the 4th/7th Dragoon Guards & East Riding Yeomanry were also attached to the regiment for initial Sherman training.

One major drawback with the new Shermans and the DD variant, however, is described by Robert B. Jarvis in *Chariots of the Lake*:

> The Duplex Drive versions of the Sherman M-4 A4 saw the British units supplied with the Sherman V with its Chrysler Gasoline 370Hp Engine, which was much more prone to catching fire when hit and 'brewing up', than was the Sherman III with its General Motors diesel engine. Hence the British tanks being dubbed by the Germans, 'Tommy Cookers'.

Sadly, many 3&8s would suffer a very unpleasant end to their lives, as a result of their vehicles brewing up in this fashion, since with their petrol engine and the ammunition carried within the tank, their home was essentially a mobile bomb.

On a lighter note, Cosy Comfort was relaxing on his bunk at Wickham Market when a sergeant stuck his head around the door. 'Comfort, I hunderstand that you plays an hinstrument?' This was correct, as he played both the clarinet and alto saxophone. 'Right, parade at the Regimental Office in your best battledress with your hinstrument at 1700!'

Cosy complied with this order and met up with Troopers Ball and the previously mentioned Kippax, armed with a trumpet. Each was handed a 13th/18th pennant and informed, 'Tonight you are the 13th/18th band!' They were driven in a truck deep into Suffolk and eventually arrived at a large house, surrounded by Red Caps (military police). They were shown to the kitchens and given a good meal before being taken to the dining room, where there were two large tables laid out with silverware. At the end of the room was a platform that housed an upright piano. 'Have you got your music?' they were asked.

Music? They'd never so much as played a note together before. 'Has anyone got a pencil?' They then hurriedly tried to find some tunes that they all knew how to play and decided in which key to play them.

Cosy Comfort with his 3&8 pennant from his evening playing for the king.

When the guests were later brought in for dinner, the young troopers were astonished to learn that their audience was King George VI, General Montgomery, General Horrocks and an assortment of other high-ranking staff officers. Somehow, they managed to play their way through the evening and at the end, each musician was handed an envelope containing a crisp five-pound note; not bad pay, considering their normal weekly wage was around £1. Cosy removed his pennant from the music stand and took it away with him in his saxophone case. His alto sax would go to war with him, wrapped in his bed roll!

In late August, the regiment returned to Linney Head for live firing. Captain Julius Neave recorded:

> In preparation for our D-Day role, we did an amusing fire practice on the beach, each squadron in turn lining the high-water line and pumping its entire load of ammunition into the cliffs in the most spectacular manner. It gave us a pleasant surprise in demonstrating fire power and was encouraging for D-Day.

While in Pembrokeshire, Cosy recalled the welcome break from rationing: 'White bread and eggs in rural Wales. The Welsh love their table, as did Buckshot Smith, the Regimental butcher and poacher extraordinaire! Soup and stew, feathers, bones and all – I have never tasted better!'

Sadly, during this training exercise, Lieutenant John Harding was crushed when his tank overturned; he had been returning to camp from Pembroke Station, when the tank skidded off the road and tumbled down a steep hill. Cosy was selected to be part of the funeral firing party. Regimental Sergeant Major Duffy Hind was sympathetic: 'Now, now, that won't do on the day lads. Let's get it right. Present Arms… Prepare… Fire, again Fire.'

Cosy recalled: 'We were right on the day and his parents stood silent by the graveside. The regiment always looked after its own.'

The 3&8s were next informed that 27th Armoured Brigade would now operate as an independent brigade. At that time, the brigade comprised the armoured regiments of the 13th/18th Royal Hussars, the 4th/7th Dragoon Guards and the East Riding Yeomanry. The brigade wore the Seahorse as their shoulder patch, affectionately known as the 'Pregnant Prawn' amongst the men. The brigade was commanded by Brigadier George Erroll Prior-Palmer.

In October, the brigade was placed under the command of 3rd Infantry Division, just a few days before the regiment's annual celebrations on Balaclava Day. In December 1943, the second phase of amphibious tank training took place down on the south coast, at Gosport, on the hards at Stokes Bay on the Solent. Here A and B Squadrons got to grips with launching their strange craft into the sea. This was carried out under the watchful eye of Instructional Wing B of 79th Armoured Division. On the first attempt, it took over two hours to launch just five tanks, and two of these would end up beneath the waves. However, within a week an LCT was able to successfully launch its full complement of tanks in just two minutes, as the tanks drove off the craft's ramp, engaged their propellers and swam away.

Young Trooper Joe 'Jock' Collins of A Squadron from Glasgow remembered: 'Then it was back to the billets to regale each other with our stories of our first day at sea in our swimming tanks.'

The Isle of Wight was used to simulate a foreign coastline and Osborne Bay on the island's north coast would be 'invaded'

The Seahorse shoulder patch of the 27th Armoured Brigade.

Loading DD Valentines onto an LCT at Stokes Bay, Gosport, during an exercise. (*Courtesy of Imperial War Museums – Image H 35175*)

repeatedly. The DD tank was to become the only item of specialist armour that the US forces elected to use in the upcoming landings, and in addition to British and Canadian units, three US tank battalions were trained: the 70th, 741st and 743rd.

Let's briefly consider some of the other variants of Hobart's 'Funnies', which would support the Hussars upon landing. There was the Crab 'Flail' tank, which would beat the ground with heavy chains with weights at the end, by means of a rotating roller, held in front of the tank by two arms. The tank could slowly creep forwards, detonating any mines in its path, clearing a lane 9 feet wide. The Crocodile tank, in addition to regular armaments, was armed with a flamethrower and towed a 400-gallon trailer of fuel, which would enable eighty one-second bursts of flame. There are stories of German soldiers surrendering in France once a couple of Crocodiles were brought forward just to deliver a firepower demonstration. A further vehicle that would prove its worth was the

DD tanks with their canvas screens raised, ready to launch from their LCT on exercise in the Solent. As viewed from the bridge of the LCT. (*Courtesy of The Tank Museum, Bovington – Image 0338-A4*)

AVRE (Assault Vehicle Royal Engineers). The AVRE was capable of throwing a huge demolition charge and its 290mm Petard mortar became known as the 'flying dustbin'. Capable of demolishing large obstructions and fortifications, the AVRE was often used in conjunction with a Churchill Crocodile flamethrower for bunker clearance. There was a host of other armoured vehicles capable of filling tank traps with a bundle of wooden poles (fascine), bridging gaps with a small box girder bridge or laying a 10-foot wide reinforced canvas path over the ground to prevent vehicles sinking into soft sand, as a few examples. The lessons of Dieppe had been well and truly learned.

At the end of December, the regiment (less A and B Squadrons, initially) moved to Hoddam Castle in Dumfriesshire, which presented a rather different climate to Wickham Market in summer. Once B Squadron had moved up to Scotland, Cosy Comfort reminisced about that period:

A DD Valentine entering the water from an LCT. (*Courtesy of Imperial War Museums – Image H 35180*)

So north to Scotland. Hoddom Castle, Ecclefechan, Annan, Lockerbie. Such names, places and people. The highs were the dances and Scottish Reels on Saturday nights in Annan. The lows – missing the lorry and walking ten miles back in the snow.

The regiment completed its move north in late January, where it would be based at Fort George near Inverness. The whole of the 3rd Infantry Division were billeted in the area, along with Force S of the Royal Navy, who were about to become close colleagues as the 3&8s prepared to fulfil their role in the upcoming invasion. However, the regiment's arrival at Inverness proved to be something of a shock, as recounted by Cosy Comfort:

A DD Sherman afloat. (*Courtesy of The Tank Museum, Bovington – Image 6220-C6*)

And still further north to Fort George, January '44. 0800 Inverness Station – the 3&8s arrive – six inches of snow. Hussars ever hopeful look for transport – what transport? Duffy squares himself to the wintery blast – 'Come along you lads, form up – we'll march!' Hussars never march – but we did! Hours later, Fort George – the Dartmoor of the north. How did the Seaforths manage the Winters in kilts?

Fort George enabled large-scale exercises to take place in the Moray Firth. It was here that the men finally met the DD versions of the Sherman tank.

Each Landing Craft Tank carried five Shermans, loaded on backwards. Captain Julius Neave:

> We would embark from the hards of Fort George, usually at night on a rising tide, and steam out to sea in a big sweep, and then the following dawn, if we were lucky and not kept on board for longer, make an assault landing on Burghead Bay. Once ashore we would move almost exactly as we should have to on D-Day itself, and then motor home to Fort George, after the exercise. It all sounds so simple now, but in fact it was far from being so! The chaos on the beach itself was on each occasion quite unbelievable, but this strangely enough was an asset for on the day itself chaos reigned, and our experience had taught us that it was a normal thing. We learned

A Landing Craft (Tank) Mk III on exercise. (*Courtesy of The Tank Museum, Bovington – Image 3455-A1*)

all we had to about waterproofing vehicles, about cooking compo rations and about the bedlam of the wireless setup, we learned the most practical clothes to wear and what 'comforts' came in really useful. We got to know the infantry with whom we would be fighting and the Navy, who would take us in. Also, we got an insight into the marshalling and loading problems, and the briefing and planning that would be necessary when we got south.

After each exercise, a vast conference would be held in Inverness attended by all the officers and run jointly by the Army and the Navy. These were notable for the complete disregard for personal feelings that the Navy seemed to hold for their subordinates, who would be slayed in the most outrageous manner in front of the assembled company. The Navy certainly knew how to put these conferences over and showed up the vagueness of the Army to a remarkable degree.

All troops stationed at Fort George and the surrounding area were paraded on 5 February for an inspection by their commander-in-chief, General Montgomery. Everyone was kept waiting for two hours on a particularly cold day, before the general arrived.

Corporal Frank Underhay, rear rank, far right.

That same day, news was received that the 4th/7th Dragoon Guards would be leaving the 27th Armoured Brigade, to be replaced by the Staffordshire Yeomanry.

This period in Scotland was marred by the unfortunate death of Corporal Francis (Frank) Underhay of A Squadron. Brigade Exercise Cupid was held on 1 March and as tanks were halfway to shore in the Moray Firth, a violent snowstorm broke, which swamped and capsized two tanks of A Squadron. The troop commander and other crewmembers were rescued, but Corporal Underhay was drowned. At his home in Rotherham he left behind a widow, Norah, and a young son of 6, also named Frank. Corporal Underhay was the only fatality during the regiment's DD training.

Chapter 4

Prelude to Invasion

Si vis pacem, para bellum – If you want peace, prepare for war.

Speaking to the House of Commons, Prime Minister Winston Churchill said of the invasion, 'And what a plan! This vast operation is undoubtedly the most complicated and difficult that has ever occurred.'

Preparations to open up a second front had actually commenced as far back as October 1941, when Churchill had appointed Lord Louis Mountbatten to lead his Combined Operations Headquarters. It was following a conference in May 1943 in Washington, DC attended by the Allied political leaders, codenamed 'Trident', that Mountbatten hosted a conference codenamed 'Rattle' in late May. This was a gathering of senior commanders from the armies, navies and air forces of Britain, the United States and Canada. Having considered all the options as to possible landing areas, British officer Lieutenant General Frederick Morgan (the Chief of Staff to the currently empty position of Supreme Allied Commander 'COSSAC') proposed Normandy as the optimal target for the invasion, which was to be codenamed 'Overlord'. Dieppe had illustrated that taking on a defended port would be indefensibly costly, and it was known that the Pas de Calais area was heavily garrisoned, being the most likely landing area, owing to its close proximity to the Kent coastline and Dover. The Pas de Calais could also be easily defended by the Luftwaffe.

Although a much greater distance away from the south coast of England, the beaches of Normandy were comparatively lightly defended and were sheltered, to a degree, from prevailing south-westerly winds by the Cotentin Peninsula. If a landing could be achieved here and a solid lodgement established, then ports such as Cherbourg and those further south in Brittany could be seized from inland. The issue of not capturing a port during the invasion did present a huge logistical problem, but this was overcome by the clever invention of what would come to be known as the 'Mulberry harbours'. These were constructed of huge, prefabricated caissons, which could be towed across the English Channel and joined together to create an artificial harbour. Two were planned to be positioned off the American and British landing areas respectively. Air superiority was also key to a successful Allied lodgement being achieved, and Normandy also offered the possibility of creating airfields, to enable the RAF and USAAF to operate more easily once ashore. Owing to the war of attrition still being fought on the Russian front and the unrelenting day and night bombing campaign over Germany by Allied aircraft, the Germans had already relocated many fighter wings and air defence systems back to the Fatherland, leaving other areas exposed. Allied air forces further reduced the Luftwaffe's capability of posing a threat to the upcoming landings by the systematic bombing of airfields, which might threaten the invasion force.

However, not to bring Normandy to the attention of the German High Command, for every sortie flown over Normandy, two would be conducted elsewhere. This was just a small part of the deception plan, codenamed Operation Bodyguard, which was designed to mislead Hitler and his generals as to the Allies' true intentions. Prime Minister Winston Churchill was quoted as saying: 'In wartime, truth is so precious that she should always be attended by a bodyguard of lies.'

In addition to reconnaissance sorties, aerial bombing of rail and road networks took place across much of occupied Europe, but this all served to hamper the Germans' ability to move men and equipment at will. In order to keep the Germans' attention focused elsewhere, Operation Fortitude was then specifically developed to convince the German High Command that they may be facing an invasion either at the Pas de Calais across the Dover Straits, or indeed in Norway. This would tie up large numbers of troops defending those areas, keeping them well away from the actual landing beaches. Under Fortitude North, a simulated build-up of troops in Scotland was so successful that Hitler held thirteen army divisions in Norway for its defence. Fortitude South set about to convince the Germans of the presence of a fictitious unit called the First US Army Group (FUSAG), which was nominally commanded by General Omar Bradley; this represented an additional eleven divisions, or 150,000 men. As the invasion approached, FUSAG was given a new commander in General George Patton, a leader whom the Germans recognised as being both capable and aggressive. The build-up of the FUSAG invasion force was bolstered by the use of fake camps, tanks, lorries, gliders and landing craft, which began to appear around south-eastern England to be spotted by German reconnaissance flights. There were inflatable fake vehicles and others constructed from cloth and plywood, but when viewed from the air or at a distance by prying eyes, they would look like the real thing. Fake news reports were created, ranging from General Patton reviewing his troops down to complaints in local newspapers about the behaviour of his soldiers. There was continual radio chatter between fictitious units who were meant to be based in Kent and East Anglia, for the Germans to intercept and monitor.

Most importantly, to give credence to the existence of FUSAG and the threat it posed to the Pas de Calais, double agents were used extensively to feed false information to the Abwehr (German military intelligence). Some German agents were captured upon arrival in Britain and 'turned' by MI5 to work for the British. However, the most notable of these spies was Juan Pujol García, known as 'Garbo'. Garbo was a Spaniard who had established himself as a spy in pro-Nazi Spain and had been accepted by the Abwehr to spy on the British. However, his real intention was to work against the Germans, and he was to become a pivotal asset to the British in feeding misleading intelligence to the German High Command. Garbo established an imaginary ring of subordinate sub-agents, who could be blamed if the veracity of any intelligence was ever questioned; Germany would eventually be funding twenty-seven fictitious agents. So pleased were the Germans with the information provided by Garbo, that he was awarded the Iron Cross. So pleased were the British with his contribution to the war effort, that he was awarded an MBE!

This was all overlaid by the 'Ultra' intercepts obtained from the secret work being carried out at Bletchley Park. The Germans, confident in the invincibility of their Enigma codes, which changed every twenty-four hours, had no idea that the British had been able to eavesdrop on their communications for most of the war. Polish military intelligence had got halfway to cracking Enigma and handed over what they knew to the British at the start of the war. Gordon Welchman and Alan Turing were two principal characters in completing that work and the breaking of the Enigma codes, which gave the British an incalculable advantage as invasion loomed.

The United States entering the war really turned the tables regarding the vast volume of men and matériel that could be fielded against the Wehrmacht. US industry and agriculture were feverishly working on the manufacture of aircraft, lorries, jeeps, tanks and vital landing craft, plus the food to feed the invasion force. Of course, the clearest challenge with taking a huge, mechanised invasion force to war was that its vehicles required fuel, and lots of it! With the proposed landing beaches being a dangerous six-hour sailing from the English coast, it presented a real logistical challenge; German U-boats and torpedo boats posed a continual threat. The problem was solved by British civil engineer Arthur Hartley, by the development of pipelines that could be laid by ships right across the English Channel to lie on the seabed, from Britain's south coast to Normandy. This incredible feat of engineering was known under the codename Operation Pluto (Pipe-lines Under The Ocean), and would provide a continual supply of fuel to the invasion force. The pumping stations at the British end were disguised as buildings made to look innocuous, such as a rural cottage, or a small business – all intended to mask their true purpose.

Amid all of the preparations for the invasion, in January 1944 the new commander of the invasion force arrived in London. The operational commander for the north-west European Campaign would be the American, General Dwight D. Eisenhower, known as 'Ike', the Supreme Allied Commander. Having already overseen the successful Allied invasions of North Africa and Sicily, Ike was an obvious choice for this critical role. British General Bernard Montgomery, or 'Monty', would be given command of the 21st Army Group, which included all the land forces involved in the invasion.

Meanwhile, across the English Channel the German command structure of the Westheer (Western Army) in occupied Europe was fractured and dysfunctional at best. Rivalries existed between senior commanders, many of which held vastly different beliefs around strategy. Concerning the armoured Panzer Divisions, Generalfeldmarschall Gerd von Rundstedt, the overall commander of the Westheer, advocated a cautious approach to the deployment of the Panzer divisions held in reserve, well inland. When the invasion came, von Rundstedt preferred to wait until the Allies had shown their hand, and could assess their intentions and strength before unleashing the full weight of the Panzer divisions to counterattack in force, crushing the Allies in a decisive battle. In contrast, as appointed General Inspector of Western Defences, Generalfeldmarschall Erwin Rommel favoured holding the Panzer reserves closer to the coast. The infantry responsible for coastal defence would hold the Allies in and around the area of the beaches, before quickly releasing the Panzer reserves to drive the invasion back into the sea. Rommel was keenly aware of the likely superiority that the Allies would hold in the skies over France and feared that attack from above could place the Panzers at a distinct disadvantage in a large, set-piece battle. Hitler, unable to support fully either approach, plus being distrustful of his senior commanders, decided to retain personal control of the Panzer divisions, such that they could only be deployed with his authority.

In June 1944, the closest armoured formation to the Normandy coast was the 21st Panzer Division. Virtually wiped out in the North Africa campaign, it was reconstituted in July 1943, but was comparatively poorly equipped with an assortment of captured vehicles.

21st Panzer Division's compliment of vehicles were the brainchild of Alfred Becker, who was an artillery officer whose guns had helped force the capitulation of Holland in May 1940. Becker had discovered some abandoned Dutch military motor transport and had the idea of using those to pull the guns of his artillery regiment, rather than horse-drawn limbers. This gave Becker the idea to extend the idea of recycling captured vehicles from Germany's enemies from the 1940 campaigns. After the development of some motorised self-propelled guns and anti-tank guns, Becker was given the opportunity to demonstrate one of his cannibalised vehicles to the Führer himself in Berlin. Becker was immediately tasked with the conversion of captured armoured vehicles, to provide them with more powerful armaments. Having taken over the Hotchkiss plant near Paris, it now became a vehicle modification centre. For example, the French Hotchkiss H-39 tank would have its turret removed, to be replaced with perhaps a 105mm Howitzer, or a 75mm anti-tank gun. These modified vehicles would enable the German defenders to engage advancing armour at range, and then rapidly relocate.

Wasting nothing, many of the tank turrets from captured tanks would be rehoused in concrete emplacements along the coast as fixed gun positions, to bolster the Atlantic Wall. French tank turrets and Czech guns would subsequently be taken to the Normandy coast.

The area around the Pas de Calais was heavily defended by Hitler's 15th Army, whereas Germany's troops garrisoned in the Normandy sector were fewer in number and generally felt to be of a lower quality than the crack German units fighting on the Russian front. Those given the responsibility of coastal defence comprised many older soldiers (whom it was hoped may have families and may have less stomach for a fight), young conscripts with only a few weeks of training behind them, or even those soldiers convalescing from wounds received on the Russian front. Added to this were the Ost (East) battalions, whose ranks were drawn from countries such as Poland, Czechoslovakia, Russia and Ukraine. Many were prisoners of war, who had chosen to serve Hitler rather than languish and possibly die in a prisoner of war camp; others were simply coerced into joining. Then there were those of German descent living in other countries, who were not German nationals, but who nevertheless wished to serve the Third Reich.

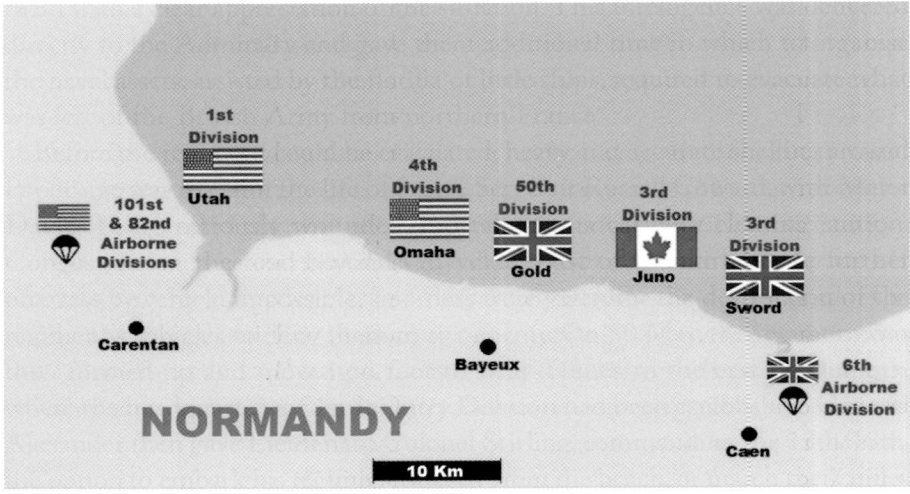

Again, it was hoped that their loyalty might be called into question when faced with the collective force of the Allied invasion.

The plans for Operation Overlord evolved over time, but the final plan would see five divisions land on the beaches of Normandy, with three airborne divisions securing the flanks; American in the west and British in the east. From the west were the American beaches codenamed Utah and Omaha, with the British and Canadian beaches being Gold, Juno and Sword.

Facing these Allied divisions, working from the Cotentin Peninsula in the West, were the German 709th Infantry Division (Utah Beach), 352nd Infantry Division (Omaha Beach) and 716th Infantry Division (Gold, Juno and Sword Beaches). Defending the area of what would be codenamed Sword Beach were men of the 736th Grenadier Regiment, commanded by Oberst Ludwig Krug. His regiment was partly composed of the 642nd Ost Battalion. The regiment had very limited transportation but would soon face the most mechanised army in the history of warfare, who unlike their German foe would rely on the horsepower of their mechanised vehicles, rather than actual horses. In that regard, despite the Germans' superiority in tank design, much of the Wehrmacht had progressed little since the first war.

Although Rommel had ordered the laying of 200 million mines along the Atlantic Wall, by June 1944, only a fraction of this number had actually been laid. In fact, in the book *D-Day Through German Eyes*, a 21-year-old Gefreiter Aloysius Damski, based in Normandy, stated, 'We used to plant scraps of metal in fields to decoy mine detectors, wire it off and put up "Achtung Minen" signs – most of the minefields in our area were false.' However, over half-a-million anti-invasion obstacles had been placed along the beaches, which was sufficient to worry Allied planners enough to move a preferred landing under the cover of darkness to landing after first light; this would present improved visibility and provide the landing craft, and amphibious tanks, a better chance of avoiding such obstacles, which were often armed with Teller mines.

The ideal conditions for the invasion could only be met on about three days in each lunar month; the Allies required a low tide at dawn to expose the German beach defences, plus a full moon to illuminate landing sites for gliders. With commanders both sides of the Channel keeping a close eye on the weather forecasts, Erwin Rommel concluded that the conditions in early June 1944 were not favourable for an invasion, so elected to travel back to Stuttgart to celebrate his wife's birthday, before a planned meeting with the Führer at Berchtesgaden on 6 June. Eisenhower and his advisors had planned 5 June as the date of the invasion, but as the date approached, all eyes would be on the weather forecast.

Chapter 5

Preparations for the Assault

I'm going to marry that girl!

Having endured training on the Moray Firth through winter, the 13th/18th ended their spell at Fort George on 16 April 1944. A and B Squadrons moved to Gosport, where they had trained a few months previously. Rather worryingly, at this late stage their new DD Shermans had yet to arrive. C Squadron and regimental headquarters relocated to Petworth Park in Sussex. Meanwhile, the trucks of the support echelons moved to Aldershot.

Leave passes enabled the 3&8s to visit their loved ones before they would turn their attentions to the task for which they had been trained. Here Enid and Jerry Bell smile for the camera, although one can only imagine at the thoughts in Jerry's mind before he left his wife; for security reasons, he was unable to share with her any details about the leading role that the regiment would play in the upcoming invasion.

At Petworth, the commanding officer, Lieutenant Colonel Moulton-Barrett, handed over command to his former second-in-command, Dick Harrap. This

A DD tank moves down the ramp of its LCT on exercise. (*Courtesy of The Tank Museum, Bovington – Image 8174–074*)

change in command was forced by health problems with the Colonel and it must have been quite a daunting task for Dick Harrap to take over command, immediately before the regiment would face its biggest test of the war so far.

The 3&8s had their final chance for a large-scale exercise before the invasion itself during Exercise Fabius IV. This involved the whole of the 3rd Infantry Division and proved to be quite a chaotic experience for the regiment, in terms of marshalling and the loading of their vehicles onto landing craft. However, it did lead to a better system being implemented for the real thing. A and B Squadrons led the invasion of beaches close to Littlehampton, which was followed by manoeuvres on the South Downs. However, owing to concerns about their highly secret DD tanks being seen and leaked, A and B Squadrons were not permitted to participate in the latter part of the exercise.

At the eleventh hour, A and B Squadrons finally received their DD Shermans and the

Trooper Bill Mawson.

The regiment's tanks moving from Petworth to Gosport. (*Courtesy of the Imperial War Museums – Image H 38985*)

crews set about modifying them and making them feel more like home. For example, it became common practice for the gun shield to be removed from inside the turret, as it made it difficult for the loader/operator to exit the tank in a hurry. Trooper Bill Mawson was the loader/operator in Lieutenant Aldam's tank in 2nd Troop, B Squadron. In addition to removing the gun shield from his tank, in order to accommodate his collection of Penguin books, he had a small shelf welded inside the tank.

The regiment participated in an inspection of the troops at Petworth Park by the king and General Eisenhower, before C Squadron and Regimental HQ moved to a camp outside Portsmouth on 1 June. All the roads leading into Portsmouth were full of tanks and vehicles of every sort.

To provide some insight into the dash and inspirational qualities of the regiment's young officers who led each troop of tanks to war, we need to look

A milkmaid delivers a pint of milk to the C Squadron crew of tank *Challenger*, on their journey from Petworth to Gosport. (*Courtesy of the Imperial War Museums – Image H 38988*)

no further than Lieutenant Tresham Hardy, MM. Tresham commanded Recce Troop of Regimental HQ as invasion loomed.

Before hostilities broke out, Tresham was a motorcycle enthusiast who competed in the Isle of Man TT Races. A popular officer who was affectionately known by the nickname 'Trash' by his fellow officers, Tresham loved racing and took part in other competitions, such as the Inter Varsity Speed Trials (Cambridge) in 1937, where he placed third. At the outbreak of war, as a Territorial Army soldier, Tresham was to accompany the Army into France with the Royal Corps of Signals as part of the BEF. Acting as

Lieutenant Bernard Tresham Hardy, MM.

The road to embarkation. C Squadron and RHQ vehicles en route to Portsmouth. The sixth man along in the beret is Regimental Sergeant Major Duffy Hind. Next to him with the goggles is Lieutenant Tresham Hardy, MM. (*Courtesy of Imperial War Museums – Image H 38986*)

a motorcycle despatch rider, he was recommended for a gallantry award, the Distinguished Conduct Medal (second only to the Victoria Cross). However, upon review this was downgraded to the Military Medal.[1]

Having successfully returned to England via the Dunkirk evacuation, Tresham Hardy was recommended to attend an officer cadet training camp, after which he was commissioned in July 1941 and posted to the 3&8s as a regular commissioned officer. The year 1941 was a busy one for Tresham, as not only was he finding his feet as a newly appointed officer with a new regiment, but he also was to marry Vivien in September. After one engagement was broken off, one day Tresham popped into a garage with his motorcar, and met Vivien, who was working at the garage. He returned to his companion waiting in the car and said, 'I'm going to marry that girl!' … and he did! (Unusually for women at that time, Vivien had

Tresham on the start line of the Syston Park Speed Trials, March 1935.

achieved a degree in Engineering, which is presumably how she ended up working in a garage.)

Moving into Gosport for embarkation, the photo opposite, taken on 3 June, shows the crew of Sherman Firefly *Carole*, Tank 71 of 2nd Troop, C Squadron. Nearest the camera is the loader/operator Fred Shaw, next is the gunner Doug Kay (in beret), the commander Fred Scamp, and holding his mug of tea, the driver, Bill Humphries. Once the initial assault was over, each of the three sabre squadrons would be provided with one Sherman Firefly for each troop of four tanks. With its powerful 17-pounder gun, the Firefly was truly a match for German armour, yet this variant of the Sherman was not adopted by American units.

Vivien and Tresham Hardy on their wedding day in September 1941.

Preparations for the Assault   45

(*Courtesy of Imperial War Museums – Image H 38995*)

The Sherman Firefly often carried a crew of just four, rather than the usual five in a Sherman, since the co-driver's compartment could be used to store the larger rounds for the tank's main armament. The tank crews would be issued with fourteen-man ration packs, with Menu A, B or C. The good news for four-man Firefly crews was that they received additional rations, compared with the five-man crews of the regular Shermans, although their workload was correspondingly higher. That said, some crews preferred to keep a five-man crew and there is certainly photographic and written evidence to show that this was the case within the regiment.

The marshalling of vehicles and the loading onto landing craft was carried out in a much more efficient manner than had been the case during Exercise Fabius IV a few weeks earlier. However, loading C Squadron's tanks took longer than usual, as they were towing waterproofed sledges, called Porpoises. These carried a reserve of ammunition, in case more was required after landing before the support echelons could resupply the squadron.

The invasion was all set to take place on 5 June, so the regiment completed loading its tanks onto their respective landing craft by 1000 on 3 June. Once all the landing craft were moored in their designation place in Portsmouth harbour, a stiff breeze sprang up and the weather began to deteriorate. On the morning of 4 June, orders were received that the invasion was postponed and as the uncomfortable landing craft began to be tossed around in the heavy swell, the 3&8s were faced with spending an additional, and very unwelcome, twenty-four hours afloat. Seasickness affected just about all the soldiers now, regardless of how many rations each crew had been issued, and few could keep their food down. There was one notable exception in A Squadron, who was described by Corporal Pat Hennessey:

LCTs of the 13th/18th head into the English Channel – their secret DD Shermans hidden under camouflage nets. (*Courtesy of Imperial War Museums – Image B 5106*)

Corporal Bob Charmbury, however, seemed to be quite impervious to the constant movement of the ship as he sat eating a tin of apricots, supplemented by spoonfuls of thick, sweet, condensed milk. He attracted much well-deserved abuse for this inconsiderate exhibition of gluttony!

Although the weather didn't appear to be much improved at dawn on 5 June, the original date for the invasion, the Hussars waited to hear whether or not they would be given the order to go. At the nearby Supreme Headquarters Allied Expeditionary Force (SHAEF), based at Southwick House, General Eisenhower and the Allied commanders were briefed by Operation Overlord's chief meteorological officer, Group Captain James Stagg. Stagg and his team of meteorologists had correctly predicted the high winds and rain that had moved into the English Channel during the previous night, but now a temporary improvement in the conditions was predicted, which might enable the invasion to go ahead for 6 June. If the forecast was wrong, Eisenhower could have an epic disaster on his hands. However, to delay would mean a postponement of at least two weeks, waiting for favourable conditions again, and the Allies might lose the crucial element of surprise. The lives of many thousands of men were in Eisenhower's hands, as he decided to put his faith in his meteorological officer and made the decision for the invasion to proceed. Around midday on 5 June, Force S of the Royal Navy received the signal to press on, and in the early afternoon the landing craft carrying the DD tanks of A and B Squadrons moved to the head of the convoy, waved off by C Squadron and Regimental HQ, who would follow on behind to the Normandy beaches.

Chapter 6

Operation Overlord

Bill, it's now 'make your mind up' time.

Operation Neptune – the naval component of the invasion – was now under way. The fleet was commanded by Admiral Sir Bertram H. Ramsay of the Royal Navy (who had previously been responsible for the Dunkirk evacuation), and comprised thousands of merchant vessels, warships and landing craft. Vessels that had sailed from ports all along the south coast of England, even as far round as the Thames estuary, now headed to a prearranged, mine-cleared rendezvous in mid-Channel, codenamed Piccadilly Circus. From here, the five forces destined for each of the landing beaches (Utah, Omaha, Gold, Juno, Sword) would set their respective courses and commence their run-in to the French coast.

The British 3rd Infantry Division was now steaming towards Sword Beach; the beach furthest east of the landing area. Spearheading its advance were A and B Squadrons of the 13th/18th Royal Hussars, with their amphibious DD Sherman

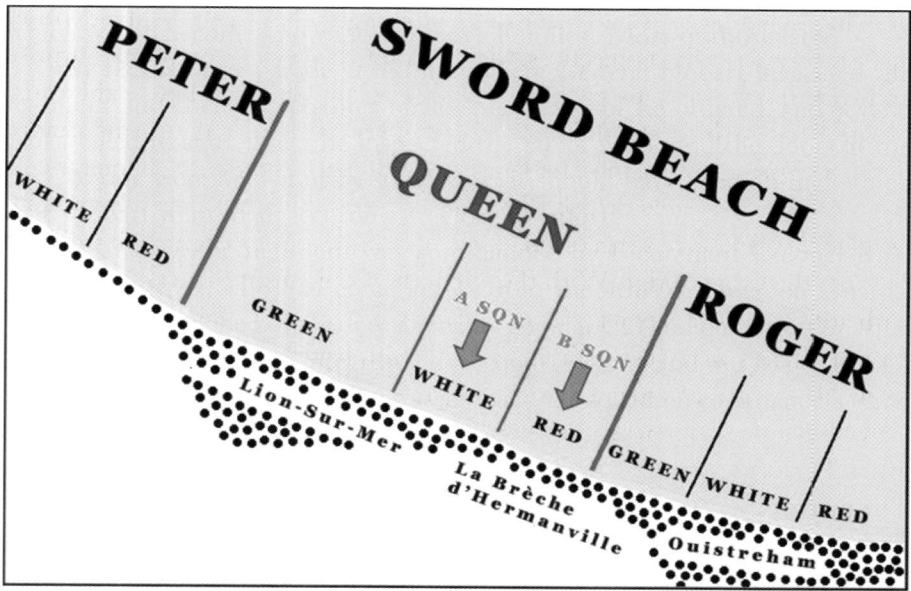

tanks. They were headed for the Queen sector of Sword; A Squadron headed for Queen White Beach, on the edge of the coastal town of Lion-sur-Mer, and B Squadron headed for Queen Red Beach at La Brèche d'Hermanville, on the edge of the port of Ouistreham. The plan was for the regiment's DD tanks to launch at 7,000 yards from the beach and commence their swim. Once ashore, they were to subdue any local opposition that was not already destroyed by the prior naval and air bombardments. They would support the assault of the 8th Infantry Brigade, who would land at H-Hour, set at 0725 hrs. The regiment's tanks were due to land at H minus 7.5 minutes, to give them time to soften up resistance opposing the infantry's landing. The regiment would be followed by mine-clearance Crab flail tanks, to begin work on clearing paths off the beach. A Squadron would support the 1st Battalion of the South Lancashire Regiment, B Squadron would support the 2nd Battalion of the East Yorkshire Regiment, and C Squadron would support the 1st Battalion of the Suffolk Regiment.

As the ships steamed through the hours of darkness, above their heads RAF bombers towed Horsa gliders destined for Normandy. These contained men of the Oxfordshire and Buckinghamshire Light Infantry, commanded by Major John Howard, and formed part of the 6th Airborne Division. Their task would be to seize and hold the bridges over the Caen Canal and Orne River by the village of Bénouville, a few miles from Sword Beach. The capture of these bridges would prevent German reinforcements being moved up from the east to threaten the landings. Shortly after midnight, once released by their towplanes, the pilots of the Glider Pilot Regiment executed a magnificent feat of flying, avoiding trees and marshland, bringing their aircraft to a halt within just a few yards of their objectives. Major Howard's men achieved total surprise and were quickly able to seize both bridges. Café Gondrée, beside the canal bridge, became the first building liberated in France. Realising the importance of these crossing points, the 21st Panzer Division did attempt to counterattack, but the only serviceable British PIAT anti-tank weapon (not a terribly accurate or reliable weapon) was successful in setting their lead tank alight, as it rumbled towards the Orne bridge. With the strength of the Allied force unknown and with anti-armour weapons in evidence, the German attack faltered, and Major Howard's men were successful in holding both bridges throughout the night, to enable the 3rd Infantry Division to get ashore on Sword.

A similar operation was also being carried out by the American 3rd Battalion, 506th Parachute Infantry Regiment at the western end of the landing beaches. The men of the 506th PIR were similarly tasked with seizing and holding two important canal bridges, east of Sainte-Mère-Église, to protect the landings taking place on Utah Beach.

In addition, during that night, the British 9th Parachute Battalion, commanded by Lieutenant Colonel Terence Otway, was charged with the destruction of the German gun battery at Merville, just east of the Caen Canal. These guns, housed in their concrete casements, posed a direct threat to the landings on Sword Beach, so a force of 600 airborne troops were sent to neutralise the gun battery. However, much of the force became scattered and only 150 men reached the planned assembly point, mostly without heavy weapons. Unable to wait any longer, Colonel Otway commenced his assault with his much-reduced assault force, which also would suffer approximately 50 per cent casualties. Without their sappers from the Royal Engineers and their explosives, the Paras gathered what plastic explosive they could muster from their Gammon bombs and did their best to destroy the guns. Once the Paras left the site to tackle their second objective of the night, a local village, the Germans did reoccupy the battery and managed to get two guns into action, although they were unable to bring down accurate fire onto Sword Beach to hamper the landings.

During the early hours of 6 June, in order to create confusion and draw German troops away from the actual drop zones to be used by the US 82nd and 101st Airborne Divisions in the west, and the British 6th Airborne Division in the east, Operation Titanic was implemented; this was part of the overall Operation Bodyguard deception plan. Titanic involved the dropping by parachute of hundreds of hessian dolls called 'Ruperts', filled with straw and sand in the shape of a human body. Each carried an explosive charge, which was used to simulate gunfire as each Rupert hit the ground. The RAF dropped these fake parachutists in four locations around Normandy, while at the same time inserting several special forces teams from the Special Air Service. The SAS teams played prerecorded soundtracks of men shouting, accompanied by rifle, machine-gun and mortar fire, to add some realism to each dummy parachute drop. They were also tasked with opening fire on any German troops who came to investigate, but would allow some to escape so that they might report the airborne assault.

To further confuse the German radars as the genuine fleet of Operation Neptune steamed across the Channel, the Royal Air Force carried out two further deception plans: Operations Taxable and Glimmer. Both of these operations involved RAF bombers dropping strips of foil, or 'chaff', which was codenamed 'Window'. The bombers would fly towards the French coast, slowly moving the curtain of foil closer and closer to the German defenders. As one group of bombers completed dropping their chaff, the next wave would take over, dropping their chaff in a relay, ever closer to France. Below, a token force of vessels moved across the Channel towing radar reflector balloons, with radio traffic designed to simulate that of a much larger invasion force. Operation Taxable was intended to make the Germans believe that their radars were showing a large force moving towards the Cap d'Antifer, north of Le Havre, and was carried out by the 617 'Dambusters' Squadron in its Lancasters. Operation Glimmer was headed straight towards the Pas de Calais – the area where the Germans most expected an invasion to take place. This was carried out by 218 Squadron using Stirling bombers. Perhaps predictably, Operation Glimmer provoked more of a response from the Germans, who sent up reconnaissance aircraft to investigate the 'fleet'.

The assault

As dawn approached, the aerial bombardment of Normandy also commenced, targeting the coastal gun batteries and other German strongholds. Over 1,000 bombers participated, dropping over 5,000 tons of bombs – the largest tonnage of bombs dropped during a single night of the war. As the fleet approached the Normandy coast, the heavy calibre naval guns from the accompanying warships also commenced firing and shelled the German positions overlooking the beaches and inland. These were joined by rocket-firing landing craft, so the 3&8s who were readying their tanks for launching had their eardrums assaulted by a cacophony of noise as huge naval shells and rockets split the air, passing right over their heads. Many decades later, when questioned about which memory was most prevalent in his mind from the assault on D-Day, Cosy Comfort stated: 'The terrific noise. You've never heard anything like it!'

Lance Corporal Patrick Hennessey of A Squadron remembered:

> On our left we heard a terrifying 'whooshing' noise and saw a veritable firework display, as the rocket firing ship went into action. Beyond her stood HMS *Warspite*, adding a loud contribution from her loud guns. We had been warned that it would be very noisy, but this still took us by surprise. As daylight slowly appeared, we could see ships of every description stretching away to the horizon on both sides of us and to the rear. It was a stupendous sight, which must remain in the memory of all who saw it. We marvelled that such a gigantic force could assemble over a period of five days and move across the English Channel, undetected.

Owing to the heavy sea conditions, the original plan for the 13th/18th to launch their swimming tanks from 7,000 yards out was reduced to 5,000 yards. Most of the other DD tank units on D-Day decided that conditions were too rough and that they would be taken directly onto the beach by their landing craft. Bill Mawson, destined for Queen Red sector of Sword Beach with B Squadron, recorded:

I still feel that our C.O. knew exactly what our feelings would be if we did not actually perform our much trained-for launch. The code-word 'Floater' was received with relief – it meant that we were back in our own little maritime element. It is incredible the trained confidence that we had in over thirty tons of metal and explosives held just above the water-surface by an apparatus of canvas and pram struts. It was not misplaced.

The two assault squadrons were planned to launch twenty tanks each. The LCT Mk III could accommodate five tanks, so four were assigned to each squadron, the flotilla being commanded by Lieutenant Commander Charles Creighton RNVR.

With smoke from the aerial and naval bombardments making landmarks harder to see in the coastal towns, both A and B Squadrons were assigned an LCP(N) (Landing Craft Personnel – Navigation). These craft would position themselves in front of each squadron commander's LCT and lead them towards the correct landing zone, by shining a light over the stern, until the beach was clearly visible. In belt-and-braces fashion, a midget submarine was also assigned to each of the two sabre squadrons to identify the correct launching position. Once launched, each landing craft's allotment of five tanks would swim towards shore in a line, one behind the other, then, once 1,000 yards offshore, would fan out to form a line parallel to the beach.

At 0615 hrs, the landing craft carrying A and B Squadrons dropped anchor and set about launching their tanks into the water. Unfortunately, Major Rugge-

A DD Sherman launches into the sea from its LCT Mk III. (*Courtesy of The Tank Museum, Bovington – Image 0200-A2*)

Price's tank (CO of B Squadron) tore its canvas screen when trying to launch from LCT 467. The major wished to jettison his tank, to enable the other four tanks to launch, but he was overruled and forced to land dry, behind the vessels carrying AVRE tanks. Meanwhile, LCT 465 successfully launched four of its tanks, before the ramp door was damaged, so the fifth tank was taken back to England.

Of the forty DD tanks of A and B Squadrons, thirty-four successfully entered the water. However, Corporal Sweetapple's tank of A Squadron was unable to drop and engage its propellers and capsized, but thankfully, the crew was rescued. Less fortunate was Captain Noel Denny's crew of A Squadron. The scheduling was so tight that the landing craft carrying the AVREs were not far behind and owing to its slow forward speed in the heavy swell, Captain Denny's tank was run down from behind by an LCT (AVRE), just 800 yards from the beach. Captain Denny was eventually plucked from the water but would be the only survivor. Sergeant Rattle's tank, also of A Squadron, would sink just 400 yards offshore, but the crew all survived.

DD tanks leave their LCTs and head for shore. (*Courtesy of Imperial War Museums – Image A 23110*)

Of the regiment's forty DD tanks, thirty-one would successfully touch down on Sword Beach, making the 13th/18th the most successful DD regiment on D-Day.[1] Be that as it may, such thoughts were far from the minds of the young Hussars approaching a hostile reception at the beach. The German defenders of the 736th Grenadier Regiment watched through their sights at what they believed to be infantry landing craft approaching the beach, and once the Hussars touched down onto the sand and dropped their canvas screens, they were very surprised to find themselves facing a row of armour. Soon all weapons were pointed at the regiment's tanks. Cosy Comfort said:

Yes, I'm sure they were surprised, but trust me, they rallied quickly! Spandaus. Mortars. Rounds hitting the hull like a kettle drum. However, I don't remember being overcome with fear, but instead was completely engrossed in executing my duties properly, so that I didn't let the rest of the crew down.

Regimental Adjutant, Captain Julius Neave, summarised the regiment's initial task as follows: 'To make the beach habitable for the infantry, subdue all pill boxes, knock out machine gun posts and suppress the opposition.'

Bill Hammond, a veteran of the BEF and Dunkirk, commanded a DD tank in 2nd Troop, A Squadron. Bill was known as 'Happy' Hammond.

Sergeant Jerry Bell's DD tank of 1st Troop, A Squadron, engages German positions on the promenade at Lion-sur-Mer. (*Artwork by Andrew May*)

Bill's co-driver, Trooper Joe 'Jock' Collins, remembered the rattle of the tracks hitting the sand as they touched down. Sat alongside driver Lenny Mills, Jock heard the metal struts of the canvas screen clatter down and the turret crew behind commence firing at German positions on the seafront. After about five minutes, water from the rapidly incoming tide started to come through the hatches and at the same time, the tank's engine spluttered to a halt. Realising that his part of the invasion was over and now getting rather wet, Jock called to Lenny to climb out and join him behind the turret of the tank. Meanwhile, the turret crew continued to keep the gun in action for as long as possible, but the 75mm gun

Bill 'Happy' Hammond.

began recoiling into the rising water. Each tank had been provided with a self-inflating dinghy, but when Jock attempted to inflate theirs, he discovered that the ripcord had broken off (or had been shot off). As the tank's gun was now under water, the rest of the crew joined Jock and Lenny at the rear of the turret. Spying a dinghy sitting on the roof of an abandoned tank 15 yards away, Happy Hammond decided to swim for it and try to secure that dinghy to get them ashore, but as he was halfway to the other tank, a wave crashed into the turret and carried off the dinghy with it. Hammond climbed onto the other tank and called for the rest of the crew to swim over and join him. Jock dived in, and did the backstroke until Hammond was able to grab his wrists and haul him aboard. Then the gunner, Roy Cadogan, was next to swim across, but Lenny Mills had vanished; it later transpired that he'd been wounded, had floated off and had been fished out of the water by a landing craft. Now only the loader/operator, Harry Hughes, remained, up to his knees in water on the back of their tank. Despite being a keen swimmer back in the UK, he ignored the encouragement of his crewmates and refused to leave their tank and swim across. 'I won't make it!' he shouted. Hughes obstinately refused to move. Jock turned to Hammond and said, 'Bill, it's now "make your mind up" time.' Since they clearly couldn't reach Hughes against the tide wearing full battledress, Hammond said, 'You're right Jock – let's go.' Jock Collins remembered doing the backstroke towards the shore and as he was facing the oncoming waves, having to take a deep breath as each one crashed over him. Once ashore, they began removing some of their soaked clothing. A landing craft carrying commandos came ashore, and Jock was tossed a dry denim suit and a pair of plimsolls, which he quickly changed into. The three remaining members of Bill's crew later managed to get a lift from one of the regiment's tanks, away from the beach and into Hermanville-sur-Mer.

Lenny Mills returned to England and was convalescing in Dagenham. It is unclear how Harry Hughes met his end, but he was not to survive D-Day; he now rests in the Commonwealth War Graves cemetery at Hermanville-sur-Mer.

Having successfully reached the beach, the commander of A Squadron, Major Derek Wormald, recorded:

> I still remember very clearly the 'brewing-up' of the leading AVRE Churchill tank as it drove down the ramp of an LCT, which beached a few yards to my left front. The turret and the contents thereof spun into the air after a violent explosion, presumably caused by a penetrating direct hit by an anti-tank shell, which detonated the explosive charges which the AVRE was carrying for the purpose of destroying concrete placements. I immediately got my gunner to engage a bunker from which I thought that the shot had been fired. His first round hit the target and the gun became silent.

As the assaulting infantry of the South Lancashire Regiment began to land upon Queen White from their LCAs (Landing Craft Assault) behind A Squadron, their commanding officer, Lieutenant Colonel Richard Burbury, stepped onto the sand carrying a flag made for him by his sister in the battalion colours. He had intended to use the flag as a rallying point, but as he made his way up the beach, encouraging his men on, he found himself in German sights and was shot in the chest, command of the battalion now changing hands to Major Jack Stone.

Further to the east at La Brèche d'Hermanville, Lieutenant Aldam's tank of 2nd Troop, B Squadron touched down on the sand. His loader/operator Bill Mawson's experiences initially mirrored those of Jock Collins, and after a short spell of firing on German positions, their tank was also soon overcome by the fast, incoming tide. Luckily, their dinghy was in good working order, and they watched with joy as it slowly swelled up and they climbed aboard in rather undignified haste, while mortar rounds and shells landed in the water around them. Bill, as a non-swimmer, was particularly relieved to see the dinghy inflate.

In front of them now were the tops of largely submerged beach defences, armed with Teller mines; these were intended to block landing craft, or to funnel them into kill zones covered by German weapons. Bill Mawson and the crew frantically used their helmets as paddles and balers, in an attempt to avoid being driven straight into the mines by the advancing waves. Royal Engineer assault teams were now beginning to try to disarm and clear the beach obstacles. Bill remembered:

On and around the obstacles were crowds of poor devils drowning, as they tried to neutralise the booby traps; the sea being so rough that clinging to the obstacles, they just went under the rising water, or an approaching craft. Curiously, the rising tide saved us as it carried our dinghy right over the detonators and onto the beach beyond.

Once on the beach, Lieutenant Aldam's crew moved into the sand dunes. When they had organised themselves a little, they spied a knocked-out landing craft aground at the water's edge, with a figure lying beside it on the sand. Upon inspection, this proved to be a naval rating, who was missing a leg, but still conscious. Having heeded their troop commander's advice about splitting the first aid box amongst them, they had plenty of morphine syringes and quickly injected the wounded sailor. Bill scavenged along the beach and located a stretcher, and they were then able, with some difficulty in the soft sand, to carry the injured man to a place where he could receive proper medical attention. The young sailor turned out to be 19-year-old Ordinary Seaman Peter Hutchins – a signaller on board the landing craft. His vessel had suffered three hits from a German 88mm gun, killing several of the crew and wounding him. Peter had just about summoned up the strength to shuffle himself to the edge of the craft, inflate his lifebelt and drop into the water. He lost his leg, but was to survive, thanks to the prompt action taken by Bill Mawson and crew.[2]

Once the casualty had been handed over, the men set about making themselves as comfortable as they could in the dunes, by digging a trench and roofing it with wading screens being discarded on the beach by arriving Bren Gun Carriers. Now into the afternoon of D-Day, as things were calming down in terms of enemy fire, Bill decided to walk out towards the receding tide and scavenge what he could from the abandoned 3&8 tanks. Tins of self-heating soup were popular items in the ration packs; a lit cigarette would be put to the fuse and bingo, instant hot soup!

Having obtained some items of food, Bill soberly passed the dead body of a fellow B Squadron member, 20-year-old Trooper Cecil Schofield from Selby in Yorkshire. (Cecil is remembered on the Bayeux Memorial.)

Bill Mawson and the rest of his crew lived in their makeshift home in the dunes until they were collected by one of the lorries from the regiment's support echelon, with a familiar face at the wheel. (A small party of lorries and light load carriers arrived on D-Day, commanded by Major John Cordy-Simpson. A second party of soft-skinned vehicles, under Captain Hannah, would not arrive in Normandy until D+10 Days.)

Also approaching the Queen Red sector at La Brèche d'Hermanville with B Squadron was the tank of Lance Sergeant Johnny Hardie of 2nd Troop.

Originally of Scottish stock, but brought up in Haslingden in Lancashire, Johnny Hardie was also another of the regiment's non-swimmers. He had served briefly with the 15th/19th The King's Royal Hussars[3] but transferred to the 13th/18th in time to join them in France with the BEF and had returned through Dunkirk.

As Hardie's tank was completing its swim to the beach, the tanks either side of it were knocked out by anti-tank weapons. Despite the obvious threat to his vehicle, he was able to direct his driver around the burning vehicles up onto the beach, and then steadfastly set about engaging the German positions to his front. Once

Lance Sergeant Johnny Hardie.

a gap had been cleared and the tanks could leave the beach, Johnny Hardie left the relative protection of his vehicle, and with complete disregard for his own safety, on foot started to direct other B Squadron tanks off the beach. At this stage in the proceedings, the beach was still a very unhealthy environment, as the Germans continued to bring down mortar fire onto it and snipers were still active in the beachfront chalets. Despite his gallant efforts to get the squadron's tanks off the beach and into battle inland, while trying to move inland himself, Johnny Hardie's own tank was to drive over a mine. In the book *Remembering D-Day*, Trooper 'Slim' Wileman recorded:

> As we progressed up the beach, we saw that one of our tanks had gone over a mine and been blown onto its side. I recognised it at once as Sergeant Johnny Hardie's tank and we feared the worst. We approached it, expecting to find the five-man crew dead inside. To our amazement, we discovered Johnny and his crew completely unharmed, sitting on empty ammunition cases in the lee of the tank, calmly drinking tea. They offered us some of the brew and we were about to join them when the beach marshal appeared and told us in real soldier's language what to do with our mugs of tea. When I asked Johnny why he and his men had stopped for tea in the middle of battle he shrugged, 'We're not infantry. We're not equipped to fight. What else could we do?' Rather sensible when you think of it!

However, not to make light of Lance Sergeant Hardie's contribution on D-Day, for his actions on 6 June, he was awarded the Military Medal for gallantry. In fact, the NCOs of the regiment were to receive many gallantry awards for their work on Sword Beach and two other recipients of the MM were Corporal Bob Charmbury (of tinned apricots fame) and Sergeant Jerry Bell, both of A Squadron.

For all the propaganda, Hitler's mighty Atlantic Wall lacked any real defensive depth and the Allied forces had swept through it in short order. Following Hitler's edict concerning the deployment of the Panzer reserves, vital hours were lost on 6 June as the Führer slept and no one dared wake him. This prevented the Panzer divisions moving towards the Normandy coast and driving the Allies back into the sea, as Rommel had planned. The Luftwaffe was also so depleted in the area that only two lonely Focke-Wulf 190s (FW109) were to take to the skies over the invasion beaches on D-Day from Jagdgeschwader 26 (JG26). They did manage to strafe Sword Beach and shot down one B-24 Liberator but could do little to stem the tide of Overlord. In contrast, the Allies had amassed fifty-four squadrons of fighters for beach cover, fifteen squadrons to protect the fleet, thirty-three squadrons to escort the thirty-six bomber squadrons and a further seven squadrons of Mustangs and Spitfires for fire control. They were an extremely brave pair of German pilots to take to the skies at all.

Only on Omaha Beach did it appear that the Overlord assault might falter. Certainly, the heaviest casualties of the assault had occurred on Omaha, as the landing infantry lacked the armoured support that had been so much in evidence on Sword. The American 741st Tank Battalion took the decision to launch their DD Shermans, but with the heavy swell found themselves being swept further east of their designated landing area, so were forced to alter their course to starboard. This alteration placed their floatation screens side-on to the crashing waves and most were ultimately capsized, with the loss of many crews, who sadly followed their vehicles to a watery grave. Of the twenty-nine tanks launched by the 741st, only two would make it ashore.

Next objectives

Back on Sword, A Squadron had successfully reached the beach with sixteen tanks. Unfortunately, following losses to enemy fire and with other tanks abandoned to the incoming tide, Major Wormald was left with just six tanks with which to support the infantry of the South Lancashire Regiment.

A key objective within Lion-sur-Mer was a strongpoint codenamed 'Trout', known as 'WN21' to the Germans, WN referring to Widerstandsnest (nest of resistance). Despite the naval and air bombardment of the coast, coupled with the Hussars' more local attempts to silence the German defenders, the assault infantry were not to have an easy time of it. Upon approaching Trout, infantry platoon commander Lieutenant Jones remembered:

> With two men from my platoon I then reconnoitred cautiously towards the rear of the central block of buildings in Lion. A shot rang out and the rifleman on my right fell, shot directly between the eyes. The bullet shattered the back of his skull and showered me with blood and fragments of brain and bone. A second shot killed the rifleman to my left. I was fortunate to retire unscathed.[4]

By 0930 hrs on D-Day, the 1st Battalion South Lancashire Regiment, supported by A Squadron's tanks, had successfully moved inland and captured Hermanville-sur-Mer and had begun a mopping-up operation in Lion-sur-Mer.

Overlooking Queen Red was strongpoint 'Cod' (WN20), which was positively bristling with anti-tank weapons, mortars and machine guns. The defenders at Cod would be responsible for many casualties among the East Yorkshire Regiment but were eventually silenced by 1000 hrs on D-Day.

Brigadier, the Lord Lovat, whom we previously met commanding 4 Commando on the Dieppe raid, had landed with his Commandos of the 1st Special Service Brigade at La Brèche d'Hermanville, behind the DD tanks of B Squadron. The Commandos were famously piped ashore by Lovat's piper, Bill Millin, to the tune of 'Hielan Laddie' on his bagpipes.

Upon reaching the lateral road along the coast, Lieutenant Douglas Coker's troop from B Squadron turned left and found themselves accompanying Lord Lovat's Commandos as they fought their way through Ouistreham; the tanks could not be recalled and supported the Commandos all the way into Bénouville. Piper Millin then strode towards the bridges alongside the brigadier, playing 'Lochanside' on his pipes, much to the amusement and huge relief of the Airborne troops in the area. After a long night, they had finally been relieved, and the Commandos and B Squadron tanks were warmly received. Lieutenant Coker's troop was to lose two tanks to 88mm guns south of Bénouville,[5] and the remaining tanks would not rally with the rest of the regiment back in Hermanville until evening.

The remainder of B Squadron supported the East York's infantry to attack and capture a command post of the German 736th Regiment, codenamed 'Sole' (WN14), to the south-west of Ouistreham. Under enemy observation during their approach, the infantry and tanks were mortared and shelled, making the going slow. Unable to locate their attached Naval Artillery Observation Officer, no naval bombardment could be brought down on the stronghold, but eventually, 76th (Highland) Field Regiment, Royal Artillery, was able to shell the target

Lance Sergeant Joseph Gillibrand's B Squadron tank moves into Ouistreham with men of 4 Commando. (*Courtesy of the Imperial War Museums – Image MH 2011*)

area. When C Company of the East Yorks was finally able to overcome the defenders at 1545 hrs, forty prisoners were taken at Sole.

B Squadron and the East Yorks then moved on to their next objective of 'Daimler' or 'WN12', which was a heavy gun emplacement south of Ouistreham. Daimler consisted of four gun pits, plus adjoining bunkers. As well as a minefield to overcome, Daimler boasted four 155mm SFH 414 French howitzers, two Flak 30 anti-aircraft guns, one mortar and six machine guns. The commanding officer of the infantry, Lieutenant Colonel Hutchinson, moved along a sunken lane with other officers in order to perform a reconnaissance of the objective. This prompted a salvo of enemy fire upon the group and the colonel was hit in the arm. The 76th Field Regiment was once again able to oblige and shelled the gun battery, and supported by B Squadron tanks, A and C infantry companies put in their attack and were able to overrun Daimler by 2000 hrs, with little loss to themselves. They were to capture seventy prisoners of war from Daimler. Many weapons were seized from the site, and it was then discovered that the Germans had been handsomely supplied with wine and Champagne, which the troops were happy to liberate!

C Squadron, having landed directly onto Queen White Beach at H + 45 minutes with Regimental HQ (RHQ), then moved inland to support the

Sergeant Stanley Diver's 3rd Troop, C Squadron tank (Tank 75) passes a DUKW amphibious vehicle in Hermanville-sur-Mer. (*Courtesy of Imperial War Museums – Image B 5025*)

infantry of the 1st Battalion of the Suffolk Regiment. Before this, owing to the terrific congestion on the beach, they were unable to move off for some forty-five minutes, and in the process of landing, were to lose ten of their precious Porpoise trailers containing extra ammunition; only five remained.

At Colleville-sur-Orne (now Colleville-Montgomery) stood the first objective of D-Day for the 1st Suffolks and C Squadron 13th/18th. This was a gun battery codenamed 'Morris' (WN16), 800 yards to the north of the headquarters of 736th Regiment, which would be their second objective of the day. The gun battery consisted of four horse-drawn Czech FH 14/19 100mm howitzers in casements. B Company of the Suffolks were poised to assault the position and although they hadn't been in the first wave of infantry to land on Sword, the adrenaline was now coursing through the men's bodies in anticipation of what was about to happen. But, as the Pioneer platoon moved up to place their Bangalore torpedoes under the wire, to blast their way into the battery, a white flag appeared. Then, to everyone's astonishment, the entire garrison surrendered, and sixty-seven soldiers filed out with their hands raised; these proved to be Polish soldiers, serving in the Wehrmacht. It appeared that the naval bombardment that they had already received had produced such a devastating psychological effect that they no longer had any stomach for a bitter fight.

The reader may have noticed that after the fish-related codenames, such as Cod and Sole, as the Hussars pressed inland, the codenames of their objectives were all British car manufacturers. With Daimler and Morris already under British control, the next objective for C Squadron was 'Hillman' (WN17), which would prove to be a very different proposition than was the case at Morris.

Hillman was the command headquarters of Oberst Ludwig Krug and his 736th Grenadier Regiment. It covered an area of approximately 600 x 400 yards and was surrounded by two heavy barbed wire fences and was garrisoned by 150 soldiers. Defences were bolstered by a dense minefield containing both anti-personnel and anti-tank mines. The Hillman complex was constructed of deep, underground concrete bunkers and commanded a virtually uninterrupted view of the approaches from the coast. It had been planned that Hillman would be bombed from the air, but low cloud cover over the target area had caused this bombing run to be aborted, leaving Hillman's garrison unscathed.

The first attack made by the Suffolks had little impact and soon faltered; although able to breach the wire with Bangalore torpedoes, the infantry came under heavy machine-gun and rifle fire, were taking casualties and were unable to advance. C Squadron's tanks were tasked with providing close support for the infantry and a Sherman Firefly tried firing at the armoured steel cupola atop one of the bunkers, which had been causing much trouble. However, their armour-piercing rounds from Sherman Firefly's 17-pounder gun simply ricocheted off! It was clear that they would need to be able to bypass the fences and minefield in order to have any hope of seizing the complex. Attached Royal Engineers from 246 Field Company under Lieutenant Arthur Heal were next ordered to try to enter the wire and clear a path through the minefield, wide enough to enable C Squadron's tanks to enter the position. Heal crawled forward with Lance Corporal Boulton and examined the minefield on his belly. He had familiarised himself with all manner of mines that he might encounter, but when he located one and unearthed it, he discovered that it was one he did not recognise. Upon further inspection, he discovered writing in English on the casing, and it proved to be an obsolete British Mark III mine, probably obtained by the Germans at Dunkirk. Heal decided that Crab flail tanks could accomplish the task faster, so two were ordered to advance to Hillman. However, upon learning that it would take an hour for them to arrive, Heal suggested that he could perform the task faster using gelignite charges to create a path 5 yards wide.[6] This was agreed with the leading troop commander from C Squadron. As this was taking place, 4th Troop of C Squadron, under Lieutenant Smith, were in open country to the east of Hillman. They came under fire from German anti-tank guns and had two tanks knocked out but were at least able to reply by destroying one enemy gun, as its crew hurriedly prepared to make it ready. In his C Squadron Diary, Major Cotter recorded that several of the squadron's men were wounded on the 6th (Corporals Collins, Murphy and Pickles, plus Troopers Owens, Shreeves, Turner and Ward); 23-year-old Trooper John Owens of Blackpool would sadly die of his wounds on 10 June.

Once the path had been cleared through the minefield, the commanding officer of the Suffolks, Lieutenant Colonel Dick Goodwin, called for a five-minute artillery barrage and as this lifted, the tanks of C Squadron began to cross the cleared minefield, closely followed by the infantry. The leading tank stopped as a corpse obstructed its path but was told in no uncertain terms to get on with it! It is gruesome in the extreme to contemplate what the weight of a Sherman tank would do to the poor man's remains, but there was a job to be done. A Company of the Suffolks worked their way forward, trying to make best use of the tanks, any dead ground and shell holes. Any movement drew fire from the Germans, and they were taking casualties, but Corporal Lawson and Private 'Tich' Hunter managed to get within 20 yards of the steel cupola. Tich Hunter then took it upon himself to advance on the cupola, firing from the hip with his Bren gun, and emptied his magazine at the German position. This stemmed any fire coming from the cupola, allowing other members of A Company to move up. Tich jumped down into the German trench, when he heard a shout of warning from Corporal Lawson, as he had seen a German rifle aimed at Tich. A round was fired, which grazed the top of Tich's head; if he'd been a taller man, he would have been dead! Lawson shot the German. The infantry began dropping grenades down ventilation shafts and then the occupants of the bunkers began to emerge with their hands raised. All firing ceased around 2000 hrs and the mopping-up process began, with around fifty prisoners being taken. During this successful assault, the only casualty suffered by C Squadron was the squadron commander's tank, which fell into a German officers' latrine and broke a track. Major Cotter was not amused! Although his war was over, Private Tich Hunter was recommended for a Military Medal for his charging of the enemy position at Hillman, but upon subsequent inspection of the facts, this was upgraded to a Distinguished Conduct Medal.

C Squadron then withdrew to a harbour area near Colleville-sur-Orne and were resupplied by the regiment's support echelon vehicles. That evening, the sky grew dark with 250 Douglas C-47s towing Horsa gliders, as the British 6th Airlanding Brigade appeared overhead, headed east of the Orne River. These were followed by Stirling bombers, dropping weapons, ammunition, food and medical supplies, all under different coloured parachutes. This display of Allied air power did much to buoy the spirits of the British assault troops witnessing it from the ground, whilst hopefully having the exact opposite effect on the German units in the area. Meanwhile, the Suffolks dug in around Hillman, in anticipation of an expected counterattack from the 21st Panzer Division – an attack that thankfully never materialised.

The following morning at 0645 hrs, the commander of the 736th Grenadier Regiment, Oberst Ludwig Krug, emerged from the bunker complex at Hillman, followed by his batman carrying his suitcases. Impeccably dressed with polished boots, he led out the remainder of the garrison of Hillman, who had remained hidden underground throughout the night.

Counting the cost

The 13th/18th regrouped south of Hermanville and began to count the cost to the regiment on D-Day. The adjutant, Captain Julius Neave, recorded thirty-two vehicle casualties; A Squadron losing fourteen tanks, B Squadron losing ten, C Squadron losing seven and RHQ losing one: almost 50 per cent of the regiment's tanks. Many crews had become 'unhorsed' on the beach and had been forced to abandon their vehicles to the sea. Captain Denny, Lieutenants Jennison, Harold, Anderson and Burgess, plus seventy-eight other ranks were missing. Initial counts identified twelve wounded and twelve killed, but once everyone was accounted for, the number of wounded grew and the death toll on D-Day would rise to nineteen.

The Roll of Honour for 6 June reads: Sergeant Charles Norris, Lance Sergeant Joseph Gillibrand, Corporal Ernest Booker, Corporal Stanley Singleton, Lance Corporal Lloyd Kershaw, Lance Corporal John Robinson, Trooper John Atkinson, Trooper William Fullbrook, Trooper Frederick Gascoigne, Trooper John Green, Trooper Frederick Hockley, Trooper Harry Hughes, Trooper Charles Lovell, Trooper Edward Miller, Trooper Robert Pickard, Trooper Cecil Schofield, Trooper Harold Smith, Trooper Matthew Telford, Trooper Norman Whittaker.

May they all rest in peace.

Chapter 7

Battle for Normandy

God wills that these good fellows must leave us so soon.

Early days

As more 'unhorsed' crews arrived in Hermanville-sur-Mer, some reassignment was necessary and Corporal Bill Hammond was given a new loader/operator in Trooper Charlie Tank, and with Jock Collins moving over into the driver's seat, received a new co-driver in the form of one Trooper Henry 'Dutch' Hollands. Henry would have been pleased to join his friend Roy Cadogan in Hammond's crew, as before Overlord, Henry had taken his little sister Barbara on leave with him to visit Roy's family. Eventually, 265 Forward Delivery Squadron arrived with replacement tanks for the regiment and soon Bill Hammond and crew were back into action.

After his spell in the sand dunes of Sword Beach, Bill Mawson remembered his reunion with the regiment in Hermanville-sur-Mer. 'Our C.O. was to be seen dressed in his only remaining clothes, a civilian white jumper with grey trousers. He was unfeignedly glad to see us; come to that, we were relieved to see HIM. Home again!'

The following day, most of the regiment moved east of Hermanville-sur-Mer, following sketchy reports of Tiger tanks moving up astride the Orne River towards Bénouville and Panzer Grenadiers in the area. C Squadron took up positions to the north-west of the bridges to cover the approaches. B Squadron and Regimental HQ moved up to strengthen the position to the south-east of St Aubin d'Arquenay. However, none of these German forces subsequently materialised, after a flurry of activity to prepare to meet this apparent threat.

By the evening, A Squadron remained in Hermanville-sur-Mer, consolidating that position. B and C Squadrons were in position to cover the bridges, with RHQ stationed to the west of Bénouville. The regiment did receive a little trouble from snipers – remnants from the Riva-Bella coastal battery near Ouistreham (WN08). They managed to capture two and had them call out in German to encourage the others to surrender, but to no avail. Another sniper would be captured during the night, but at the end of 7 June, the commanding officer,

DD Shermans of B Squadron move through St Aubin d'Arquenay. (*Courtesy of The Tank Museum, Bovington – Image 0179-F6*)

Lieutenant Colonel Dick Harrap, was pleased to record in his diary that they had received no losses this day, in terms of vehicles or personnel.

On 8 June, reports were received of self-propelled guns and infantry of the 21st Panzer Division advancing northwards, east of the Orne River. However, the only minor engagement to take place concerned Recce Troop with three enemy snipers south of Ranville, all three of whom were killed. The following day, C Squadron captured two more Germans from the Riva-Bella battery who had been lurking in the bushes. A Squadron was finally released from Hermanville-sur-Mer and the regiment was once again complete in the Bénouville area.

As 10 June dawned, RHQ's early-morning wake-up call came in the form of a stick of bombs dropped in their area by the Luftwaffe, who were beginning to fly a few sorties over Normandy. No damage was done, but a wounded airman was brought in from a crashed Junkers 88 who was able to supply useful information about the enemy's bomber bases. Next, the regiment received a salvo of enemy mortar rounds (known as a 'Stonk'), which wounded two medical orderlies, and killed a man in A Squadron. While sitting beside their tank drinking tea, Major Wormald's gunner, Trooper Frank Surey, was hit in the temple by

Two crewmembers of C Squadron's 2nd Troop Sherman *Cameo* rest as others write letters home. (*Courtesy of Imperial War Museums – Image B 5425*)

a mortar fragment and was killed. This prompted the crew to dig a pit about 2 feet deep under the tank in which to live by day and sleep in comparative comfort at night, with overhead cover provided by the tank. However, the major's signaller, Sergeant Charles Mason, elected to make his nest in the turret of the tank, where he would sleep for the remainder of the war on 'listening watch'.

One German weapon that was frequently aimed in the Hussars' direction was the Nebelwerfer (literally, 'fog thrower'). This was a six-barrelled mortar, which had a range of about 5 miles. Tanks would often kick up a lot of dust through the warm, summer months, which would draw the attention of the Nebelwerfer crews. Its rocket projectiles would screech towards their intended target, with a terrifying, howling noise, giving it the nickname of the 'Moaning Minnie'. They were to make the 3&8s' lives most uncomfortable at times and were responsible for many dead and wounded.

Battle for Normandy 69

(*Courtesy of the Imperial War Museums – Image NA 15590*)

Saturday, 10 June turned out to be a very wet day and at 1230 hrs, the commanding officer set off in the rain to attend an Orders Group (O Group) and reconnaissance for a B Squadron operation that afternoon.

On the east side of the Orne River, in an area held by the British 6th Airborne Division, B Squadron formed up with one section of Recce Troop to support the 7th and 13th Airborne Battalions.[1] Moving off at 1600 to the east of Ranville, the Paras and tanks advanced across the open terrain; their primary objective was to link up with 3 Parachute Brigade, who were cut off from the remainder of the airborne division. In their path were three known positions occupied by soldiers of the German 858th Grenadier Regiment, part of the 346th Infantry Division, who were deployed in the vicinity of Bréville. The Stuart tanks of Recce Troop were led by Lieutenant Tresham Hardy, MM, followed by B Squadron's Shermans. Moving past Bréville Woods to the north, in an elevated position on their left flank, the tanks were now in the sights of well-concealed German anti-tank guns up in the treeline. Before anyone knew what was happening, Lieutenant Hardy's tank was hit and it burst into flames; he was killed instantly. Before the Hussars were able to identify the guns' positions and return fire, the Germans had got off several more accurate shots.

The gunner in Corporal Hind's tank from 1st Troop, B Squadron was Trooper Gil Masters, who remembered how their tank was struck by one round, and before they could bail out, was hit by a second shot and caught fire (known as 'brewing up'). Corporal Hind and Trooper Masters managed to bail out, but the loader/operator, Trooper Davies, was seriously burned on one arm and both the driver and co-driver, Troopers Moyse and Pell, were both wounded and badly burned. This was Gil's first encounter with anti-tank guns and both he and his commander took cover in the long grass, until it was safe to emerge.

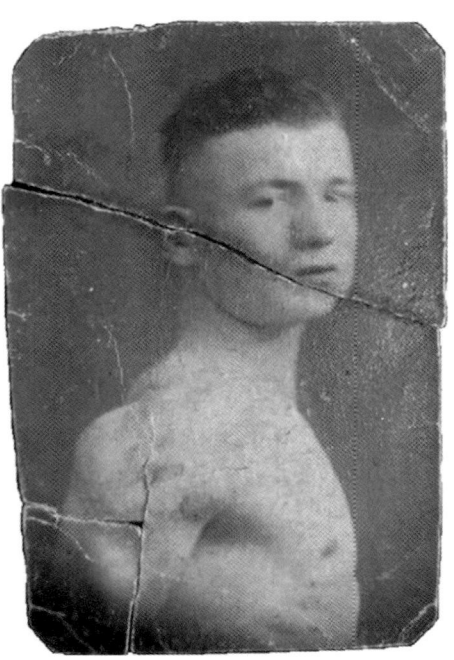

The tatty photo of John Cunliffe, carried in his brother Len's wallet.

B Squadron suffered several casualties, including Lieutenant Coker, and had two men killed.

Trooper John Cunliffe was the driver of one of B Squadron's Shermans. Back home in Widnes, both he and his brother Len were best friends and good amateur boxers. John's driver's compartment took a direct hit, such that there were no remains to be recovered. With no grave, John is remembered on the Bayeux Memorial. Len would carry John's photo in his wallet his entire life, as a constant reminder of the dear brother and best friend that he lost.[2]

Lieutenant Hardy, MM, and seven others from Recce Troop lost their lives. One of those killed was Trooper Fred Sayce, who had joined the ranks of his Local Defence Volunteers back in his hometown of Shrewsbury, before joining the 3&8s. When their Stuart tank was struck, both Fred and his tank commander, Sergeant Reginald Blake, managed to escape the burning vehicle and were 30 yards from the vehicle on foot when a shell exploded behind them, killing them both instantly. Fred was just 20 years old, and his family received a letter of condolence from HQ Squadron's commander, Major John Cordy-Simpson.

A Squadron's commander, Major Wormald, had listened to the day's events over the radio and recorded in his Squadron Diary: 'It seemed to me that this was another case of an advance over open ground with an open flank, which might have been covered by smoke!'

Overall, the operation was to achieve its objective by 1800 hrs and the 3rd Parachute Brigade was reunited with its division; the enemy was estimated to have taken a hundred casualties, with a similar number being taken prisoner. However, the ambush from Bréville Woods had knocked out two Stuart tanks of Recce Troop and four Shermans of B Squadron. Cosy Comfort, who'd been there with B Squadron, said of this action: 'It was like a fairground duck shoot! The tanks went up in flames, one after the other.'

Trooper Fred Sayce.

By contrast, the next day was a quiet one and although the regiment's tanks were dispersed to watch over a number of likely approaches by German forces, no enemy advance was sighted.

Trooper Frederick Sayce and Lieutenant Tresham Hardy, MM, now lie side by side in the Commonwealth War Graves Commission cemetery at Hermanville-sur-Mer.

1st Troop of C Squadron was to spend the day bodyguarding General Montgomery at his headquarters at Creully.

On 12 June, the whole regiment moved east of the Orne River and came under the command of 6th Airborne Division. A Squadron were ordered to prepare for an operation supporting airborne troops for an assault on Bréville the following day. Major Wormald first went to liaise with the 12th Parachute Battalion, who were due to carry out the attack and to carry out a general reconnaissance of the area. He next paid a visit to a Commando company, who had set up their headquarters in a local château. This was commanded by a distinguished Commando officer, Major Peter Young (who was awarded the Distinguished Service Order, a Military Cross and two bars to his MC; in short, he was awarded the Military Cross for gallantry on three separate occasions during the war). Major Young gave his appraisal of the enemy disposition and explained his own positions over a glass of brandy! This was interrupted by the sound of approaching Sherman tanks form the direction of Ranville and Major Wormald was soon informed that Major General Richard 'Windy' Gale, commanding 6th Airborne Division, had decided that the attack should be launched that evening, since he believed that Bréville represented a dangerous gap in the perimeter of his bridgehead.

Upon meeting the general at the assembly point at 2138 hrs, he quickly explained his plan in about two minutes to Captain Peter Lyon, Major Wormald's second-in-command of A Squadron (the same Captain Lyon whom we last met as the Widow Twankey in *Trooper Aladdin*). The general then told them to 'Get on with it!' as he wanted firing to commence at 2145 hrs. Therefore, four troops and Squadron HQ raced to an orchard, to the north of Bréville, where they planned to soften up the defences and shoot the Paras into the village. Major Wormald jumped up onto the leading tank and directed each troop to their respective firing positions, before rejoining his own vehicle. All were in position and firing commenced, as planned, at 2145, each tank pouring the maximum weight of fire it could into the objective. The Shermans in the squadron each boasted two Browning machine guns, plus the 75mm main armament (or the 17-pounder gun, in the case of each troop's Sherman Firefly). This all amounted to no less than forty machine guns and twenty 75mm/17-pounder guns, all firing into the village simultaneously, providing quite a firework display for the Paras to witness. Their main armaments were firing high-explosive 'impact fused' shells, which detonated on the slightest contact with any trees and undergrowth, producing an airburst that was quite lethal to any enemy infantry sheltering in slit trenches below, or anti-tank gun crews, unless they'd had the foresight to build substantial overhead cover. This concentration of fire lasted an entire fifteen minutes, before the 12th Paras launched their assault on the village. 4th Troop, under Lieutenant Garlick, were then tasked with supporting a company of Paras to destroy a known strongpoint in the village, which they quickly accomplished. In the process, Lieutenant Garlick's tank was struck by a round from a 75mm anti-tank gun, which passed straight through the tank's mantlet and lodged in the turret without detonating. It destroyed the radio set, but thankfully did not cause any casualties. A very lucky escape!

The squadron's tanks were then called upon to support the Paras in clearing some woods east of Bréville. In the process, Sergeant Rodwell's tank fired on and destroyed a 75mm anti-tank gun. Once the engagement had ended, a further five 75mm anti-tank guns would be captured intact. From a squadron commander's point of view, this was virtually a textbook assault, much as they had rehearsed back in England. The 3&8s suffered no casualties, but unfortunately casualties had been high amongst the airborne troops; many had been wounded once the area started to receive increasingly heavy enemy artillery and mortar fire. A Squadron withdrew back to the regimental harbour near Ranville just before 0300 hrs, except for 4th Troop, who would spend the night with the 12th Parachute Battalion. The strength of German forces around Bréville had not been known in detail, but when the bodies of the German soldiers were collected, there were found to be around a hundred left dead in the area.

While this was all taking place, B Squadron had been supporting the infantry of the Black Watch on an assault of the Château Saint-Côme, south of Bréville, which Colonel Dick Harrap had felt was a most unsuitable task for his tanks and would be proved right, as three Shermans would be knocked out during the assault. Licking their wounds, B Squadron also rallied back with the regiment at Ranville.

During their first week in Normandy, the regiment had already lost several tanks to German anti-tank guns. The Wehrmacht entered the war with their gun crews, Panzerjäger (tank hunters), armed with a 37mm gun – the 37mm PAK (Panzerabwehrkanone – literally anti-tank gun). However, this proved ineffective against modern armour at that time. Arms manufacturer Rheinmetall-Borsig AG were therefore commissioned to find the solution, and developed the 50mm PAK, but even this didn't carry enough punch to stop a Russian T-34 tank. Next came the 75mm PAK, which quickly proved itself to be efficient on the Eastern Front, and several variants of this would be developed. The 75mm PAKs could be easily towed by a small armoured tractor, be horse-drawn if required or could be mounted on captured armour from Alfred Becker's Paris plant, and were used extensively during the Normandy campaign. The loss of six of these to the Germans during the Bréville attack is significant, as it was becoming increasingly difficult for German units in Normandy to receive replacement weapons and ammunition, since the RAF and USAAF had managed to reduce the amount of rail traffic down to about 30 per cent of its 1943 volume through their extensive targeting of the French rail network.

Even more devastating than the 75mm PAK was the 88mm PAK, which came into service in 1943. Originally used as an anti-aircraft gun, it was realised that the 88mm Flak was perfectly equipped to dispose of modern armoured vehicles. Weighing over 3,500kg, the 88 PAK was towed by a 3-ton tractor or was mounted onto a tank chassis as a self-propelled gun, such as the Jadgpanther. The shortened recoil of the 88 meant that it could be fired from its wheels, enabling it to relocate at speed. Cosy Comfort recalled his thoughts about the 88 PAK:

> Always it was the 88 – the Boche[3] super gun that lurked behind bush or cottage, from the beaches of Normandy to Bremen in May. It was to rule our lives, movements and most important of all – our health! It was always there to a tank man, a continual threat.

Such was the threat posed by the 88 PAK, that many reports of anti-tank guns would state that it was an '88', although in many cases the Hussars would have been facing the 75mm PAK, which could easily 'brew up' a British Sherman. In games of 'Housey-Housey' (bingo), instead of the traditional call of 'Two Fat Ladies', for armoured units it was replaced with a chorus of '88 – Driver Reverse'!

Similarly, many sightings of German armour would be recorded as being 'Tiger' tanks – the Panzerkampfwagen VI. Although some Tigers were present in Normandy, especially in the battles taking place in July and August, a much more common vehicle was the Panzerkampfwagen IV (Panzer IV), the Panzer V (Panther) or indeed any of Becker's cannibalised vehicles.

The next three days were spent operating out of the Ranville area, although no further engagements took place, other than the occasional stonk received from enemy mortars and artillery, injuring a few troopers. The poor weather had cleared on the 13th, enabling the Allied air forces to resume providing aerial cover to the ground troops in Normandy, with rocket-firing RAF Typhoons and USAAF Lightnings actively hunting German units. German paratroop officer Martin Pöppel recorded: 'No vehicle on the road is safe from the fighter-bombers and Lightnings. It's become virtually impossible to travel the roads by day.'

On the morning of 16 June, RHQ was shelled by German artillery, wounding three and killing 23-year-old Trooper John Perry from Nuneaton. Lieutenant Garlick's 4th Troop of A Squadron, under the temporary command of Captain Noel Denny, were sent to report to the commander of 153rd Infantry Brigade (of the 51st (Highland) Division), to try to cut off a reported withdrawal of enemy troops from Escoville. This was personally ordered by the general commanding the Highland Division and accepted under protest by Colonel Harrap. The Regimental Diary records:

> We have been frittering away tanks and men on such penny packet jobs too long, and few people seem to have any conception of Tank and Infantry co-operation, or the role of the Sherman tank gun as opposed to any other tank.

The 4th Troop were unsuccessful in trying to dislodge a group of four Panzer IVs, three armoured cars and a self-propelled gun of the 21st Panzer Division, all manned by Polish troops. Their only success was Corporal Bob Charmbury's tank shooting up a German field gun.

Colonel Harrap had gone to advise the commander of the 153rd Brigade as to the employment of his tanks and agree a plan whereby his A Squadron tanks would deploy with the 1st Battalion of the Gordon Highlanders to the south-east of Escoville. On his return journey from this conference in a jeep with the infantry brigadier, intent on conducting a reconnaissance, Lieutenant Colonel Richard Harrap rounded a corner in Hermanville-sur-Mer to find himself confronted by a German Panzer IV tank and was subsequently killed by machine-gun fire. He was buried at the 3rd Infantry Division cemetery at Colleville-sur-Orne on 17 June but was later moved to the cemetery at Douvres-la-Délivrande. His burial in Colleville was attended by Brigadier Prior-Palmer, his staff, the commanding officers of the Staffordshire Yeomanry and the East Riding of Yorkshire Yeomanry, plus thirty representatives of the 13th/18th. Colonel Harrap would be replaced as commanding officer by Major the Earl of Feversham, with Major Rugge-Price as his second-in-command (2ic). Captain Lyon assumed command of B Squadron, with Captain Gale taking over as 2ic of A Squadron.

Sunday, 18 June saw more shelling of the regiment's positions, resulting in the death in A Squadron of Trooper Cecil Murley; he was just 18 years old. Cosy Comfort recalled: 'The shriek of shells and distant thud of a Nebelwerfer... and here comes its

Colonel Harrap's final resting place at the Commonwealth War Graves cemetery at Douvres-la-Délivrande.

mortar bombs. Earth flies everywhere. The stench of dead cows, legs pointing skywards like miniature hot air balloons waiting for take-off.'

In the evening, three troops from C Squadron supported different units of the 153rd Brigade in operations around Hérouvillette, to the south of Ranville. Here, 2nd Troop, supporting the 1st Battalion the Gordon Highlanders, participated in a skirmish at close quarters in woods, killing twelve Germans, capturing a further six, knocking out a machine-gun position and seizing an 81mm mortar.

Other than getting regularly stonked by German mortars and artillery, no significant actions followed over the next few days, until 23 June, when the regiment would record its most successful action against enemy armour during the whole course of the war. Still east of the Orne River and now supporting the 152nd Infantry Brigade, of the 51st (Highland) Division, the regiment deployed between Escoville and Sainte-Honorine La Chardronette. C Squadron provided left flank protection to the east, behind Escoville, with A Squadron facing St Honorine, with B Squadron between the two. A Squadron were to support the 5th Battalion of the Cameron Highlanders to seize the hamlet of St Honorine. The Camerons made a silent approach on St Honorine at 0300 hrs, but once spotted were met with a hail of heavy small arms, machine-gun and mortar fire and subsequently failed to break into the hamlet. At 0330 hrs, Major Wormald was sent for by the infantry brigadier and instructed to support the Camerons and was given the impression that the infantry were already in the hamlet. Therefore, A Squadron moved up into St Honorine, which they did in the darkness without loss. Having studied aerial photos of the area, each crew commander knew which position he was meant to occupy, and the tanks fanned out. To their surprise, they found none of the Camerons in the hamlet and only a small number of them in a nearby orchard. As the light conditions improved, Major Wormald realised:

> As dawn broke it was noticed that some of the chaps who were occupying the slit trenches beside the tanks were wearing the wrong shaped helmets. With a little encouragement they soon left, and we remained in occupation of our positions. The Procedure was not to be found in a Tactical Textbook and the result was a great surprise – to both sides!

A Squadron would remain in position for an hour, without any infantry support. When the infantry managed to move up and take up defensive positions, they were to suffer heavy casualties from well-concealed enemy machine guns, plus heavy shelling, which also began to rain down on the 3&8's RHQ position further back. The Germans attempted a counterattack but were driven back with some difficulty.

Meanwhile, Captain Wardlaw and Trooper Urquhart of C Squadron HQ were manning an observation post up a tree, south of Escoville, and were linked to RHQ by telephone via a wireless Jeep, parked below. They reported that they had observed enemy tanks moving northwards across La Butte de la Hogue, an area of open, cultivated farmland, devoid of trees. They could see enemy tanks, self-propelled guns, plus an assortment of other vehicles… first twenty, twenty-five… thirty-five… finally a count of forty-three vehicles in all, which formed up behind the ridgeline. These now turned north-west and commenced their move in the direction of St Honorine. The very moment that the enemy vehicles came within range, A Squadron opened fire and quickly managed to knock out the Germans' two lead tanks. At 0715 hrs, enemy infantry of the 125th Panzer Grenadier Regiment, of the 21st Panzer Division, were sighted moving up from the direction of Cuverville. The attached Royal Artillery forward observation officer called in medium artillery, which halted and dispersed their advance, knocking out several more tanks in the process. One German tank crew, closest to A Squadron, bailed out of their burning vehicle and advanced under a white flag to surrender. However, with no infantry evidently available to accept this gesture, the German crew changed their minds and made a hasty retreat!

At 0940 hrs, the C Squadron observation post was then able to identify enemy shelling being fired from the steel factory area of nearby Colombelles, so artillery fire was requested, which rapidly quietened down those responsible. The convoy of German vehicles now split into two groups and some retired eastwards and took up a hull-down position in front of 2nd Troop of C Squadron, commanded by Lieutenant Norris; 2nd Troop quickly opened fire and destroyed one tank and set several soft-skinned vehicles on fire. The other group had turned north and were to provide A Squadron with an ideal target and they were successful in claiming a further eight tanks destroyed. Sergeant Cooper, temporarily on attachment from C Squadron, was to score four hits with his Sherman Firefly's 17-pounder gun. Firing at maximum range, B Squadron were to score another tank destroyed and despite the significant losses inflicted on the 21st Panzer Division, the regiment were to receive no tank losses.

The Hussars next witnessed a considerable amount of movement by enemy tanks and self-propelled guns, but this appeared to be with the intention of luring them into giving away their positions. It seemed that the Germans weren't sure if they were being engaged by tanks or anti-tank weapons. However, the 3&8s had anticipated this and held firm.

Eventually, the enemy vehicles retired south, but to add to their woes, were followed up from the air by rocket-firing RAF Typhoons, which took a toll on the remnants of the German convoy.

In addition to those German vehicles knocked out by artillery fire or the RAF, the regiment would claim thirteen tanks, two half-tracks and several soft-skinned vehicles destroyed. A Squadron recorded ten tanks destroyed, B Squadron one tank and a half-track, with C Squadron stopping two tanks, one half-track and several soft-skinned vehicles. Quite a haul!

At around 1600 hrs, a lull in activity enabled the regiment to replenish its ammunition. At 1715 hrs, A Squadron reported enemy beginning to form up on their right flank, attempting to hide their movements by laying a smokescreen. Once again, the artillery guns were called upon to deal with the threat, which proved most effective in scattering the German advance.

The regiment withdrew from their forward positions at dusk, moving at a walking pace, to avoid throwing up dust and inviting a stonk from German troops, keen to avenge the day's events. The 3&8s had dealt their foe a bitter blow, difficult as it was for them to receive replacement vehicles with the Allies dominating the skies overhead. French Resistance cells were also now actively doing their best to frustrate the Wehrmacht's ability to move men and matériel into Normandy, through acts of sabotage.

A Squadron spent the night in harbour in an area of pasture, formed up into a rectangle, with the squadron HQ at the top. All tanks were facing outwards in all-round defence, with their main guns loaded with high-explosive shells and aimed at the ground 50 yards to their front. Browning machine guns were set up on ground mountings, beside sleeping pits under the tanks. This represented quite a fortress, but no enemy were to approach during the night to test its firepower.

On 27 June, Lance Sergeant Bill Hammond, with 2nd Troop, A Squadron, was part of a deployment at Longueval, north of Colombelles, standing guard over the Orne River to prevent German troops attempting to move north along the opposite bank. Then, 2nd Troop would be stonked from a Nebelwerfer crew, sited in Démouville to their south-east, wounding the troop commander, Lieutenant Peter Hunter. Several decades after the war, Bill's driver, Trooper Joe 'Jock' Collins, remembered the day's events:

> We got there first thing in the morning and as the day progressed, nothing appeared to happen. Everyone dug in around us – each corner of the field and we sat in the tanks waiting for something to happen. The day wore on and nothing took place and we decided about midday that I should go down to a farm not too far away and collect a Dixie of milk and we could make some chocolate drink on the Primus stove.
>
> I left the members of the crew, took the Dixie with me with a view to carrying out this exercise. I went down to the farm which was badly damaged from the previous action and the old buzzard of a French farmer

took Francs from me for the two or three pints of milk that I asked for. I felt this was a lousy deed, having just liberated his farm in the action the day before. But nevertheless, as I made my way towards the tank, at that moment of time I heard the firing of a Nebelwerfer, a six-barrelled German Howitzer. I ducked down in the lane that I was coming up and within seconds a series of explosions took place in the vicinity of where the tanks were sitting.

I gathered my wits, collected the milk and rather urgently made my way back to the tanks, knowing it took some time to reload these Howitzers. I arrived back there in time to see the various members of the crew climbing out of the slit trenches where they'd dived in on top of the infantry.

We sat around for a few minutes – things seemed to have calmed down and it was then we decided to make our drink. We lit the Primus stove, put the milk on top to boil and were just settling down when this Howitzer went off again. I made to go under the tank but another member, Dutch Hollands, who was sitting nearer the Dixie was going under first. I then extracted myself and ran round the right-hand side of the tank. But I could tell from the noise of the bombs from this Howitzer that they were getting nearer, so I jumped between the tracks and the bogeys and because of my size I was able to squeeze in there and wait for the outcome of what was to follow. There was a series of explosions again, all around the tanks, and I could tell from the smell of the cordite and the explosion, one had landed very near to the tank. I waited for a few seconds, with a thumping heart I ran round to the front, went underneath to climb through the escape hatch into the co-driver's side and looking towards the rear I could see Dutch Hollands lying there with blood on his head.

After a few minutes when everything seemed to quieten down again, we then got out to see how badly Dutch was and we discovered that he had been killed in the explosion from the mortar which had landed in front of the tank.

This is when you reflect and say to yourself, I could have gone under the tank but for the fact that Dutch was blocking my way and here we lost another comrade, who was a very, very pleasant guy – sense of humour and very attached to his duty. At this moment Dutch is buried in Normandy and it's my intention when I return there on the 50th Anniversary of the Normandy Landings to go to the Cemetery in 1994 and reflect and say a prayer at the graveside.

It was unfortunate indeed, that having taken shelter under the tank, Henry should have been hit by shrapnel and killed. Trooper William Henry 'Dutch'

The final resting place of Trooper William Henry 'Dutch' Hollands at Douvres-la-Délivrande. (*Artwork by Andrew May*)

Hollands was to lose his life at just 20 years of age. It is hard to imagine how devastating this news would have been to his family back in Fulham[4] when the official telegram was received from the War Office announcing his death. Before long, they were also to receive a letter from Henry's tank commander, Lance Sergeant Bill Hammond:

> Dear Mr & Mrs Hollands,
> This short letter is very difficult for me to write. It has taken me a long time to make up my mind and I pray that old wounds are not opened as a result of this.
>
> I was Henry's Crew Commander when he was killed, and I would like to say he was one of the best. As a worker and a pal he was tops. It hurt me terribly to lose him and I might well understand how deep your grief must be. If the Army was made up of the stock that was Henry's then maybe the War would already have been won. One day I will go back and visit the place where he was put to rest.
>
> God wills that these good fellows must leave us so soon and I suppose we must not reason why.
>
> My own brother was lost on a Berlin raid this year, and like your son he can never be replaced.

We are trying our hardest to end the war at the earliest possible date, and thus end forever all strife and heartbreak that War inevitably brings.
Yours very sincerely
W. Hammond

The Hollands family were later sent the campaign medals issued to their son for his service with the regiment. He was awarded the 1939–1945 Star, the France and Germany Star, and the 1939–1945 War Medal; all of these are still in the greaseproof paper in which they were issued, unworn to this very day.

Tuesday, 27 June ended with the return from England of three missing A Squadron crew from D-Day: Sergeant Marke and Corporals Gammon and Sweetapple.

The regiment would remain in the area of Ranville and Sainte-Honorine La Chardronette into July and on the 2nd of that month, A Squadron at St Honorine would be stonked again from the direction of Démouville. This time a prompt artillery bombardment was directed onto Démouville, which had the desired effect.

On 4 July, the regiment (less A Squadron) crossed back over the bridges and were taken out of the line to rest at the coastal town of Luc-sur-Mer. It was the first time in a month that they would sleep under a roof. A Squadron was finally relieved at St Honorine by the 148th Regiment, Royal Armoured Corps at 0015 hrs on the 5th and joined the rest of the 3&8s. After a dusty drive, their first task was to get themselves cleaned up. Since D-Day, ablutions had consisted of a canvas bucket filled with cold water and if nature called, one would have to go on a 'recce' armed with a shovel! The men took a brief, well-earned rest and commenced spring-cleaning the interior of the tanks on the morning of the 6th. However, at midday, they were informed that their holiday was to end the next day, when they would be required to support the 59th (Staffordshire) Infantry Division in General Montgomery's latest attempt to capture the city of Caen.

Operation Charnwood

The original plan for Overlord was that Caen would be in British hands by the end of D-Day, which perhaps in hindsight was rather ambitious. Realising Caen's strategic importance, the Wehrmacht was intent on repelling the Allied advance into the city. Once released by Hitler, additional Panzer units were rushed into the Caen sector. Opposing Montgomery's first large assault in early June, Operation Perch, were the Panzer Lehr Division and the 12th SS Panzer Division Hitlerjugend, in addition to the 21st Panzer Division. Panzer Lehr (Lehr meaning 'teach') was drawn up from instructors from various Wehrmacht

Panzer training units and ranked amongst the best Panzer divisions within the German Army. They were well equipped with Panzer IVs and Panzer Vs (Panthers), although they would lose several tanks from aerial attack on their enforced 90-mile drive from Chartres to Caen. The 12th SS Panzer Division Hitlerjugend were largely drawn from the ranks of the Hitler Youth movement and had been fully indoctrinated with Hitler's ideology. Although the majority of its junior ranks were just 18 years old, they were very motivated and well equipped with Panzer IVs and Vs. They would prove themselves worthy adversaries in many engagements.

Montgomery had planned a classic pincer movement involving two complete corps, sending forces east and west of Caen, with the intention of either finding a weakness in the defences in the flanks, or taking the city from the south. Unfortunately, Operation Perch was not to achieve its objectives and Caen remained in German hands.

A violent storm raged in the English Channel between 19 and 22 June, destroying the Mulberry harbour in the American sector and damaging the British harbour at Arromanches-les-Bains, which served to delay the much-needed build-up of troops and equipment. This gave the Wehrmacht vital time in which to move more Panzer units into Normandy, although many of these units would also lose tanks to Allied aircraft or mechanical failure on their long journeys. Newly arrived were the 9th SS Panzer Division and 10th SS Panzer Division – experienced units from the Eastern Front. Also, the 2nd Panzer Division, 1st SS Panzer Division Liebstandarte SS Adolf Hitler and the 2nd SS Panzer Division Das Reich. When Montgomery launched Operation Epsom in late June, his attempt to outflank the defenders around Caen to the west would meet stiff opposition and was also destined to fail.

General Montgomery's next attempt to crack the problem of Caen would be Operation Charnwood. Three Anglo-Canadian Infantry divisions were to engage the Germans in a straight, frontal assault to the north of Caen. After their brief spell out of the line, the 3&8s formed up and departed Luc-sur-Mer at 2300 hrs on 7 July and moved through the darkness to arrive at their assembly area at 0200 hrs on the 8th, ready to support the 176th Infantry Brigade. Opposing them would be the young soldiers of the 12th SS Panzer Division Hitlerjugend. As the Hussars took up their positions, Lancaster and Halifax bombers of the RAF's Bomber Command flew overhead and would drop 2,350 tons of explosives on Caen, north of the Orne River, in an attempt to soften up German resistance. Lance Corporal Patrick Hennessey of A Squadron remembered:

> We heard a thunderous sound and looking up, we saw the sky black with aircraft. Wave after wave of RAF bombers flew in across the coast, right

over our heads, and began a ferocious and systematic bombardment of the city of Caen, only a few miles away. We had a grandstand view from where we were and watched in horrified fascination as the bombs rained down and clouds of smoke and flame arose from the stricken city.

Six squadrons of RAF de Havilland Mosquitos also attacked specific targets in the surrounding villages, accompanied by the naval guns of HMS *Rodney*, positioned off the coast.

With A Squadron in Brigade Reserve with the 7th Battalion of the South Staffordshire Regiment and RHQ in Le Mesnil wood, B and C Squadrons would form up in the vicinity of the Château de la Londe, facing the hamlet of La Bijude and the village of Épron. B Squadron left their forming up position west of the château and following a creeping barrage laid on by the 15th Field Regiment, Royal Artillery, advanced with infantry of the 6th Battalion the North Staffordshire Regiment towards La Bijude, north of Épron. It was some time before B Squadron could locate the Germans, as the area was obscured by smoke and dust from the artillery barrage. However, B Squadron were to report the objective captured by 0515 hrs. They had planned to swing right to tackle some entrenched positions to the west of La Bijude, but confusion reigned, and they were unable to encourage the infantry to move into the hamlet from the lane to the west to consolidate it.

Nevertheless, the 7th Battalion of the Royal Norfolk Regiment commenced its assault on Épron, supported by tanks of C Squadron, who were stationed to the east of the château. While in this position, they were heavily mortared, which wounded Sergeant Cooper, when his tank received a direct hit. Their tanks then moved up to La Bijude, where the Norfolks were held up by machine-gun fire. At this moment, Lance Sergeant William Short's tank turret was struck by what was believed to be an 88mm shell and the sergeant was killed. C Squadron's commander, Major Cotter, then had his tank knocked out by a 'bazooka', possibly a portable Panzerschreck (literally 'tank's fright'), wounding Lance Corporal Little. The tank was abandoned and the bazooka dealt with by Captain Akers-Douglas, who had assumed command. Although forced to dismount, Major Cotter remained with the attack, trying to rally the infantry forwards. Lieutenant Uttley was to have a very lucky escape when his turret received two glancing blows from long-range anti-tank fire, without damage. Captain Akers-Douglas was less fortunate when his tank was hit, as both he and his driver were wounded. By 0838 hrs, it was reported that Épron was captured, with two companies of the Norfolks on the objective, plus 1st and 2nd Troops of C Squadron to consolidate the position.

However, as time elapsed, it became apparent that the report of Épron being seized was far from accurate and in fact, the assaulting troops had yet to even enter the northern end of the village. This news came as quite a shock to the brigade commander and Major Earl of Feversham, who had both believed that their units had achieved their objective before 0900 hrs. Instead, following continued hard and confused fighting, the village remained in German hands into the afternoon.

After a reconnaissance was carried out from La Bijude by the commanders in a tank, an attack was planned for 1700 hrs, involving the use of Crocodile flamethrower tanks and Crab flail tanks. This was subsequently postponed until 2030 hrs, then while B Squadron provided suppressive fire, the remainder of the Norfolks moved up with C Squadron's reserve troop, plus one troop of A Squadron attached. One of the C Squadron tanks was knocked out at short range, but the crew managed to bail out, unharmed. Following what Julius Neave was to record as 'impressive use of Crocodile flamethrower tanks', Épron was captured and the regiment retired to the area of 'Cazelle' (Cazelles), by the château to their north. Sergeant Charlie Rattle would later report to his A Squadron commander that to the south-west of the village, he had discovered approximately forty British and Canadian bodies, unarmed and dead. He could only conclude that they had been taken prisoner by the Germans and murdered.

At the end of the day's action, B Squadron had accounted for six Panzer IVs knocked out, but had lost three tanks themselves, and only suffered one casualty wounded. C Squadron had lost three tanks, with the death of Lance Sergeant Short, plus had suffered Captain Akers-Douglas and five others wounded. Considering the ferocity of the day's fighting it is remarkable that the regiment should only suffer one fatality. In contrast, Major Wormald had recorded in his diary: 'I recall that on the road entering Épron, it was quite difficult to avoid driving over dead German bodies.'

At 0300 hrs on the 9th, RHQ requested that two troops of A Squadron would be required to support the position at La Bijude against an armoured attack, so 3rd and 4th Troops moved out at 0430 hrs to perform this task. No news was received and at 0745 hrs, a squadron leaders' conference was held to outline the plan for the day. The enemy entrenchments to the west of Épron that had not been attacked the previous day would now be assaulted by the infantry of the 6th North Staffs. Once taken, they would advance south to capture the village of 'Couvre Chef' (Couvrechef). They were to be supported by two troops of B Squadron, once again, with two troops of A Squadron protecting their exposed left flank; 3rd Troop would lay a smokescreen. The B Squadron tanks were to move at a walking pace to the rear of the infantry and provide covering fire as required. The advance was to follow a creeping artillery barrage, laid on by the 5th Field Regiment, Royal Artillery. The start time of 1000 hrs would be postponed to 1030 hrs, but it appeared the gunners were ignorant of this fact and were unaware of the start line 500 yards to the west of Épron and commenced their barrage at 1000 hrs. The North Staffs infantry at the eastern end of the entrenchments were to receive many casualties from 'friendly fire' but all attempts to cancel the barrage failed. It wasn't until the gunners had completed their programme that the infantry was able to advance on Couvre Chef. Owing to this delay, 3rd Troop of A Squadron were running out of smoke shells, so more had to be brought up quickly to enable them to continue protecting the left flank of the attack. Nevertheless, B Squadron tanks were on the edge of their objective by 1300 hrs, but there was confusion as to whether any friendly infantry had managed to enter the village, so the tanks were unable to fire into the objective. Nevertheless, the village was finally reported captured by 1330 hrs.

It was then decided to send a troop of tanks to 2 miles south to place an observation post, watching the main road into Caen from the west, to report any enemy withdrawals. Concerns were raised about the lack of intelligence in relation to any enemy forces that may still be in this area, so it was decided to send a more potent force of two troops of tanks, supported by a Bren Gun Carrier platoon. A Squadron's 3rd and 4th Troops were given this task, under the command of Captain Gale, and they were in position by 1600 hrs. In the meantime, the remainder of the regiment had moved up to consolidate Couvre Chef.

As the afternoon wore on, nothing of interest was observed by the forward A Squadron tanks and at 2000 hrs, the regiment was ordered to retire back to Cazelle. News was received from other units in the area from 27th Armoured Brigade that their objectives had also been achieved and that Caen finally appeared to be within the grasp of the Allies. Operation Charnwood had been a battle of attrition and despite some spirited fighting by the young soldiers of the 12th SS Panzer Division, they were to suffer heavy casualties and were forced to retire out of the city and to the south of the Orne River.

The city of Caen (certainly north of the Orne) was now in British hands and the regiment would spend the next week based around Cazelle and Château de la Londe, carrying out important administrative tasks to keep their tanks in good working order. It was an opportunity to take baths and relax, and even a mobile cinema was brought in on 12 July. The regiment also received their new commanding officer, Lieutenant Colonel Vincent Dunkerly, whom they'd been expecting for a few days. Following his appointment, Major the Earl of Feversham became his 2ic, with Major Rugge-Price and Captain Lyon returning to their original roles. Captain Gale transferred to C Squadron, after Captain Akers-Douglas was wounded during the battle for Épron.

Captain Julius Neave and Major the Earl of Feversham headed out in a Jeep to survey the ground over which the regiment had recently fought. Julius Neave recorded:

> We went down past La Bijude and Épron, and found the shambles awful. There were quite a number of civilians creeping back, presumably from Caen, and it was a very pathetic sight. The story is that during Thursday night's monster bomber attack, the population collected in the cathedral for a service. After the attack, the cathedral was the only place practically speaking left intact and they all emerged singing the Marseillaise – much to the discomfort of the Boche! It isn't possible in Épron and La Bijude to tell which was a house or which just a wall. No sign of life of any sort and a vile smell of dead Boche, cows, horses etc. [Major Cotter] Deleval's tank was sitting in the middle of Épron with a neat hole from the bazooka in the side of it and the whole bottom blown out. We set off for Caen, a couple of miles away. Eventually we got into the town, having made numerous detours, and the sight was really staggering. There can be only a few people at this stage of the war who have seen the results of our own bombing at close quarters, and this was 2,300 tons in an hour in an area a mile square. It was like H.G. Wells or worse, and piles of debris were just everywhere. We could however distinguish streets and buildings, unlike Épron, and the cathedral, apart from the windows, was reasonably intact but it was pretty grim. The inhabitants seem to have been pleased to see us, but I felt personally pretty sorry for them and can't quite understand their feelings. They weren't involved in '14–18' and saw no fighting in '40. The Boche bought all their produce and kept them going on much as normal, and now the 'Forces of Liberation' have completely flattened them down and left them virtually destitute.[5]

On the 13th, the squadrons went out onto the ground they had just fought over to inspect German tanks and equipment and to reconstruct the battles as a TEWT (Tactical Exercise Without Troops). The colonel and Major the Earl of Feversham attended a brigade conference the next day at the headquarters of 27th Armoured Brigade to discuss lessons learnt from the battle. On 15 July, both would perform a reconnaissance, east of the Orne, for the next big operation of General Montgomery's, Operation Goodwood. On the 16th, Colonel Dunkerly attended an O Group at the headquarters of the 3rd Infantry Division, then his squadron leaders were briefed on plans for the operation.

Operation Goodwood

General Montgomery's plan was an attempt to break out of the Orne bridgehead, capture the German-held Bourguébus Ridge and to push south-east towards Falaise. It would be the biggest tank engagement fought by the British Army during the war and the main assault would involve three armoured divisions – the 11th Armoured Division, the Guards' Armoured Division and the 7th Armoured Division.

Montgomery's intentions were:

> to engage the German armour and wear it down to such an extent that it is of no further value to the Germans as a basis of the battle. To gain a good bridgehead over the Orne through Caen and thus to improve our positions on the Eastern flank. Generally, to destroy German equipment and personnel, as a preliminary to a possible wide exploitation of success.

Although considered by the planners to be 'good tank country', the battlefront was narrow and was only wide enough for two tank squadrons (forty vehicles) to operate, so each division would be required to advance in sequence. The role of the British 3rd Infantry Division (with 27th Armoured Brigade under command) would be to attack the German forward enemy defences and secure the left (eastern) flank of the attack, with the 51st (Highland) Division performing a similar role to secure the right flank (western). The three armoured divisions would thus be able to pass through the corridor created. However, moving so much armour across the bridges and into the Orne bridgehead would be impossible to conceal from the Germans.

A secondary goal of the operation would be to keep most of the German Panzer divisions committed to the Caen sector, thus reducing resistance to Operation Cobra to the west; the capture of Saint-Lô by American forces. Saint-Lô had proved a tough sticking point for the Americans and the timing of the operations were to coincide, so that the Wehrmacht could not adequately defend against both operations. The capture of Saint-Lô would enable the Americans to break out of the Cotentin Peninsula and exploit this success to push south, behind the German units in Normandy and into Brittany, against comparatively light opposition. Not that their task was an easy one, since they were operating in the close terrain of the bocage, with its sunken lanes and dense hedgerows; some of the worst tank country imaginable. This led to the development of the Rhino tank, whereby steel girders from the German beach defences would be recycled to create hedge-cutters, which when welded to the front of a Sherman, would enable US units to rip their way through the bocage hedgerows, enabling a much quicker deployment of tanks than having to wait for bulldozers or engineers to blast a hole in a steep bank.

At 0100 hrs on 17 July, the regiment commenced its journey east of the Orne to their assembly area at Hérouvillette. There was terrific congestion on the roads, as the enormous volume of armoured vehicles was funnelled over the bridges at Bénouville and shoehorned into the small British bridgehead. Julius Neave recorded: 'The crush east of the Orne has to be seen to be believed. There isn't an orchard or field empty.'

It would take the Hussars five hours to cover the 8 miles to Hérouvillette, arriving three hours later than planned. At 1500 hrs, the squadron commanders conducted a reconnaissance of their area of attack with officers of the infantry brigade, which was followed by a 27th Armoured Brigade O Group at 1800 hrs. The regiment's start line would be from the village of Escoville, nicknamed 'Stonkville' by Julius Neave, owing to the daily weight of mortar fire that the area seemed to attract. Sergeant Jerry Bell from 1st Troop, A Squadron would receive the unwelcome news that he was not to participate in the upcoming action, as his tank would be on guard duty at General Montgomery's headquarters.

The 3&8s were to be reunited with their old friends from D-Day, the 8th Infantry Brigade. A Squadron would once again support the 1st Battalion South Lancs to attack the farm at Le Pré Baron before approaching Touffréville from the north. B Squadron with the 2nd Battalion East Yorks were to capture the village of Touffréville, and C Squadron and the 1st Battalion Suffolk Regiment were to capture the village of Sannerville. Major Wormald was surprised by the changes he witnessed with the South Lancs battalion, since only three of the original officers from D-Day were still with them, their commanding officer having been killed on the initial assault. The casualties they had suffered over the six weeks since landing in France meant that they were only able to muster around thirty men per company – less than one third of a regular, full company's compliment.

Opposing the British forces would be the German I SS Panzer Corps and LXXXVI Army Corps, representing a formidable force with which to engage. Anticipating that a British operation of this type was likely from the Orne bridgehead, the Germans had prepared the defences 10 miles deep, with four defence lines, and the forward villages were turned into veritable fortresses, bristling with anti-tank weapons. Therefore, aerial bombing had been arranged by the Allies in an attempt to soften up the German positions in front of the advance. On 18 July, Julius Neave recorded that at 0600 hrs heavy Lancaster bombers of the RAF flew overhead continuously for forty-five minutes, bombing the villages of Cuverville, Sannerville, Démouville, Giberville and the Colombelles factory area. B Squadron's objective of Touffréville was also meant to be bombed, but on their own initiative, the RAF had moved their bombing line south of the village, for fear of accidentally bombing friendly forces. However, leaving this strongpoint intact and not having communicated this decision to the Army was to leave the 3&8s with a much tougher challenge on their hands. A huge artillery barrage then followed, which would continue for twenty minutes, before B-26 Marauders flew in, scattering fragmentation bombs over the 16th Luftwaffe Field Division, and Boston fighter-bombers attacked German gun positions. Hundreds of American Flying Fortresses then bombed gun positions to the south-east of Troan and the Bourguébus Ridge. The result of this heavy bombing would mean that the leading British units would encounter many German troops who were still dazed from the concussion of the bombs and artillery rounds detonating around them and were unable to offer any resistance. Further within the German defences, the mighty Tiger tanks of the Heavy Panzer battalions had suffered several destroyed during the aerial bombing. One Tiger had taken a direct hit and nothing could be found of its crew, whilst the blast of a near miss had flipped another of the 58-ton monsters over like a child's toy. It was hoped that the success of this bombing mission would enable the 11th Armoured Division to punch its way through the corridor and quickly secure the Bourguébus Ridge.

At 0745 hrs, A and B Squadrons of the 13th/18th moved up through Escoville to their start line. A Squadron would follow a creeping artillery barrage, which would move forwards at the speed of 100 yards every five minutes. The farm at Le Pré Baron was captured with relative ease, whilst B Squadron deployed onto the open, rolling farmland of La Butte de la Hogue to their right, to the north-west of Touffréville. Two companies of the South Lancs infantry were to have moved up ahead of A Squadron through wooded country, to orchards at the northern edge of the village, but for two hours no information as to the situation was received, despite frequent requests to the commanding officer of the infantry. In order to remedy this situation, Corporal Bob Charmbury was sent forward with tanks from 2nd Troop, A Squadron to link up with the infantry to provide an up-to-date situation report. The first infantry Privates who Corporal Charmbury happened upon seemed to have no idea what was happening and while he was ferreting around the area trying to locate someone of authority, he was shot in the head by a sniper. Although not fatally wounded, he was forced to retire from the operation and his war was over!

After much confusion, Major Wormald and Captain Lyon managed to track down a company commander from the infantry. Eventually a plan was approved by battalion HQ to send another infantry company forward, which were supported by 2nd and 3rd Troops of A Squadron, using their Browning machine guns to fire into the wooded area. It transpired that their Browning fire had made the German positions such a hostile environment that they had vacated the area and the South Lancs company were not fired upon as they advanced.

As this was happening, Major Wormald was watching events through his binoculars, from his tank parked on some scrubland that was thought to have been cleared by the infantry.

> I was tapped on my left shoulder and looking round was surprised/alarmed to see a German soldier. However, there was no need for alarm because he very politely asked (in English) whether it would be possible for him to be taken prisoner, as he was tired of the war. A suggestion with which I was pleased to agree. I was also pleased that he was a medical orderly and not a fanatic member of the Hitler Jugend with a grenade.

Cosy Comfort, moving out onto La Butte de la Hogue with B Squadron, encountered more Germans who wished to surrender: 'Twenty Boche infantry, hands on heads, advance towards our tank. I wave my revolver, "To the rear you Bastards!" Too late, their own mortars have their range, right amongst them!'

Cosy's crew next came across a stationary 3&8 tank with engine trouble, so pulling up alongside, Cosy was given the short straw and told to assist them. Having completed his task, with the Sherman engine roaring back into life, Cosy tried to remount his own tank, but they were spotted on the flat, open terrain. Machine-gun fire began striking the tank's hull, followed by the shriek of incoming mortar rounds. Cosy dived headfirst into the turret, but his right leg was still out. Suddenly he felt a burning sensation and felt sick; that last mortar round was a hit! Some nine hours later and now into darkness, Cosy peeped under the field dressing on his leg: shrapnel in the calf and knee. He was moved to a First Aid Post and his leg received a fresh dressing. The orderly handed him a chunk of metal from his leg as a souvenir. A label was tied to his battledress, and he was in the system. A 15cwt truck ferried him back to the Field Ambulance station, complete with a marquee, low lighting and wounded everywhere on stretchers. Once moved into a gap on a stretcher, lying there Cosy remembered: 'My neighbour was very, very silent… dead!'

Bleary-eyed medics went about their business, Cosy's leg was redressed again and then he was taken to the beach and put aboard a tank landing craft, its deck now a mobile hospital ward full of wounded, all on stretchers, some of them German. Cosy was given warm tea and soup, but no food. 'Sorry mate, forbidden!' Once back in England he would be taken to hospital in Basingstoke before an onward train journey to a hospital near Widnes, to begin a three-month period of convalescence. At least there were the first clean sheets in weeks and kind nurses. It then occurred to him that he'd left his beloved saxophone, wrapped up in his bed roll, back in the tank!

Back at Operation Goodwood, fighting for the village of Touffréville continued all morning, since the German garrison had been spared the attentions of the RAF. The deadlock was finally broken, once Crab flail tanks had cleared a path through a minefield, which was quickly exploited by the B Squadron tanks of Lieutenant Franks and Lance Sergeant Johnny Hardie, who raced into the village centre, enabling others to join them and capture the objective.

With Touffréville captured, the 1st Suffolks, supported by C Squadron's tanks, pushed on to capture the village of Sannerville, which unlike Touffréville now lay in ruins following the aerial bombardment. What remained was a moonscape of bomb craters, rubble and a fine grey powder, which made the digging of slit trenches impossible for the infantry, as the sides would simply crumble and collapse; when it began to rain, this became a clinging, grey paste. Then 2nd Troop moved to high ground north of Sannerville to cover the infantry's movements into the village. However, A and D companies of the Suffolks were able to enter the village without difficulty and the other troops moved up onto the high ground to join 2nd Troop. Following a request from the Suffolk's colonel, 3rd Troop was then sent in support of C Company, to orchards north-east of the village to deal with some active snipers, whilst 4th Troop moved into the village to assist with 'mopping-up' activities. Several prisoners were taken from the orchards and with the arrival of the tanks, more Germans were driven out of a nearby hedgerow. With Sannerville in British hands, D Company pushed on to dominate the ground between the villages of Sannerville and Bannerville and requested armoured support to accomplish this. D Company collected several prisoners, who were very willing to give themselves up, and when A Company passed through into Bannerville itself, they discovered more dazed Germans, who were rounded up. They also took possession of six Nebelwerfer mortars and three large artillery pieces. A well-concealed 88mm gun sited in an orchard near Bannerville proved problematic for a while and the infantry were unable to get near it, but the 17-pounder gun of one of C Squadron's Fireflies soon silenced it. While this was happening, five German tanks or self-propelled guns concealed to the south-east engaged the C Squadron tanks, knocking out four Shermans before making good their escape to the south. They would claim the lives of 19-year-old Trooper Eric Spaven, plus 33-year-old Lance Corporal Richard Woodcock. Nine others were wounded in this engagement. AVRE vehicles were later able to recover two of the tanks. By 1730 hrs, all companies of 1st Suffolks had moved up to Bannerville, and C Squadron of the Hussars was soon able to withdraw and rejoin the remainder of the regiment.

At the front of the main attack, leading units of 11th Armoured Division had progressed well, having pushed south beyond Démouville, and had crossed the main road running west–east and were headed towards the village of Cagny. That morning, Major Hans von Luck was returning to his Kampfgruppe, as part of the I SS Panzer Corps, after three days of leave in Paris. Finding the chaos following the Allied bombardment, he took command of a Panzer and set off to see for himself what was happening on the front line. Upon discovering that dozens of British tanks were already across the main road and advancing on his position, he approached the young officer commanding a Luftwaffe anti-aircraft battery. He ordered the young commander to commence firing at the tanks, but he refused, stating that his job was to engage aircraft only. Incensed by this response, von Luck produced his service pistol and aiming it at the officer said, 'Either you're a dead man or you can earn yourself a medal.' The four 88mm flak guns were quickly repositioned to the north-west of Cagny, their gun barrels lowered, and with an uninterrupted view to their north began to engage the British tanks; 'good tank country' would become a perfect tank killing ground. Unfortunately, C Squadron of the Fife & Forfars obligingly provided the Luftwaffe crew with plenty of vehicles to aim at and they continued firing on the British tanks until they ran out of targets. The following Guards' Armoured Division would also receive heavy losses in this area, and it is reckoned that the Luftwaffe 88m flak battery commandeered by Major von Luck was largely responsible for halting the British advance and had claimed an estimated forty British tanks.

Operation Goodwood would ultimately fail to break through to Falaise but did succeed in holding two Panzer corps in the Caen sector, so that neither could oppose the successful American breakout from the Cotentin Peninsula to the west.

For his role in halting the British advance during Operation Goodwood, Hans von Luck would be awarded the Knight's Cross of the Iron Cross and was promoted to Oberstleutnant (equivalent of lieutenant colonel).

At least the 13th/18th Royal Hussars (QMO) had achieved all its objectives for Goodwood and the villages on the left flank of the British advance had been secured. Unfortunately, in the early afternoon RHQ was heavily stonked, killing the technical adjutant, Captain Anthony Lyon-Clark, with Technical Quarter Master Sergeant Turner losing a leg.[6] Each squadron was released in turn from the villages they were occupying, to harbour south of 'Stonkville' – Escoville. Not surprisingly, in the late afternoon they were heavily stonked here, once again, while the support echelons went about the task of replenishing each squadron's tanks with ammunition, fuel and stores. The opening day of Operation Goodwood had cost the regiment five killed (Captain A. Lyon-Clark, Sergeant

D. Murchison, Lance Corporal P. Lewis, Trooper E. Spaven and Trooper D. Smith). Fourteen other men were wounded (including Peter 'Cosy' Comfort and Bob Charmbury), with the loss of four tanks.

RHQ had processed ninety-four prisoners of war, with a further 176 surrendering to a section of Recce Troop.

On 19 July, the regiment's tanks would secure the ground captured the day before and assumed counterattack positions, but nothing happened other than Captain Julius Neave recording what a nuisance the mosquitos were. Neave shared his thoughts on the little pests: 'Bloody mosquitos again – perfectly pestiferous – I am covered in bites and so is everyone else.'

On the 20th, torrential rain began to fall, making tracks all but impassable. Living quarters under the tanks and the infantry's slit trenches began to fill with water, creating quite a miserable environment for everyone and despite efforts to divert the flow away, it was impossible to halt the advance of this enemy.

On 21 July, the Regimental Diary simply reads: 'Rain continued with increased fervour, nothing to report.'

On the 22nd, the regiment was routinely stonked with heavy calibre shelling, wounding three men. B Squadron was particularly badly shelled and Corporal Kenneth Pendlebury was killed, along with 20-year-old Trooper Stanley Bannard, who had followed Jerry Bell into the regiment. His photo was to appear in the local Northampton newspaper as his death was announced, although he would never return to the village of Bugbrooke.

Over the coming days, the regiment readied itself for Operation Spring, which involved the II Canadian Corps with 7th and Guards' Armoured Divisions under command. The 27th Armoured Brigade was to be held in reserve in a counterattack role and the 3&8s would spend thirty-six hours in the general area of Le Mesnil Frémentel, north-west of Cagny. Operation Spring commenced on the same day as the American Operation Cobra to the west, and German High Command were confused as to which was the main operation, but owing to the importance of the Caen sector, to keep the Allies held in Normandy, they chose to focus their attentions on Spring for the first two days, which ultimately enabled Cobra to be successful and allowed the American breakout

Trooper Stanley Bannard.

94   DD Sherman Tank Warriors

Kenneth Pendlebury and Stanley Bannard lie together at the Commonwealth War Graves Commission cemetery at Ranville.

from the Cotentin Peninsula. The 3&8s were not called forward and Julius Neave remembered the general lack of activity:

> Really a boring and bloody day. Spent most of it under the tank and dodging the mortars and shells. Whenever we got out, which we did periodically to walk around and see Squadrons etc., it always seems to start again.

Indeed, Major General Miller's book records:

> On the night of the 25th the sky was set aglow with a panoply of chandelier flares, and the Regiment was bombed with high fragmentation bombs, followed by a quick concentration of heavy calibre fire, which caused the loss of one Stuart tank, killing the troop Sergeant[7] and wounding Lieutenant Cornwell and one other rank. Intermittent shelling continued through the following day, and the area was altogether very unhealthy.

They would be relieved by the 144th Regiment Royal Armoured Corps and moved off on the afternoon of 26 July and would leave the Orne bridgehead for the final time.

Operation Spring was also to be 27th Armoured Brigade's final operation, as news was gloomily received that the brigade was to be disbanded. The Staffordshire Yeomanry was to return to England for further specialist training on DD tanks. The future of the East Riding Yeomanry was as yet unknown, but the 13th/18th were to come under the command of the 8th Armoured Brigade, which had a good reputation from the North African campaign against Rommel's forces; the 3&8s would be replacing the 24th Lancers. With great reluctance, the 3&8s removed their coveted 'Pregnant Prawn' Seahorse shoulder patches and sewed on the Fox's Mask badge of the 8th Armoured Brigade. Julius Neave recorded: 'It is all very depressing as the "Pregnant Prawn" had become well known in the Second Army particularly east of the Orne.'

The Fox's Mask shoulder patch of the 8th Armoured Brigade.

Some good news was that their own commander, Brigadier Erroll Prior-Palmer, would assume command of their new brigade and would bring many of his staff with him. The regiment would also be joining their old friends, the 4th/7th Dragoon Guards. Rumours abounded that the 27th Armoured Brigade had been written out of the order of battle, because the planners didn't believe that they would still represent a cohesive fighting force this far into the Normandy campaign.

The regiment crossed the river bridges and moved west to Coulombs, a small village to the south-east of Bayeux. Here the colonel gathered the regiment together behind an orchard and spoke about the changes that were taking place. As replacement vehicles were now being received from the Staffordshire Yeomanry, all of them would need to have their signs repainted, ready to join the 8th Armoured Brigade. Any of the original, surviving DD tanks from D-Day were now retired and replaced. The regiment believed that they had at least five days out of the line in which to maintain and replenish their vehicles, but a warning order was received at 1800 hrs on 28 July that the regiment should be ready to move at 2000 hrs. This was simply not possible, as most of the tanks were far from ready to move, without even any ammunition stowed. The time was subsequently revised to 2200 hrs, before finally being pushed out to 0630 hrs on the 29th. It seemed that the 3&8s' brief period of rest was already over, and they set off south to harbour at La Senaudière, midway between Bayeux and Villers-Bocage.

Operation Bluecoat and Mont Pinçon

Following on from the success by the First US Army, as it broke out of the Cotentin Peninsula to the west, Operation Bluecoat was organised at short notice to exploit this situation. 'Ultra' intercepts at Bletchley Park had indicated a weakening of the German line between the Caen sector to the east and the American area of operations to the west, as German divisions were redeployed. The operation's intended objectives were the capture of Mont Pinçon, the highest point in Normandy, plus the centre of Vire, which acted as a hub for a network of many roads emanating out through the bocage country.

The challenge to the 3&8s of operating their tanks in this terrain is summed up in the A Squadron Diary:

> The country was typical of the 'Bocage'; small fields, large hedges, some with deep ditches and some sunken tracks. Good country of the use of the German Panzerfaust[8] handheld anti-tank hollow charge weapons, which they had used to devastating effect against British tanks, particularly when our tanks were without close infantry protection, sitting alone on an objective.

Not for the first time in British military history, senior commanders incorrectly believed that the advance would be rapid in the face of weakened opposition. However, as the diary goes on to note: 'Each Battalion commander did not seem to anticipate the "walk-over" advance that had been forecast by their superior Commanders, based upon intelligence reports.'

Indeed, many local engagements were fought over the opening days of the operation by the infantry battalions, supported by the regiment, costing the infantry many casualties and the 3&8s several wounded and five deaths.

Corporal Patrick Hennessey recalled:

> By now we were meeting members of the Maquis; the French Resistance movement. They were excited and bloodthirsty. We managed to communicate with them and found them overjoyed that we had arrived and more than ready to impart useful information concerning the movements of the hated Boche.
>
> From time to time we halted for a day or two, in reserve, when we would take the opportunity to clean up the tanks and carry out essential maintenance. The supply echelons would come to us with fuel, ammunition, rations, and, most important of all, the mail!

Each day began around 6am when the crew member who was on guard duty would light the cooker to make tea and then go round waking the rest of the crew. We would struggle out of our blankets, wash and shave (every day!), tackle a breakfast of tinned bacon and baked beans and pack the tank ready for movement. Radios were switched on and tested to make sure they were all on the net, gun sights and ammunition checked. The drivers and co-drivers would start and run the engines. Meanwhile, the crew commanders were summoned to a briefing by the Troop Leader, who had already attended a Squadron Commander's Orders Group. Armed with map boards, talc and chinagraph pencils, the three of us NCOs would gather round the young officer, who would tell us of our action during the day to come. Synchronise watches, any questions, move off in twenty minutes.

Back to our tanks to brief the crews, last minute stowage and load guns with HE ammunition in anticipation of soft skinned targets and move off to meet our Infantry on time at the start line.

On 2 August, both A and B Squadrons were to support the 69th Infantry Brigade to advance from Cahagnes to Amayé-sur-Seulles, which had been an unachieved objective of the 56th Infantry Brigade the previous day. B Squadron tanks would support the infantry of the 5th Battalion of the East Yorkshire Regiment on the right, with A Squadron supporting the 7th Battalion of the Green Howards to the left. A Squadron would move first. The Green Howards were to occupy the village, with A Squadron's tanks covering from a ridge of high ground to the north. Intelligence reports indicated that there were few, if any, enemy forces remaining in the village. Captain Peter Lyon moved A Squadron up to their start line and in order to move at speed, 2nd Troop were given the task of ferrying the leading company of the Green Howards into the village, with the battalion's Bren Gun Carrier platoon protecting their right flank. With the Company HQ sat atop Troop Commander Lieutenant Peter Hunter's tank, each other tank carried a platoon of thirty men, plus their kit, which was quite a balancing act while moving cross-country. A forward observation officer from the Royal Artillery was also made available to bring down an artillery barrage onto the objective, if required. The remainder of the squadron moved out, with 3rd Troop left of the road into the village, 4th Troop protecting their exposed left flank and 1st Troop heading to orchards to the right. Upon approaching the orchards, 1st Troop came under significant enemy fire and engaged the Germans to their front with their full weight of firepower. Along with their accompanying carrier platoon, 2nd Troop also came under machine-gun fire, so the infantry rapidly dismounted the tanks and went to ground. Artillery was requested onto the orchards and village and within moments, shells began screaming onto their targets. Once the artillery lifted, 1st Troop ceased firing into the orchards and a good number of German soldiers emerged from within with arms raised in surrender. They were instructed to move to the rear, and willingly obliged. Meanwhile, the leading infantry company, 2nd Troop and the carrier platoon were still in the sights of machine guns, so a second artillery stonk was requested. Once this lifted, with added support from Captain Lyon's tank and 1st Troop, the advance into the village now made better progress and before long, A Squadron's tanks were in the village and consolidating their positions. The advance of the other tank troops was largely unopposed, although they were not accompanied by the infantry and would therefore hold the village without infantry support for several hours. Danger still lurked in the surrounding countryside and Lieutenant Elliott was wounded in the head by a sniper's bullet. A bazooka round also struck Corporal Davies's tank, wounding its crew. Sadly, one of them, Trooper Albert Dodson, was to die of his wounds the following day.

Corporal Patrick Hennessey remembered:

We had halted in the area of a crossroads, when the second-in-command of the squadron, Captain Peter Lyon, called me over to his tank. I climbed up and spoke to him as we studied his map, I was standing on the side of his tank and he leaning out of the turret. I jumped down and was walking back to my own tank, when I heard the unmistakable sound of Schmeisser sub-machine-gun fire. Captain Lyon lay slumped across the top of his turret, shot through the head.

Captain Peter Edward Lycett Lyon, MC, son of Major Edward Lycett Lyon of the 18th Royal Hussars, now lies within the Bayeux War Cemetery.

By 1800, the Green Howards had consolidated Amayé-sur-Seulles and the nearby orchards, watched over by 3rd Troop and 2nd Troop, which had moved up onto the ridge to join them. Eight German officers and fifty other prisoners had been captured.

Meanwhile, B Squadron had commenced their advance at 1500 hrs with the East Yorks' infantry but had been held up for some time at a tank obstacle. They eventually arrived at their objective at 1900 hrs and would capture a further fifty prisoners.

The real thrust to capture Mont Pinçon was to commence on 5 August. This feature, looming over the surrounding countryside, had been a thorn in the side of the Allies since they had landed in Normandy, since it commanded an uninterrupted view for miles around. The 129th Infantry Brigade, supported by the 13th/18th, were to operate to the west and south-west of the feature, which

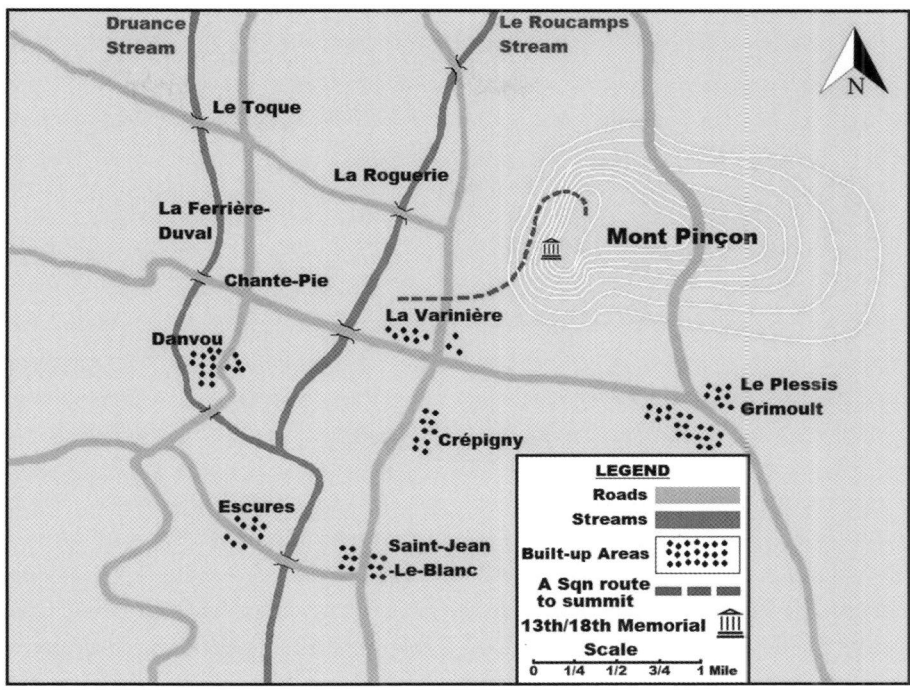

presented the steepest slopes to the summit. At 0800 hrs, B Squadron's tanks were to carry the leading companies of the 4th Battalion Wiltshire Regiment (4 Wilts) through Escurès towards their objective of the village of Saint-Jean-le-Blanc. Meanwhile, A Squadron would operate to their north on a parallel route, in support of the 5th Battalion of the Wiltshire Regiment (5 Wilts), with an objective of the village of La Varinière. C Squadron were in reserve with the 4th Battalion of the Somerset Light Infantry (4 SLI).

However, in front of the infantry battalions and tanks was the relatively narrow Druance stream, which stretched roughly from north to south across the terrain. Since the Druance acted as a tank obstacle, the bridges across the stream were naturally of primary importance and unfortunately for the attacking force, the German defenders on the summit of Mont Pinçon had a grandstand view of all of their movements and could call down artillery and mortar stonks at will.

When 4 Wilts approached their bridge over the Druance, they found it destroyed, its banks sowed with mines. Their Pioneer platoon did a sterling job of removing the mines and constructed a ford out of brushwood in under thirty minutes. However, once C Company did manage to cross, they had to contend with a steep, wooded gradient to their front. German infantry lay well concealed within the undergrowth and began to inflict heavy casualties, to such an extent that there were junior NCOs leading the remnants of their platoons; their officers or section commanders were dead or wounded. By late afternoon, the Pioneer platoon had succeeded in constructing a prefabricated bridge over the stream, despite being under almost continuous Nebelwerfer fire, which enabled B Squadron's tanks to advance to the far side of the stream and provide better fire support to their infantry. Despite the German troops also suffering heavy casualties, they fought relentlessly with well-sited machine guns and when 4 Wilts finally entered Saint-Jean-Le-Blanc and began to dig in to consolidate their position, only dead Germans were to be found; none of the Germans wanted to give themselves up and all the survivors had withdrawn. As this was happening, German troops were seen to be forming up down the hill, complete with tanks, intent on mounting a counterattack. A forward observation officer from the Royal Artillery was able to call in a bombardment of accurate heavy artillery, which quickly dispersed them.

However, despite this apparent success and the casualties suffered by the infantry companies of 4 Wilts, at dusk it was decided that the area around the village was too heavily defended and both B Squadron and 4 Wilts were ordered by 129th Brigade's commander, Brigadier Gerard Mole, to retire back across the Druance stream to Danvou. They would be needed the next day to support the assault on Mont Pinçon itself.

Meanwhile, during 5 August, 5 Wilts and A Squadron 13th/18th were to secure the crossroads at Chante-Pie, then a bridge over Le Roucamps stream between there and La Varinière, before pushing on through La Varinière to assault the dominating feature above – Mont Pinçon. The advance commenced at 1300 hrs and despite crossing the Druance stream and D Company having seized the crossroads, 5 Wilts and A Squadron would meet fiercely determined opposition further down the road and were unable to cross the next stream towards La Varinière. The conditions were hot, dry and dusty and the movement of the tanks would typically invite another mortar stonk, much to the chagrin of the infantry. As one infantryman had commented: 'Contrary to popular belief, I think the infantryman dislikes armour supporting him in attack. It is magnetic in its attraction of enemy fire.'[9]

Positioned some 200 yards from the stream, they would be shelled repeatedly throughout the evening, causing many casualties to the infantry. Indeed, 5 Wilts were to suffer the loss of their popular chaplain, The Reverend Jimmy Douglas, along with the officer commanding D Company, Major Richard Thomas. C Squadron were meant to have ferried infantry of 4 SLI on a route to the south towards Le Plessis-Grimoult, but finding the roads congested with tanks of the Guards' Division, this plan had to be abandoned and the tanks moved to the rear of B Squadron.

The regiment harboured west of the Chante-Pie crossroads for the night, joined by B Squadron at 0400 hrs, who had remained with 4 Wilts until the depleted battalion had reached Danvou in the early hours; despite becoming the reserve battalion, they were destined to suffer yet more casualties during the night from shelling. Having personally reconnoitred the bridge which had held up the 5 Wilts' advance, Major Wormald gave orders for Royal Engineers to clear the mines, to ensure that a bridgehead could be established on the east side of the stream, to give them a solid footing the next day.

Major General Ivor Thomas commanded the 43rd (Wessex) Infantry Division, and his orders for 6 August were that the 7th Battalion of the Hampshire Regiment (7 Hants), part of 130th Infantry Brigade, would assault Mont Pinçon from the north, with a view to drawing focus away from 129th Infantry Brigade's assault to the west and south-west, where they had failed to break through to the main objective the day before. The 129th Brigade would operate with two battalions leading, 4 SLI on the left with B Squadron's tanks, 5 Wilts on the right, supported by A Squadron; 4 Wilts were in reserve behind 4 SLI. Owing to the number of casualties sustained on 5 August, the depleted A and B companies of 5 Wilts would now form a combined company, with a joint force of C and D companies also forming up behind, before they reached their start line. With the 7 Hants' attack taking place to the north, 5 Wilts and A Squadron formed up, ready to cross the stream and bridge. H-hour had been pushed back from 1200 hrs to 1400 hrs, following the Wiltshire infantrymen furthest right being attacked by German troops in the morning. At 1350 hrs, a creeping artillery barrage and smokescreen descended on the east side of the stream, moving east at 100 yards every five minutes. This would cover the movement of 5 Wilts wading the stream and A Squadron's tanks crossing the bridge, which they were unable to reach on the 5th. Lance Sergeant Bill Hammond's tank led 2nd Troop over the bridge and initially the advance was working well, until 5 Wilts were about halfway to La Varinière. The German defenders had used the smokescreen to their advantage and had moved to adopt positions to the right flank of the attack and then opened up with a terrific weight of fire, scything down the men of the leading combined company. The Germans threw literally everything they had at the Wiltshires, and it was certainly a very unhealthy place to be. The 5 Wilts' commander, Lieutenant Colonel 'Pop' Pearson, attempted to rally his leading platoons. As he strode forward, walking stick in hand, he was shot dead by a sniper lurking in a tree; the sniper was promptly shot dead by one of Pearson's corporals. Chaos reigned and with the infantry disorganised with mounting casualties, their advance was halted for a time. With their Major Milne captured by the Germans, the 5 Wilts' adjutant, Captain Peace, took over command of the faltering attack.

Meanwhile to their left, B Squadron tanks moved up 4 SLI from Le Toque to La Roguerie ready for their attack up the steep incline. The B Squadron tanks were unable to accompany them on to their objective, since, as the A Squadron Diary records: 'On this flank the terrain was considered to be impossible to tanks.'

An O Group took place at 1230 hrs, with H Hour set for 1500 hrs for the advance by 4 SLI. B Company would lead on the left side, with D Company following, and A Company on the right, with C Company behind. In the hot August afternoon, the leading companies began their advance up the steep slope, the men in shirtsleeves. As soon as the battalion was exposed in open countryside, the Germans opened fire with an estimated dozen machine guns, from well-concealed positions above. The leading platoon of A Company was almost completely wiped out and the Red Cross armbands worn by the stretcher-bearers, who tried to reach the casualties, seemed to draw German fire. None of the gun positions could be identified and 4 SLI would remain hugging the ground for the next six hours, unable to move without drawing fire.

Back with the assault by 5 Wilts and A Squadron, following an artillery stonk being directed onto the village, the infantry finally managed to advance towards the houses at La Varinière, where white flags started to appear, and the German defenders began to emerge to surrender. Over a hundred prisoners would be captured by 5 Wilts, who's battalion was now reduced to around seventy-five men. However, they had La Varinière secured within twenty minutes and began to dig in around the crossroads there. Captain Peace was wounded by an enemy shell, so Major Roberts of 4 SLI was ordered to move to La Varinière and take over command of 5 Wilts. As this was taking place, Major Milne arrived out of breath, at a gallop, having managed to escape from his German captors to rejoin 5 Wilts!

At this stage, C Squadron's tanks were deployed to protect A Squadron's right flank. Orders received at 1800 hrs from Brigade stated that 5 Wilts should hold the crossroads, whilst 4 Wilts would pass through their position to assault Mont Pinçon itself. However, 4 Wilts were some distance away at Le Toque and Lieutenant Colonel Dunkerly didn't want to lose the initiative. Corporal Patrick Hennessey had identified a narrow track, which looked as though it may lead to the summit, so the colonel ordered A Squadron to send up a patrol to see if they could exploit this track. It was a bold move, since without infantry support, they might well encounter German infantry armed with Panzerfausts along the way, or indeed the feared 88mm gun waiting for them at the top. But Captain Noel Denny (who had replaced Captain Peter Lyon as Squadron 2ic) moved up the track with Lieutenants Elliot's and Jennison's troops. Corporal Patrick Hennessey recalled:

> I was just about to head up this path when all of a sudden from my left, another Sherman appeared and came racing across my bows with a friend of mine, a chap called Corporal Hammond, leaning out of the turret, roaring with laughter and waving at me; and away he went up the track and I had to follow him. We both started racing up this track, as if it was something of a game. I was furious with Hammond for going in front, in this piratical fashion, but away he went crashing up to the top.

Near the bottom of the track, with a steep drop either side, they passed some quarries, which would claim Corporal Davies's 17-pounder Firefly as it slid down the bank and overturned. Sergeant Rattle's tank was also fired upon and had its track blown off by an armoured piercing round, so he was forced to drop out of the race to the summit. Part way up the climb, the tanks of 2nd Troop fired smoke rounds ahead to mask their approach and before they knew it, they emerged onto the summit of Mont Pinçon at 1830 hrs, virtually unopposed all the way up. Captain Denny remembered: 'Contrary to expectations, it was much more pleasant at the top than at the bottom of Mont Pinçon, as it was a lovely summer evening.'

It appeared that the German defenders had their armour committed elsewhere and were preoccupied with the attacks going on to the north and east of the feature. The 7 Hants attack seemed to have drawn the Germans away from the western end of the summit and the 3&8s had managed to successfully exploit an Achilles' heel in the German defences. As the seven A Squadron tanks took up positions in all-round defence, 4 SLI could see the Hussars' tanks up on the summit.

Royal Engineers had been busy clearing mines from the road around La Roguerie, which enabled a troop of B Squadron tanks to move up to support 4 SLI on the open hillside. The tanks were able to identify and deal with a few German positions before a heavy mist began to descend over the hillside, obscuring their movements to the German defenders and leaving 4 SLI now in a position to advance. The infantry companies now broke cover and commenced their heavy slog up the steep hill, carrying all their ammunition and equipment. C and D companies passed through A and B and led the way, managing to pass through the German defences undetected in the mist and emerged to join the regiment's tanks on the summit. Once dug in, the infantrymen were hot, sweaty, dusty, utterly exhausted and hungry, but dressed in their shirtsleeves would soon begin to shiver in the cold mist enveloping the summit, without even the comfort of a hot drink.

During an artillery stonk back down the hill, Major Wormald's tank had become immobilised and an armoured recovery vehicle was sent to attend to it. As that was moving into position, it ran over a mine, badly wounding two of its crew, who had been perched on the front of the major's tank. As Major Wormald was helping to bandage the two casualties, Colonel Dunkerly arrived and urged the major to join his forward troops up the hill. His hands covered in blood, the major explained that he had a slight mobility problem at present, which did not seem to impress his commander. However, he was soon successful in hitching a ride with another of the squadron's tanks to the summit and the squadron fitters were not long in delivering a replacement vehicle for him and his crew.

Once A Squadron had moved off to scale Mont Pinçon, C Squadron were no longer required to guard their right flank, so were sent to probe the terrain east of La Varinière, towards Le Plessis-Grimoult, to the south of the feature. Beyond La Varinière, 1st Troop, under the command of Lieutenant Coates, ran into some soft ground and their tanks became bogged down; 2nd Troop were dispatched to help them, but only two of the tanks could be recovered. One tank was attacked by the enemy, killing two troopers, and other 'unhorsed' crewmembers were forced to return on foot. The dismounted troops were caught in an ambush on their return journey, costing another trooper killed and two others wounded, before they finally managed to reach friendly lines.

Before long, A Squadron was joined by both B Squadron and RHQ on the summit and they organised themselves into defensive positions. The men of 4 Wilts had now passed through the 5 Wilts position below and followed the 4 SLI path to the top, and they began to dig in also. German voices could be heard shouting through the mist, but they seemed to be oblivious to the location of the regiment's tanks, a short distance away. Captain Noel Denny recorded:

> We were told a few weeks later that the fog was our salvation, as a large German counterattack, which had formed up and would almost certainly have succeeded in driving us off the position, lost the way in the fog.

Down below, C Squadron under Major Sir Delaval Cotter, would spend the night in support of 5 Wilts around the La Varinière crossroads. In the morning, they were forced to fight off a determined German counterattack, which got to the stage of the infantry of both sides throwing grenades at one another. However, the Germans were eventually beaten off and thanks to the Royal Artillery having guns set on prearranged targets, another group of Germans forming up was successfully stonked and forced to disperse.

The dawn on the summit brought with it German shells, but thankfully there were few casualties. At 0530 hrs, B Squadron tanks with 4 SLI moved out to secure the eastern end of the summit ridge. In order to accomplish this, B Squadron commander, Major Anthony Rugge-Price, elected to walk 20 yards ahead of Lieutenant Hugh Franks's lead tank, following a compass bearing in the thick mist; he insisted on this distance, so that the tank's metal hull wouldn't interfere with his magnetic compass. He had performed a very brave act indeed since there were still German infantry on the eastern end of the ridge. As they swept the remainder of the summit area, they collected a few dispirited prisoners along the way.

The 3&8s were shelled until relieved at midday by two squadrons of the 4th/7th Dragoon Guards. Next, the 214th Infantry Brigade were deployed to relieve what remained of the infantry battalions on the summit; 4 SLI was relieved by the 7th Battalion Somerset Light Infantry and 4 Wilts was relieved by the 1st Battalion of the Worcestershire Regiment. The regiment's tanks carried the infantry of 4 Wilts and 4 SLI back down the hill to a rally point near Danvou-la-Ferrière. C Squadron harboured nearby at 'La Quesnee' (Le Quesnoy), once released from La Varinière, and finally the battered remnants of the 5 Wilts companies were relieved by the 5th Battalion of the Duke of Cornwall's Light Infantry.

As such a pivotal objective within the battle for Normandy, Mont Pinçon would be added to the regiment's battle honours. Today the memorial to the 13th/18th Royal Hussars (QMO) stands on its summit.

The fighting in the general area of Mont Pinçon was far from over, however, and the regiment was back in the thick of it on 9 August. Now supporting the

battalions of the 151st Infantry Brigade, the 6th, 8th and 9th battalions of the Durham Light Infantry, they would advance towards Saint-Pierre-la-Vieille to the south-east of the high ground, which sat astride another significant road junction. Once dominating the ground for 2 miles to the south of Le Plessis-Grimoult, the plan was for the tanks of the 4th/7th Dragoon Guards, supporting the 69th Infantry Brigade, to pass through their positions, onto Saint-Pierre-la-Vieille. In addition, 9 DLI would provide a firm base in reserve at Le Plessis-Grimoult, with A Squadron. C Squadron with 8 DLI would advance on the right, with B Squadron supporting 6 DLI on their left. Again, with the advance following a creeping artillery barrage, C Squadron and 8 DLI met comparatively light opposition, with the usual machine-gun fire noticeably absent. However, they were to be shelled routinely as they advanced and although C Squadron lost only one tank during their advance, sadly, the squadron 2ic, Captain John Wardlaw, was to lose his life. He was particularly unfortunate, as he was halfway to closing his turret hatch when a shell exploded in a tree above his head, killing him instantly. B Squadron and 6 DLI also achieved their objective, but at much heavier cost. The adjutant, Captain Julius Neave, recorded: 'Unfortunately, we have had some fairly heavy casualties in tanks. C losing one and B eight! B's were from Bazookas [2], 88mm Armour-piercing [3], mines [2] and one badly bogged.'

Also commenting on Captain Wardlaw, he stated: 'He had done magnificently since arrival. Nothing worried him and he was most unlucky.'

Another casualty of the advance on Saint-Pierre-la-Vieille was Lance Sergeant Johnnie Hardie, MM, in B Squadron. He too was to succumb to a high-explosive shell bursting above his head while looking out from his tank turret but was fortunate to survive the incident. He would be evacuated through the battlefield medical system and his service book records that he was 'HOME' on 13 August.[10] Not all of the pieces of shrapnel were removed from his head by the medics, leaving him with a bumpy and itchy scalp for the remainder of his life, acting as a constant reminder of his narrow escape from the Grim Reaper!

By late afternoon, the infantry dug in north of Saint-Pierre-La-Vieille and both B and C squadrons were initially required to remain in support, since bad road congestion behind at Le Plessis-Grimoult (which had held up B Squadron earlier in the day) delayed the arrival of anti-tank guns to support the infantry. In the evening, the 4th/7th DG with their accompanying infantry passed through and a steady stream of German prisoners began to filter back, estimated at between 200 and 300 in the Regimental Diary. They appeared quite willing to surrender and seemed very relieved that their war was over. As the complete regiment harboured to the south of Le Plessis-Grimoult, Colonel Dunkerly attended an O Group with the headquarters of the 69th Infantry

Brigade. In the morning, A Squadron would be required to support the 5th Battalion of the East Yorkshire Regiment in an attack on high ground to the west of Saint-Pierre-La-Vieille, while the remainder of the regiment would remain in the harbour area as a counterattack reserve. Heavy shelling continued throughout the night.

At 0400 hrs, Major Wormald joined the commanding officer of 5 EYR for a reconnaissance of the terrain for their attack up to the village. In the A Squadron Diary, the major rather ominously recorded:

> Thick fog. Plan extremely loose. Artillery support bad and attack unlikely to be successful. The ravine was similar to that which had held up the 5th Wilts, west of Mont Pinçon. Deep, wooded and a tank obstacle. The approach to the ravine was across open country as was the country beyond the ravine, leading up to a ridge containing the village, which was the objective. In the thick fog we could only give fire support for the infantry until they entered the ravine. There was a road bridge on the left of the immediate area of the attack which we intended to cross as soon as the infantry emerged on the far side of the ravine. We were then to lead them into the objective, with maximum 'suppressive' fire.

The attack commenced at 0800 hrs with the infantry moving down the forward slope towards the ravine, their movements hidden by a blanket of fog. The A Squadron tanks were deployed across the open hillside, waiting for the infantry to emerge up the other bank of the ravine before they would cross the bridge to support them on the far side. However, the men of 5 EYR would meet stiff opposition and did not reappear on the far side of the ravine. By 0900 hrs, the fog was lifting, leaving the A Squadron tanks exposed on the open hillside. A Squadron was fired upon and three Panzer V Panthers were identified on the high ground above them. The 3&8 tanks responded with high-explosive shells and smoke, and 3rd Troop observed two Panther crews abandon their vehicles, and the third was believed hit, as no further shots were received from it. Positioned on the right-hand side of the slope, 2nd Troop's commander, Lieutenant Peter Hunter, MC, could not be contacted over the radio. Corporal Patrick Hennessey remembered:

> Major Wormald came up on the air to say that he could get no response from the Troop leader of the other troop, which was up forward with us, although his tank was in view and not very far away. I was told to go across and find out what was the matter. We drew up just behind the other tank and I told Trooper Cocoran, the co-driver, to go and have a look. He was

not keen, but we watched him as he made his way to Lt Hunter's tank. He scrambled on to the side of the tank, took one look into the turret, and came rushing back to us.

'Christ!' he said, 'they are all dead in there – what a bloody mess.' What had happened was that an 88mm shot had penetrated the turret, in which it had ricocheted round and round, killing all the turret crew and ending up in the co-driver's back. Suddenly, we saw some movement from the driver's hatch of the stricken tank, and out of it climbed a very shocked and distressed Trooper Shuttleworth, who was the only survivor of that ghastly episode.

Other than the driver, the whole crew were dead, including 20-year-old Trooper Russell Burgoyne from West Hoe in Plymouth and Trooper Frederic Brown.

For the rest of the morning, A Squadron continued to fire into the German positions and laid a smokescreen, until at midday, 1st Troop managed to cross the bridge. They engaged some pockets of German infantry and destroyed two self-propelled anti-tank guns. However, the attack had largely petered out and although another assault was planned with a reserve company at 1700 hrs, this never took place. The Green Howards relieved 5 EYR, and the East Yorks retired to the north side of the ravine. Once released, A Squadron harboured to the north alongside the 5 EYR battalion headquarters.

Trooper Russell Burgoyne.

A spirited defence of Saint-Pierre-La-Vieille by its German garrison held up plans the following day. In the evening, Colonel Dunkerly attended an O Group with the 151st Infantry Brigade and an attack was planned for C Squadron at first light, provided that the 4th/7th Dragoon Guards achieved their objectives overnight, with infantry of the 231st Infantry Brigade. On the morning of 12 August, the attack would first be postponed to 1000 hrs, then to 1300 hrs. Finally, at 1330 hrs, 9 DLI commenced their attack on La Villette, to the east of Saint-Pierre-La-Vieille, supported by C Squadron. B Squadron, firing from a firm base behind, helped to shoot the infantry into the village, despite heavy enemy fire coming from the north and east. C Squadron had one tank brewed up, but the crew managed to escape unharmed. Another tank was hit, wounding the attached forward observation officer from the Royal Artillery. As 2nd Troop's tanks advanced on the village, Trooper Doug Kay proved his gunnery skills in Sergeant Scamp's Sherman Firefly, *Carole*, by taking on and destroying first a Panzer V Panther, then a Panzer VI Tiger. This action highlighted that the Firefly's 17-pounder gun truly was a match for even the best German armour. A ground-mounted 88mm gun was also silenced before 2nd and 3rd troops achieved their objectives, meeting only light resistance once the attack had gained some momentum. Some Bren Gun Carriers of 9 DLI moved into La Villette to take up defensive positions by 1500 hrs, but they had been quite badly shot up earlier in the battle, so the C Squadron tanks remained in the village awaiting the infantry to arrive on foot, before they could be relieved. They were finally able to withdraw at 2130 hrs.

A pocket of German troops in an orchard had been proving a nuisance and seemed reluctant to move off, so A Squadron, who had been held in reserve back on Mont Pinçon, was ordered to deal with the problem. Captain Denny led 1st and 4th troops forwards, to support 6 DLI onto this position. They commenced their attack on the orchard at 1730 hrs and were able to deal with the problem quite swiftly, capturing a few prisoners in the process. The infantry had moved in and consolidated the position by 2100 hrs, allowing the tanks to withdraw.

That evening, the whole regiment withdrew to Clamesnil, south of Villers-Bocage, arriving around midnight. They were to enjoy four days out of the line, which was their first proper rest since they had moved off to participate in Operation Goodwood on the night of 17 July.

On 14 August, the regiment were to receive a high-ranking guest. The Regimental Diary records:

> Lieutenant General Horrocks, who has recently taken over 30 Corps, came over to talk to the Regt and 4/7 DG. Congratulated us on our efforts and put us in the bigger picture. Situation at the moment is that the American and Free French armour are in Argentan and pushing north to Falaise. Canadians are also attacking southwards from Potigny with Polish Armoured Division. 12 Corps are also pushing S.E from Thury Harcourt. The RAF are strafing daily with considerable success and altogether the German 7th Army is beginning to look fairly uncomfortable with only an 18-mile gap through Falaise to get out from. Our future is apparently to strike eastwards from Conde sur Noireau with a US Corps on the right, directed on Paris, 30 Corps centre and 12 Corps left.

Chapter 8

The Breakout from Normandy and Operation Market Garden

We had the smell of success in our nostrils.

As the regiment enjoyed a few days' well-earned rest at Clamesnil, on 16 August they would receive forty-three new faces who had been drafted in from the headquarters of the now late 27th Armoured Brigade. This helped bring the 3&8 squadrons back up to strength and new tanks were also received to replace the recent losses.

Falaise

Meanwhile, with the success of Operation Cobra and the rapid advance of General Patton's US 3rd Army south from the Cotentin Peninsula, Hitler devised a plan to send the majority of his armour in Normandy west, to cut off Patton's forces in the south. Hitler did not appreciate the critical condition of his Panzer units in Normandy, most of which had been fighting continuously for many weeks and were unable to make good the losses suffered through this fighting. Hitler's new commander, Generalfeldmarschall von Kluge (following von Rundstedt being relieved of his command), was ordered to send eight Panzer divisions west, which von Kluge objected to and requested that the forces in Normandy be permitted to fall back to a new defensive line along the Seine River. Hitler would not hear of it and insisted that his plan, codenamed Operation Lüttich, was to be carried out. However, only four divisions could be made ready and Operation Lüttich commenced around Mortain on 7 August, intent on cutting straight through the American-held territory, to the west coast near Avranches. Hitler's generals knew the plan was madness but could not go against the wishes of their supreme commander. Of course, thanks to 'Ultra' intercepts from Bletchley Park, plus aerial reconnaissance, US General Bradley had a very clear idea of German deployments and was able to anticipate the movements of von Kluge's Panzer divisions. It quickly became apparent that Operation Lüttich could not be successful and fully realising that his forces were being encircled in Normandy, von Kluge finally managed to persuade the

Führer to relent, and the German Army began to move east, in a race to escape the jaws that were closing around them.

With Allied forces pressing in from each side and being harassed from the air during the hours of daylight, German losses in men, weapons and transport began to mount up. By 19 August, the remains of the German forces in Normandy were now hemmed into the Dives valley, beyond Falaise, with the British 2nd Army blocking them from the west and north-west, the Canadian 1st Army from the north, the US VII Corps pressing from the south-west, the US XV Corps from the south and the French 2nd Armoured Division from the south-east. The newly arrived 1st Polish Armoured Division had moved onto the heights of Mont-Ormel in the east, directly in the path of the fleeing Germans. Only a narrow corridor now existed across the Dives River between Trun and Chambois, with just two crossing points remaining open: a bridge at Saint-Lambert-sur-Dives and a ford to the south-east at Moissy. Burning tanks and vehicles littered the roads through the Dives valley, as Allied attack aircraft hunted the German convoys, trapped in this burning cauldron. Artillery units shelled the German formations at will and soon there were thousands of German corpses, plus many dead horses from their horse-drawn transport and cattle littering the valley floor. The Allies threw the full weight of their firepower at the fleeing Germans. Some German units had managed to escape from this pocket before the Polish armour had moved to block their last avenue of escape and during the night of 19/20 August, the remaining Germans tried to organise their breakout from the valley under cover of darkness. Major General Maczek's Polish troops fought the Germans as hard as they could, as they attempted to move through the Polish positions on Mont-Ormel. Fierce fighting took place throughout the night, with considerable loss to the Polish division, and although they inflicted heavy losses on the enemy, many Germans would still manage to force their way through and escape. At one stage the Polish were entirely surrounded by German forces and could only be resupplied with ammunition from the air. As darkness gave way to daylight, the columns of fleeing Germans became clearly visible and those unlucky enough not to escape during the night once again became the focus of attack aircraft and artillery as the slaughter continued. By 22 August, any German forces to the west of Allied lines were either in captivity… or dead! Estimates of the number of Germans who were trapped in the pocket of the Dives valley are up to 100,000 soldiers. Of those, between 10,000 and 15,000 were killed, 40,000 to 50,000 were taken prisoner, and 20,000 to 50,000 escaped the encirclement.[1] As maggots fed on the decaying flesh in the hot summer weather, swarms of flies descended on the Dives valley and the water was considered contaminated for years to come.

Upon visiting the area, General Eisenhower is quoted as having said:

The battlefield at Falaise was unquestionably one of the greatest 'killing fields' of any of the war areas. Forty-eight hours after the closing of the gap I was conducted through it on foot, to encounter scenes that could be described only by Dante. It was literally possible to walk for hundreds of yards at a time, stepping on nothing but dead and decaying flesh.

Further west of Falaise, the 13th/18th moved to a harbour area south of Sainte-Honorine-la-Chardonne on the morning of 18 August. News of German forces being on the run from Normandy was well received and a new phase of the campaign seemed imminent. The regiment moved to the west of Putanges-le-Lac the following day, in readiness to protect the left flank of the 11th Armoured Division as it advanced. However, the retreating Germans had blown bridges over the Orne River, so the advance was slowed as Royal Engineers constructed a Bailey bridge[2] over the Orne at Putanges. For 20 August, the A Squadron Diary records the following, as the regiment advanced:

At 1500 hrs we were on the road again to Sentilly, four miles west of Argentan and were now beginning to pass all sorts of enemy equipment which had been wrecked, by RAF or destroyed by the enemy in retreat. Four Tigers and five Panthers and numerous horse-drawn vehicles of all types were observed.

Following some mopping-up operations along the way, the regiment arrived at a château near Bailleul, north of Argentan, which had been used as a German corps headquarters (dubbed 'Dead Horse Château' by C Squadron's Major Cotter). Captain Julius Neave recorded:

I have seen more dead Boche since last night than during the whole of the campaign, and the chaos on the roads of burnt-out vehicles, dead horses and men, and the smell are awful. The château has been strafed thoroughly by our aircraft and the shambles is unbelievable. The Boche Corp Commander's caravan caused some amusement and I have the Corps Commander's bath and an electric iron! The whole place stinks to high heaven and I think there must be Boche all around longing to give themselves up. About 50 Boche walked in this evening with two officers. None of them know anything and haven't for a week and are really pleased to give themselves up. We have put them on to clearing up the mess, particularly burying dead horses. Another 500 Boche have walked in and the Yanks, who are also around, say they have collected hundreds all day. The 6th Durham Light Infantry have just reported that they are in a wonderful position and can see more hundreds walking towards them.

On the 22nd, Neave noted in his diary:

> Today I have a 'ride' for the first time I think since 1940 – on one of about 200 Boche horses left at the ruined château. RSM Duffy Hinc put on an impressive display of horsemanship. Have seen more carnage today than yesterday and we shall be glad to get away from it.

That day, C Squadron moved to the north-east of Argentan into Chambois with 8 DLI and continued to collect German prisoners. Some of these were SS personnel and some, it was discovered, had attempted to mask their identities by dressing in civilian clothes.

The long-awaited breakout from Normandy

On the 23rd, the long-awaited breakout from Normandy began for the regiment, as they were tasked with clearing the Forêt de Breteuil to the east. The area was discovered to be clear of enemy and despite congested roads, the 3&8 tanks would cover 43 miles that day. French people welcomed them enthusiastically all along their route. This was to prove a typical 'hurry up and wait' exercise, as the regiment would now be held up on the south side of the Seine River for five days, before they could eventually cross to the other side. This finally took place in the late afternoon of 28 August at Vernon, over a Class 40 Bailey bridge, before the regiment harboured about 3 miles north of the river, having rejoined the remainder of 8th Armoured Brigade. While waiting to cross the river, the regiment received the news that Paris had been liberated on 25 August. Allied forces, now north of the Seine River, would chase the remnants of the German Army fleeing from Normandy back towards the Fatherland.

The regiment moved out of the Gasny area on 29 August and were delayed as Royal Engineers made good a badly cratered road ahead. Once on the move again, reports were received of a German rearguard in the village of Fourges, directly in the path of their axis of advance. A vanguard, led by Captain Noel Denny, performed a left-flanking manoeuvre with Stuart tanks of Recce Troop through a wooded hillside. Meanwhile, B Squadron tanks worked their way around to the right of the German position. Recce Troop came under anti-tank fire and three of their Stuarts were knocked out. B Squadron was also fired upon, brewing up one tank. After a considerable weight of fire was returned, it was discovered that a 75mm PAK had been the culprit. A Squadron then advanced into the village and reported it as clear, before moving on to Bray-et-Lû, where another anti-tank gun stopped their advance.

Rearguard activity had continued throughout the day, with snipers and well-concealed anti-tank guns delaying the advance. Having been in reserve at Fourges, 2nd Troop of C Squadron had taken the lead as they approached Saint-Clair-sur-Epte and came under accurate anti-tank fire. Corporal Frederick Pink's tank was hit, killing the commander. Seven 3&8s had lost their lives on the 29th, with several others wounded. However, the regiment had advanced 15 miles and Brigadier Prior-Palmer was delighted with their overall progress.

The regiment moved into brigade reserve the following day. Their route north was changed, following reports of Tiger tanks in Gisors, but all was quiet until the leading tanks from B Squadron were engaged by the enemy at La Houssoye. Two B Squadron tanks were knocked out, at the cost of three more young troopers dead,[3] and another tank damaged. However, the gun responsible could not be located and at 1900 hrs, B Squadron were ordered to withdraw, and the regiment harboured for the night outside La Houssoye. On the 31st, once it was established that the route ahead was now clear of enemy, the regiment made good progress. They were able to motor north, without incident, and arrived at Oresmaux in the evening, about 6 miles south of Amiens. Captain Julius Neave recorded:

> It has been a new experience to enter villages at high speed on tanks, when the Boche only left ten minutes previously. The excitement and enthusiasm of the population was immense, and flowers, flags and kisses were showered about.

Colonel Dunkerly attended an 8th Armoured Brigade Orders Group, where he was informed that the Guards Armoured Division and 11th Armoured Division had captured Amiens and would push on to Arras the following day, with 8th Armoured Brigade protecting their left flank in the areas between Doullens and Ivergny, as they advanced.

On 1 September, the regiment crossed the Somme River. As the brigade advanced north, the 4th/7th Dragoon Guards on the 3&8's left were engaged by enemy anti-tank guns and tanks. However, they were successful in knocking out several anti-tank guns and armour, capturing many prisoners along the way.

The Resistance fighters of the FFI (Forces françaises de l'Intérieur) reported to the 3&8s that some enemy troops had been seen hastily withdrawing into woods outside of Lucheux, trying to make their way from Doullens back to Arras. A Squadron was dispatched to clear the woods and while the remainder of the regiment stood to, the regiment's tanks came to the attention of Allied aircraft above. Captain Julius Neave recorded in his diary:

> We received a personal attack from four Typhoons with cannons and machine guns – fortunately, no rockets. It was extremely frightening, and they fairly peppered the RHQ tanks. The yellow smoke came out like a flash – tons of it – and fortunately they soon stopped.

As this was taking place, A Squadron's foray into the woods had begun to drive the Germans out and dozens of them began to emerge to give themselves up. They had collected around eighty prisoners and RHQ tanks would now escort them to nearby Bouquemaison, as the regiment pressed on towards Ivergny. As the RHQ tanks advanced, more Germans emerged from the undergrowth to join the column and their numbers continued to swell until they reached the village. They were met with chaotic scenes in the village, as the tanks were mobbed by the villagers in celebration, while others attempted to mob the German prisoners, jeering and spitting at them. The local FFI wanted to shoot the prisoners there and then, and it was with great difficulty that they were prevented from doing so. As the Hussars needed to press on, an agreement was made that the prisoners would be locked in a barn and guarded by the FFI until military police arrived to take charge of them. The regiment moved off, but as Julius Neave recorded in his diary: 'As soon as the FFI thought we were out of sight, they set fire to the barn which even if understandable, was sickening to us, contrary to every wartime convention.'

On this day, another unfortunate incident would take place, described by Corporal Patrick Hennessey:

> We pulled into an area on the side of the road to allow another squadron to go past us and take over the lead. The tank commanders were called for a briefing, the crews remaining in their tanks. After the conference, we returned to our tanks and climbed aboard to brief the crews. In one tank, as the commander slipped through his turret hatch, his gunner turned in his seat to face him, and in so doing, his foot hit the firing switch of the 75mm gun.[4] He must have left his firing switch on because the gun fired, and the shot hit the tank in front. It struck the top of the turret just as Lieutenant David Jennison was climbing in and killed him outright. This tragedy deprived us of a very popular young officer who, not long before, had been awarded the Military Cross. The remainder of his crew, although badly shocked, were un-injured. If the shot had hit only six inches lower,

the whole tank could have gone up in flames. The gunner who made that fatal error must have lived with the memory of it for the rest of his life.

However, the Germans were in retreat and Patrick Hennessey recorded the sensation:

> Dreadful as were the sights we saw, this particular period of relentless pursuit of a stricken army was the most exciting and exhilarating time I have ever experienced. I could understand the fierce pride and elation which must have been felt by the young German soldiers in 1940 as they swept across Europe behind the retreating Allies. Now it was our turn, and we pressed on, hard and fast. There were some who tried to make a stand to fight it out, but they were quickly overcome and taken prisoner. They were at a great disadvantage as their organisation had completely broken down. They had no re-supply of fuel, ammunition, or rations, and they were at the mercy of the RAF from the air and us on the ground. It has truly been said that there is no greater boost to morale than success in battle. We had the smell of success in our nostrils, but we were never free from danger. Before the Germans pulled out from a farm or village, they would, if they had time, leave booby traps and mines. Booby traps and anti-personnel mines were most prevalent in empty farm buildings. Any innocent looking object, such as a jug of milk on a table, a half open door, or an overturned chair, in fact any object which may temp the unwary to handle it, could trigger the most lethal explosion.

Captain Eric Cox, of the 8th Armoured Brigade Signals Squadron, recorded this episode, when locating a suitable building to use as a mess:

> This foray was to a small, remote, single-storey house ideal for our Mess for a night or so. Bertie, short for Major Berthoud, the OC of the Brigade HQ Squadron, with the mess sergeant and myself did a reconnaissance of this building. It seemed ideal, and I was just going to check out the inside kitchen when Bertie called me for advice on a back door. The mess sergeant, meanwhile, went into the kitchen and on opening the oven, set off a booby trap that cost him his life. It was a small explosion, but its position was critical and lethal. Had Bertie not called me at that instant, it would have been my life, as I would certainly have checked out that oven. There were no external wires as it had been set to explode on opening the oven door and was virtually fool proof. Our Brigade Padre was on hand and as he had done so often before, took over the disposal action.

On 2 September, several prisoners were captured by various units of the 3&8s during mopping-up operations in local villages. Sergeant Bill Hammond captured two German artillery officers and two junior ranks in a Citroën car at Bouquemaison. The car was handed over to the squadron fitters and would later be used by the regiment's officers to visit Brussels on leave.

On the 3rd, the regiment moved through Lens and was met by a very enthusiastic local population. Moving up into northern France and towards the Belgian border, the regiment was returning to areas they had occupied in 1940 and some were able to call in on old friends. Tuesday, 5 September provided an opportunity for Major Wormald and his new 2ic, Captain Stancomb, to visit Monchy-le-Preux, a few miles east of Arras, where A Squadron had been billeted for much of the Phoney War. They visited the Leroux family's farm, which had hosted the squadron officers' mess and were warmly greeted by their old friends.

Eric Cox, 8th Armoured Brigade Signals Squadron.

With C Squadron leading, the regiment crossed into Belgium on 6 September and would advance 50 miles through Tournai, and arrived at Ninove. The journey through Tournai brought back memories to Captain Stancomb of his fighting retreat with Lieutenant Wormald in May 1940, when as young troop commanders they'd been forced to ditch their vehicles in the river, to deny them to the advancing Germans. Such a rapid advance north in 1944 now certainly kept the fitters busy, as several tanks suffered shedding rubber from their road wheels.

The regiment entered Brussels on the 7th. Corporal Patrick Hennessey described the scene:

> We came at last to Brussels. The Guards had been there before us, but the welcome we received was rapturous. We had great difficulty in driving through the streets, which were lined with cheering crowds, many of whom climbed on to the tanks and showered us with gifts and bottles of wine, cakes and flowers. Girls were climbing up and kissing us, there was laughter, tears and music. We were surprised and delighted at our reception, and we thoroughly enjoyed the adulation!

A Stuart 'Honey' tank is greeted by Belgian townsfolk. (*Courtesy of The Tank Museum, Bovington – Image 4774-C5*)

Bill Mawson recalled that it was reported over their tank's radio that a pretty girl was climbing onto their tank. Bill was able to report that this was confirmed, and as she was stood astride the turret hatch, it appeared that underwear was in short supply in this part of Belgium. Young lads at war!

After a harbour at Gelrode for the night, the following day the regiment continued its advance to the north-east of Brussels, through Aarschot and Diest, and then crossed the Albert Canal in Beringen. Once over the canal and entering a wooded area north of coal mines, they began to receive stonks of both mortars and artillery, plus they had passed several brewed-up Shermans at the side of the road from leading units, which had clearly fallen victim to anti-tank fire. Several hundred prisoners were rounded up in this area, and the regiment harboured for the night at the mining town of Beverloo.

As everyone was having breakfast on 9 September, the support lorries of A1 Echelon in the rear at Beringen were attacked by a force reckoned to be at least 200 strong. Prisoners taken later claimed that they were part of a 300-strong force from the 723rd Grenadier Regiment of the 719th Infantry Division. Twenty-year-old Trooper Albert Belson was killed, and Lance Corporal Cubbitt wounded. After helping to carry Corporal Cubbitt, Trooper Jackson took a Bren gun and identified at least twenty enemy forming up near the canal. He fired into this party and managed to force them to withdraw. Meanwhile, Trooper Scargill managed to drive his lorry out of danger, before adopting a firing position in the upstairs window of a nearby house with a Bren gun and commenced firing at any enemy movement. He would capture two prisoners!

Throughout the engagement, the defence of the lorries was ably organised by the commanding officer of A1 Echelon, Major John Cordy-Simpson. Even decades after the conflict, wartime veterans of the 3&8s would speak of Major Cordy-Simpson with the utmost respect and reverence, and he was clearly a popular and respected commander. 'John the Boche', as the troopers referred to him, since he often spoke of 'The Boche', would be awarded the Military Cross and the attack at Beringen is mentioned in his medal citation:

> On another occasion, at BERINGEN, on the ALBERT CANAL, the Echelon was attacked by a large party of enemy who had infiltrated behind the lines. Although they succeeded in destroying a number of vehicles Maj. Cordy-Simpson very soon organised parties of men to deal with them. These parties he personally led and very quickly drove the enemy from the Echelon with heavy losses and thus prevented them from fulfilling their primary role of blowing the BERINGEN BRIDGE. The fighting spirit and disregard for danger shown by this Officer had been an inspiration to all ranks in the Echelon and has instilled into them the highest ideals of service. His personal leadership has played a vital and essential part in any measure of success which the Regiment may have obtained.

C Squadron sent their 2nd and 4th troops to restore the situation, which resulted in 19-year-old Trooper Joseph Robinson being mortally wounded, Trooper Bone wounded and a further six going missing, presumed taken prisoner. Trooper Robinson would die of his wounds the following day.[5] However, before being driven off, the Germans had succeeded in destroying fifteen fuel and ammunition lorries, plus a further twelve belonging to the 4th/7th Dragoon Guards. A jeep was also destroyed, along with a cargo of eggs, butter and gin belonging to the A Squadron officers!

On 10 September, B Squadron were sent out from Beverloo to conduct a reconnaissance of the town of Bourg-Léopold, since it appeared the Germans had withdrawn in the face of the rapid Allied advance. A few anti-tank weapons had been left in an attempt to delay the Allies, but B Squadron quickly destroyed two 75mm PAKs, plus another smaller-calibre gun. Trooper John Brookes of B Squadron remembered: 'Captain Bobby Neave – pistol in hand, walked up the road and instructed the Germans with an anti-tank gun to surrender … and returned with prisoners!'

The few prisoners captured confirmed that only a small rearguard remained in the town. On the 11th, Bourg-Léopold was captured without too much difficulty, with B Squadron once again present as infantry cleared the houses. German troops were sighted in woods to the north-west of the town, so artillery was laid on to deal with them. Otherwise, the regiment remained in the Beverloo area, using these few days to clean, refit and replenish the tanks. On the 12th, the 3&8s had the opportunity to use the colliery baths and were delighted at the opportunity to get themselves properly cleaned up. Trips to Diest, Louvain and Brussels were arranged to allow the men some time to relax, since the last big battle of the war (it was hoped), Operation Market Garden, was due to commence in the coming days.

On 16 September, Colonel Dunkerly attended a lecture on the upcoming Operation Market Garden, hosted by the commander of the 2nd Army, Lieutenant General Miles Dempsey, and the commander of XXX Corps, Lieutenant General Brian Horrocks. The following morning, he attended an O Group with 8th Armoured Brigade, followed by another O Group with 129th Infantry Brigade, where he was joined by Majors Rugge-Price and Cotter from B and C squadrons respectively.

Operation Market Garden

Operation Market Garden would be an attempt to shorten the war by several months, by dropping three Airborne divisions into Holland (Netherlands), to capture and dominate a 64-mile salient into German-held territory. This would involve the dropping of the British 1st Airborne Division around Arnhem, the US 82nd Airborne Division around Nijmegen and Grave, and lastly, the US 101st Airborne Division in the area of Eindhoven. For the airborne element, 'Market', the paratroopers would seize and hold nine strategic bridges over the Meuse and Rhine rivers, plus the surrounding canals. This would pave the way for the 2nd Army to exploit this success for the land assault, 'Garden', and create a bridgehead on the north side of the Rhine, as a launch pad into northern Germany.

On returning from a short spell of leave in Brussels, the regimental adjutant, Captain Neave, recorded:

> The traffic on the way there and back was simply staggering, and it is only too obvious that the coming battle is to be stupendous. There was enough bridging equipment that I passed to bridge the Channel and also, I saw the echelons of three Airborne Divisions!
>
> Half the world (2nd Army) was in Brussels and there is no doubt at all that we are having a lull before the whale of all storms. Let's hope to goodness that it is the last, as it looks hopeful of being so.

The Guards' Armoured Division would lead the way into Holland, with 8th Armoured Brigade following. The great day arrived on 17 September and Julius Neave recorded:

> Great expectancy over the weather – however, it held and the Air boys dropped OK. It is vital to us that they get to the bridges intact, or else we shall have to assault each river in turn, being ferried over on rafts – we long for an early sitrep [situation report].

As the Guards made their way north towards Eindhoven, they were to meet stiff opposition at Valkenswaard from remnants of the 9th and 10th SS Panzer divisions, armed with self-propelled guns. The Guards did manage to fight their way through, and news came that the Eindhoven landings had been a success and that the Guards had linked up with the US 101st Airborne.

The regiment had been held at Hechtel, just over the Belgian border, until 21 September, when their move north began. As A Squadron passed through Valkenswaard, Corporal Patrick Hennessey remembered:

> We passed the burnt-out remnants of the Shermans of the Irish Guards. They had run straight into a strong force of anti-tank guns and had lost 8 or 9 tanks in a very short space of time, before the RAF's rocket-firing Typhoons could sweep down and restore the situation. We found them a very valuable asset! Having seen what had happened to the Irish Guards, we thanked our lucky stars that we had not been leading on that occasion. It was imperative to keep the whole Corps moving up the main route. Signs on the road read, 'Don't Stop! If you must stop – get off the road. If you can't get off the road – Don't stop!'

The Nijmegen road bridge over the Waal. (*Courtesy of The Tank Museum, Bovington – Image 7277-A1*)

The A Squadron Diary records that an 88mm anti-aircraft gun responsible for engaging the Irish Guards' tanks was positioned further up the road but was set up in the ground role. Travelling in single file along one road, the Guards' tanks would have presented an easy target and couldn't deploy into surrounding fields.

The Nijmegen road bridge was reported as captured by the Guards and they were now to press on towards Arnhem, to try to link up with the hard-pressed British paratroopers. The 8th Armoured Brigade would now ensure that any remaining German units south of the Waal River were dealt with or taken prisoner.

The regiment moved north as far as Nijmegen, except for A Squadron, who were east of Eindhoven with the 12th Battalion of the King's Royal Rifle Corps. The 3&8s were tasked with defending the bridges in the Nijmegen area on both sides of the river, since counterattacks were expected from the east.

Now moving ever closer to the Fatherland, the Luftwaffe were provoked into action. Captain Neave recorded:

> Quite a lot of enemy activity tonight, more bombers than we have had since Normandy. They were going for the Meuse–Escaut canal bridge, which they missed but caused casualties for 231 Brigade. We must expect more of this with 20,000 vehicles on one road, going over at least half-a-dozen very important bridges.

It was around this time that Peter 'Cosy' Comfort's convalescence ended, following his being wounded during Operation Goodwood back in July. He remembered:

> Report to Catterick on draft for Burma with other Tankies. 'Where the hell are you lot going?' a passing Lilywhite[6] Captain spotted us. 'You're not you know!' A wand is waved, saved by the bell. The Regiment has spoken – our family always claim their sons!

Cosy would therefore travel to Eindhoven and was then reunited with the regiment. His first task was to find his old crew in B Squadron to be updated on what had been happening in his absence. However, after locating his old troop, he was informed that a few days after he had been wounded, his entire crew had been killed. For three full months back in England, he'd had no idea that all of the men he'd trained with, had laughed and joked with, had landed with on D-Day and had fought with during the opening weeks of the Normandy campaign, were dead. He could have had no idea that getting wounded had likely saved his life. This naturally came as a huge shock and in an act of self-preservation, Cosy compartmentalised this news and pushed it to the back of his mind. He was assigned to Recce Troop in RHQ and began a new life in Stuart tanks. Cosy never contacted any of the families of his crew after the war, would never discuss the friends he'd lost, and treated it, in his own words, as a 'closed book'. However, the survivor's guilt never left him and throughout his life, he would suffer bouts of depression, which he would refer to as the 'Black Dog'.

Although the Guards' Armoured Division had been held up at Elst, halfway between Nijmegen and Arnhem, a plan was devised whereby the regiment's A Squadron tanks would rush up to Arnhem, supported by infantry, and ensure that the bridge was in Allied hands; this was to be known as Operation Phukkit. However, it was known that elements of the 9th and 10th SS Panzer divisions were active in the area and the whole plan seemed incredibly risky. It was unknown, at that stage, whether or not the Arnhem bridge was in Allied hands. Much to the relief of the Hussars, the whole scheme was eventually cancelled. Major Wormald recorded in his diary on 24 September:

> At 0200 hrs a message was received from KRRC that the Squadron was now to be under command of 43rd Division and in support of the 4th Dorsets. This implied that Operation Phukkit was 'off'. (Thank God – It had seemed to me that our Brigadier had been a little optimistic in assuming that 'A' Squadron with the 12th/60th KRRC could achieve what the whole of the Guards' Armoured Division had failed to achieve. On

the other hand, they had not made the attempt with our tactical plan or in the dark!)

The weather was now extremely wet and cold, but despite the poor conditions, a large force of German aircraft attacked C Squadron. Although an unpleasant experience, since nothing heavier than machine guns were fired at the tanks, they did not cause any casualties.

In order to send reinforcements to support the Airborne Division's bridgehead in Arnhem, A Squadron moved up with the infantry of 4 Dorsets, plus Polish paratroopers, to Driel, just to the south of the Neder Rijn. In the end, only the Dorsets made an assault crossing after dark. However, owing to poor landing points on the north bank, few of the Dorsets made it to British lines and many, who had drifted downstream, would ultimately become prisoners. It was estimated that there were only around 1,000 operational Paras left in the Arnhem area, with the remainder of their division either captured, wounded or killed. The 130th Brigade would also ferry across much needed stores and ammunition during the night, supported by the regiment's tanks, which would fire at any targets that presented themselves, in an attempt to keep the Germans busy.

Unfortunately for the British 1st Airborne Division, their drop zone had been adjacent to units of the II SS Panzer Corps, which had managed to escape from France and Belgium. An artillery regiment, a battalion of heavy mortars, three battalions of flak guns, two battalions of Panzer grenadiers and thirteen battalions of infantry were in the area, guaranteeing that the British Paras were in for a very rough time! By the night of the 25th, it had become clear that the airborne bridgehead at Arnhem was no longer tenable, with increasingly strong German counterattacks, which risked cutting off the Paras from the river. Therefore, a decision was made to extract them from the north side, using assault boats and amphibious DUKW vehicles. An artillery barrage was laid on to harass the German troops, while 13th/18th tanks participated in a deception plan to make the Germans believe that the activity was actually intended to send reinforcements north. Fortunately, it rained heavily, which helped mask the noise of the Paras making their way south to the river. Surprisingly, well over 2,000 troops were rescued and brought safely back to the south bank of the Neder Rijn.

The Island

The regiment, less A Squadron, was released from 130th Brigade on 27 September, but the constant rain made most of the roads unserviceable and movement cross-country out of the question. While retiring, some tanks of C Squadron would become bogged, requiring a recovery operation at night, uncomfortably close to enemy positions. Causing everyone to remain alert, a party of six determined Germans swam down the Waal River from the east, intent on blowing up both bridges at Nijmegen, and were very successful in destroying the rail bridge but only caused minor damage to the road bridge, which was quickly reopened to traffic. Once able to cross, the regiment moved from billets in Oosterhoot to Weurt, south of the Waal. This would remain their location for an extended period in an area known as 'The Island', the bridgehead north of the Meuse River near Nijmegen and south of the Neder Rijn at Arnhem. A Squadron's troops, still deployed further north in the Homoet and Driel area near the Neder Rijn, would receive regular visits from their squadron commander. However, movement in a scout car only seemed to draw a stonk in response from the Germans across the river, which did not prove popular with the infantry in the area. Therefore, Major Wormald elected to visit his tanks on foot. On one occasion, as he was approaching 1st Troop near Driel, a Focke-Wulf 190 of the Luftwaffe flew past him at low level, only 20 yards away. The major drew his revolver from within his battledress blouse and fired several shots at the pilot, and to his immense surprise, saw the aircraft land soon afterwards. Upon returning to his squadron HQ, he was informed that the pilot had walked into an area occupied by C Squadron and had been wounded by a bullet that had grazed his forehead!

On 7 October, Lieutenant Colonel Dunkerly was forced to return to England, via Eindhoven, for treatment in hospital for a paralysed wrist. He had commanded the regiment since early July, but following his departure, Major the Earl of Feversham assumed command once more. Again, Major Rugge-Price would become his 2ic, as Captain Stancomb assumed command of B Squadron.

The Island was not popular with the men as the ground was saturated with water from the almost continual rain. Owing to this situation, an interesting occurrence near Arnhem was recorded by Major Wormald in the A Squadron Diary:

> Due to the water-logged nature of the ground, 4th Troop's location was now only accessible via the flood bank of the river, which was in full view of the enemy holding the far bank. Movement along the 'Bund' could only be undertaken under cover of darkness and silently. That is to say, at walking pace. Therefore, Lieutenant Alistair Watt, the Troop Leader, was walking in front of his tank. In order to get off the 'Bund' the tanks had to descend a very narrow and steep incline. At this point Alistair was walking backwards. I was at the bottom of the ramp, waiting for the Troop. Suddenly Alistair disappeared into the ground and, in a muffled and spluttering

voice, was heard to call for 'Help'. On investigation, it was seen that he had fallen into an open cesspit, in which he was endeavouring to swim/paddle in order to avoid drowning. There was no way in which he could extract himself from this predicament; a rope was required. The only rope available was the tow rope on his tank. This was removed from its stowage position as quickly as possible, by his crew. One end was lowered to Alistair and the other attached to his tank which then slowly extracted him from his rather nasty 'deathbed'! I then instructed him to risk the possibility of drawing the enemy's attention to himself and to proceed over the 'Bund', to take his clothes off, throw them in the river, and to go for a swim. This I think he did and after which, still 'ponging' a bit, he resumed his duties as Troop Leader!

Trooper Doug Kay, with the 8th Armoured Brigade's Fox's Mask badge clearly visible on his sleeve.

Moving into the second half of October, opportunities became available for officers and men to take forty-eight hours' leave in either Antwerp, Brussels, or Louvain (Leuven). Corporal Patrick Hennessey remembered this time:

> A few of us at a time were allowed to go back to Brussels, where we enjoyed egg and chips, ice cream, which we had not seen in England for years, and a haircut and shave from a professional barber. We were also exposed to a degree of hero-worship, which we found to be much to our liking, if a bit embarrassing.

While in Brussels, many troopers took the opportunity to have their photographs taken, so they could send their portrait home.

The general lull in fighting for the Hussars also provided an opportunity for the tanks to have additional protection added, in the form of spare track plates welded onto the fronts and turrets of tanks. Sergeant Causebrook, with the Light Aid Detachment from the Royal Electrical & Mechanical Engineers,

The Breakout from Normandy and Operation Market Garden

Doug Kay (right) enjoying a very welcome beer in Brussels with fellow members of C Squadron.

led a capable group of mechanics, who were held in high regard by the tank crews, as they fixed and maintained their fighting vehicles.

On 23 October, a brigade football tournament was organised and although making the final, the 13th/18th were beaten by 147 Field Regiment, Royal Artillery.[7]

This was followed by a holiday on 25 October, to celebrate the regiment's Balaclava Day.[8] This was celebrated at Winssen, according to tradition, as far as the situation would allow. The officers versus sergeants hockey match was narrowly won by the sergeants, with a score of 1:0. In the inter-squadron football tournament, RHQ beat B Squadron. In the evening, a formal ball was held at the casino in Nijmegen. Three-hundred Dutch girls attended and had an opportunity to dance for the first time since the Wehrmacht had invaded Holland in 1940.

Chapter 9

Into the Fatherland

Enemy contact – I have collided with a Tiger.

On 8 November, the regiment's tanks left the area of Molenhoek/Mook on the Meuse River and travelled west to Grave, where their vehicles were loaded onto tank transporters. They were on the move for seventeen hours on congested roads and struggled to keep the transporter drivers awake. Despite the weather being cold, windy and snowing, they pulled off the road and harboured for the night. After breakfast, they completed the final 14 miles of their journey to Brunssum on the Dutch/German border, where the troopers would temporarily be billeted in civilian houses. The tanks were joined by their support echelons the following day and the regiment was ready to commence the next phase of its war, although the weather and the condition of the ground would not make the following months easy.

From his diary, Captain Julius Neave recorded on 9 November:

> A bloody day, biting cold wind and buckets of rain in heavy, long-lasting showers. These conditions were the norm throughout October and November, making the terrain largely impassable. Tanks would typically become bogged the moment they left the road. Accompanying Flail tanks cannot operate with the additional weight of their end-connector, adding to the problem.

After more than six months of fighting, since landing on Sword Beach on D-Day, the regiment was finally about to enter the Fatherland and did so at 0330 hrs on 12 November 1944. The 3&8s entered Germany with their old friends from Operation Bluecoat, the 129th Infantry Brigade. Relieving elements of the US 102nd Infantry Division, the sabre squadrons took up positions to the west of Geilenkirchen. A Squadron moved to Staha with 5 Wilts, B Squadron to Gillrath with 4 Wilts, C Squadron to Teveren with 4 SLI, whilst RHQ based themselves at Niederbusch, just inside the Dutch/German border.

On 18 November, Operation Clipper saw the 43rd Infantry Division attack Geilenkirchen. B Squadron were to attack Bauchem, a mile west of

The tanks of A Squadron during their indirect shoot onto Bauchem. (*Courtesy of Charge!, the museum of the Light Dragoons*)

Geilenkirchen, with the infantry of 5 Dorsets of the 130th Brigade. A and C squadrons supported this assault, with the tanks lined up in the indirect shoot role. Both squadrons would fire 2,000 rounds each from their main armaments over a period of three hours at a range of 6,600 yards into the objective. By the end of the assault, Huge piles of empty shell cases littered the ground right along the line of tanks.

Captain Julius Neave recorded:

> Bauchem was fired upon with 'everything we've got!' … including an artillery barrage and A & C Squadrons forming up in a line to perform an indirect shoot, firing 4,000 rounds of 75mm into the objective, which proved to be very effective.

The assault went well and B Squadron and 5 Dorsets captured the objective without difficulty and took 150 German troops into captivity. The overall assault by 43rd Division was successful and was a positive start to operations within Germany. However, if anyone was in any doubt whether there was now a clear road to Berlin, events on the 19th were different. Again, B Squadron were in action with 5 Dorsets and tasked with clearing woods between the villages of Hatterath and Tripsrath. The ground was sodden and as soon as tanks deployed off the roads, a large number of them became bogged. Heavy mortar fire and shelling was received and when darkness arrived, the infantry had been able to make practically no progress at all from their start line. They were forced to consolidate their positions and once B Squadron's tanks could be extracted, they retired back to Gillrath. The attack by B Squadron and 5 Dorsets was repeated on the same woods the following morning, but this time starting from the west of the woods, the assault was successful. Casualties were light among the infantry and other than one tank running over a mine and another receiving a strike from a heavy shell, there were none in B Squadron. Despite the roads becoming almost impassable, the woods were cleared and in Allied hands by 1300 hrs.

Owing to the difficulties with trying to move tanks cross-country over treacherous, waterlogged ground, on 22 November another indirect shoot was organised, targeting the villages of Straeton, Erpen, Pruth and Waldenrath. Tanks from RHQ and B Squadron would expend a further 2,000 shells. An enemy OP (observation post) was suspected in the village of Utterath, so permission was granted for two troops of A Squadron to carry out an indirect shoot onto this location. This had the effect of setting three fires ablaze in the village and caused the church tower to collapse. The A Squadron Diary recorded:

> This seemed to irritate the opposition, who then spent several days trying to knock down the church tower in the village of Tipsrath, about half-a-mile to our left. They also engaged this village with volleys of Nebelwerfers about three times each day. It was a pretty unhealthy location!

Indeed, Tipsrath became an even more unhealthy location when an attack by the 10th SS Panzer Division took place on the afternoon of 26 November, attempting to retake the village. The infantry of 5 Wilts were supported by 2nd and 4th troops of C Squadron to repel the Germans, and their supporting fire was so successful that the Wiltshires only received four casualties yet captured sixty prisoners.

The wet conditions continued to cause problems for both infantry and tank crews alike. Captain Julius Neave recorded:

> Mud continues to be heavy going in the everlasting rain and the tanks struggle to support the Infantry and when the Duke of Cornwall's Light Infanty (DCLI) were counter-attacking, the 4/7 squadron sent to support them had 100% of its tanks bogged in the mud.

The A Squadron Diary also records the plight of the infantry in the Geilenkirchen area:

> They, poor people, could not dig slit trenches because they filled up with water and, therefore, they had to build mud castles, to provide some protection against artillery and mortar fire.

Captain Noel Denny of A Squadron receives his Military Cross from the commander-in-chief. (*Courtesy of Imperial War Museums – Image B 12517*)

Cosy Comfort paid tribute to their accompanying infantry: 'Thank God for our brave infantry, BUT exchange places with us? "Not bloody likely mate, you wouldn't get me in one of those tin boxes!"'

For 30 November, the Regimental Diary records that their newly promoted commander-in-chief, Field Marshal Bernard Montgomery, visited Geilenkirchen to conduct an investiture at 30 Corps. Here, those members of the regiment who had been decorated with gallantry awards, many of which dated back to actions during the D-Day assault, would receive their medals. Amongst those presented were the Distinguished Service Order (DSO) for Major Sir Delaval Cotter and Major Derek Wormald. Captain Noel Denny and Captain Robert Neave received the Military Cross (MC). Non-commissioned officers also received their awards of the Military Medal (MM).

The following morning, Field Marshal Montgomery visited the HQ of 8th Armoured Brigade and was introduced to Lieutenant Colonel the Earl of Feversham, the current CO of the 13th/18th, plus one representative of each squadron. It is mere conjecture to wonder whether the Germans had learned that such a high-ranking visitor was in town, but that afternoon activity by the Luftwaffe increased and bombs were dropped on Geilenkirchen and Gillrath and shelling continued into the night.

Monday, 4 December saw the regiment move out of the line and back across the border into Holland, to a small village outside Maastricht called Ulestraten. This was just a rural village with few amenities, but leave opportunities to Brussels continued, plus the first lucky few would be granted leave to return to England. Plans were in full swing for Operation Shears, which was designed to drive the Germans back 10 miles north of Geilenkirchen. However, with continued foul weather and difficult, waterlogged terrain, plans were eventually cancelled. The regiment was nominally given the role of defending Maastricht, although in reality there was little to do, other than to reconnoitre defensive positions. In order to keep the troopers match fit, Exercise Linney Head was carried out in two phases, which involved all squadrons on 8 December with infantry of the 157th (Highland Light Infantry) Brigade, and battalions of 156th (Scottish Rifles) Brigade supported by A and C squadrons on the 14th.

The regiment was due to retire to Eindhoven to continue their spell out of the line and had despatched advance parties to organise billets. However, the German offensive in the Ardennes Forest back on the Belgian/Luxembourg border[1] caused a considerable stir, resulting in orders being amended to remain in position and defend Maastricht against possible airborne landings. This proved short-lived, as an intelligence officer from 8th Armoured Brigade arrived shortly before midnight with orders to move back into Germany the next morning. Therefore, the regiment crossed back into Germany on the morning of the 20th and took over positions in villages to the north-west of Geilenkirchen, relieving tanks of the Grenadier Guards. The morning was foggy, which allowed a daytime handover without any interference from the enemy. With the Germans fighting hard in the Ardennes, it was felt that this sector might prove to be a likely area for the Wehrmacht to try to launch another offensive. With each squadron's troops stationed forward in isolated positions without infantry support, there was concern that enemy infantry might attempt to infiltrate Allied lines during the hours of darkness. The A Squadron Diary describes the measures taken to combat this possibility:

> At night the Troops manned ground mounted Browning machine guns in slit trenches, near or under their tanks, and in addition, they manned the turret of a Guard Tank, the gun of which was loaded with an HE [high-explosive] round and aimed at a point on the ground about thirty yards away, on the most likely axis of approach by the enemy.

Each night the position near Hastenrath, occupied by A Squadron's 4th Troop and Squadron HQ, would have its defences bolstered by the laying of booby traps on the light railway track leading towards their tanks. An early Christmas present would be delivered during the small hours of 25 December, when an enemy patrol stumbled straight into these devices, resulting in the guard tank firing both its main armament and Browning machine gun. This woke the other troopers and officers, who 'stood to', but the patrol quickly withdrew, leaving behind one dead and two wounded soldiers. The remainder of the enemy patrol next wandered into a position held by infantry of the King's Own Scottish Borderers at nearby Birgden and were duly captured. Ironically, when questioned it transpired that their objective had been to capture a British prisoner!

On Christmas morning, Captain Julius Neave commented: 'The Regiment dutifully "Stood To" at 0700 in bright, clear and frosty weather. The ground is now as hard as rock and I think the tanks could go anywhere.'

In the village of Gangelt, Corporal Patrick Hennessey remembered: 'It was so cold in Gangelt that we had to put straw on the ground to prevent the tank tracks from freezing to it.'

However, traditional Christmas celebrations would have to be put on hold for a few days, as the Hussars guarded their front-line positions. They were finally relieved by the Sherwood Rangers Yeomanry on 27 December and retired a short distance back into Holland at Schinnen. Here they managed to enlist the help of a couple of bulldozers to create 'dug-in' positions for the tanks. The 8th Armoured Brigade would become part of 12th Corps reserve

Regimental Christmas Card 1944 – a Sherman of Regimental HQ stands guard.

and were responsible for the defence of an area of high ground just inside the Dutch/German border.

The 17-pounder Sherman Firefly had proved so effective since Normandy that now each troop of four tanks would contain two of these, rather than one. Each squadron, at full strength, would therefore boast twenty tanks; half with 75mm guns and half with the more powerful 17-pounder. Although not all of these new tanks had yet been delivered, the 17-pounder gunners were sent to Lommel Ranges back in Belgium for gunnery practice. Unfortunately, this meant that they were away for a regimental holiday on New Year's Day, where a belated Christmas was celebrated.

Corporal Patrick Hennessey recorded:

> Roast pork was served for Christmas Dinner and we were visited by our new Commanding Officer, Lieutenant Colonel The Earl of Feversham.
>
> Christmas gifts for the Hussars came in the form of a new type of uniform, called the 'Tank Suit'. It was a one-piece garment, zipped each side from ankle to chin, with a chest protector and hood. It was windproof and waterproof and had one drawback – it was flammable. Nevertheless, it was very welcome, because it was extremely cold to travel in a tank in those days.

On 3 January, their new corps commander, Lieutenant General Neil Ritchie also paid a visit to the regiment with the brigade commander, Brigadier Erroll Prior-Palmer. A number of training courses had been laid on within the regiment, especially with a view to training more tank commanders. The general was able to inspect a number of these classes, before joining the regiment's officers for lunch. (The 30 Corps commander, General Brian Horrocks, had been sent to deal with the German threat in the Ardennes.)

The training courses continued, with squadrons taking it in turns to visit Lommel Ranges for firing practice, until 9 January, when orders were received

Doug Kay (right) with a crewmate and two Dutch girls, in whose house they were billeted.

to move the following day. The regiment moved the 5 miles to Schinveld on icy roads, having to proceed slowly, otherwise the tank tracks acted as skates on the frozen surface. They spent a couple of days here, in a very congested and uncomfortable position, before moving on to Ulestraten on the 12th, where they were greeted by two V1 flying bombs, one of which exploded to the rear of the C Squadron cookhouse. Although it caused considerable damage, the only casualties were Corporal Prince and Trooper Allan being slightly wounded.

With the ground now frozen and covered with snow, preparations began for the next large operation, codenamed Blackcock (named after the Scottish Black Grouse). This was intended to clear German troops from the Roer Triangle to their north, formed by the towns of Roermond and Sittard in Holland, and Heinsberg in Germany. Remaining unseen in the snowy terrain was now a problem, so white camouflage for both the tanks and helmets was sought, to help the tanks blend in with their frozen environment. The regiment was kept on two hours' notice to move throughout 17 and 18 January but was finally given orders to advance on the 19th, when they would enter the Roer Triangle from the west, via the villages of Susteren and Echt. A Squadron led the way, supported by a company of infantry from the Royal Scots, followed by RHQ, with B and C squadrons behind with their turrets traversed to provide flank protection on either side. The weather was very cold, with sleet, rain and a high, biting wind. A Squadron commenced their advance just before first light towards Pepinusbrug, and then planned to move on to the town of Waldfeucht in Germany. However, accurate intelligence on German positions was difficult to obtain and it was unclear as to whether or not either location was held by German troops. The minor road along which they were to advance was raised and edged on both sides by deep ditches. Having seen how tanks from the Guards Armoured Division had been easily shot up during Operation Market Garden, Major Wormald had arranged with their attached artillery officer, Captain Taylor, that smoke should be readily available to cover the squadron's flanks, if required. This soon became unnecessary, as it began to snow heavily just before the start line was reached and visibility was reduced to just a few yards. As a precaution, though, the tanks' 75mm guns were loaded with smoke rounds, traversed to alternate flanks and aimed at a range of 200 yards, so the squadron could quickly deploy its own smokescreen. This proved to be a prudent decision, because as A Squadron approached Pepinusbrug, it stopped snowing and visibility increased to several hundred yards. Almost instantly, the 'crack' of armour-piercing shots was heard and initially it was not known on which flank the enemy guns were located. A round soon struck the ground to the left of the squadron commander's tank, so he ordered 'Fire smoke left'. Captain Taylor also quickly ordered for artillery smoke to be fired, but before the smokescreen could be laid, the enemy had fired nine shots at A Squadron. They succeeded in knocking out three tanks of 3rd Troop, killing gunner Trooper Thomas Barnard and wounding Lieutenant Garlick. The survivors bailed out, some into freezing water in the roadside ditch, but were provided with new tanks and were able to rejoin the squadron later in the day. With smoke now masking the squadron's movements, the tanks ahead of 3rd Troop continued their advance into wooden terrain, crossing a bridge, which they were surprised to find was not held by German troops.

Held up by the knocked-out 3rd Troop tanks on the narrow road were two troops of A Squadron, a Company of Royal Scots in Kangaroos (armoured personnel carriers), a troop of AVRE tanks, a troop of Crab flail tanks, plus the remainder of the regiment. Then, 1st Troop of A Squadron, closest to the roadblock, was ordered to fill in the ditch, which was accomplished with some helpfully stacked nearby logs, and soon the remainder of A Squadron, the infantry Kangaroos and the AVRE tanks were able to bypass the obstruction. However, as Captain Julius Neave had previously commented upon, the Crab flail tanks with their extra weight were having difficulty operating in this environment and became bogged down, blocking the way once more. Although the smoke had cleared, the blizzard had returned, so attempts were made to clear the road. Unfortunately, the tracks on the first brewed-up tank had seized and couldn't be moved, but as this was taking place, the blizzard lifted, exposing the tanks. Once again, the German guns resumed their firing. The squadron commander's tank fired smoke towards what was hoped was the right direction and Captain Taylor was again able to call in smoke rounds from the artillery guns. Attempts to remove the blockage were abandoned and the squadron commander joined the rest of his troops.

Meanwhile, with the road to Waldfeucht blocked, the remainder of the regiment were forced to retrace their route west and took another road heading east to Koningsbosch, to the south-west of Waldfeucht. About halfway to this village, C Squadron was engaged by more enemy self-propelled guns. During ongoing engagements with the enemy, both enemy self-propelled guns and tanks were sighted. Both 1st and 3rd troops bore the brunt of the fighting, with two of 1st Troop's tanks being hit and brewed up and 3rd Troop losing three tanks. In these engagements, along with four men becoming wounded, both Sergeant Stanley Diver and 20-year-old Trooper Ronald Mason were killed. Before his death, Sergeant Diver had reported one self-propelled gun destroyed by his tank, and two other guns were claimed by Sergeants Miller and Smith respectively. Discovering that the road behind them had been cut off by the enemy, C Squadron rallied at last light and assumed a harbour position near Koningsbosch, along with the 7th/9th Royal Scottish Fusiliers. The tanks were carrying five days' worth of rations with them, however, which were now shared with the infantry, who had little food. They would share a bitterly cold and uncomfortable night together.

RHQ and B Squadron retired to Geleen for the night. A Squadron harboured in woods near Koningsbosch in close 'herringbone' formation, with its troopers settling down in the pits dug under their tanks, also with a long, very cold night to look forward to. On settling down for the night, Major Wormald remembered:

> I heard a voice saying, 'Hello Derek, are you there?' The voice was unmistakably that of the Commanding Officer, Lt. Col The Earl of Feversham. Apparently, the Rear Line between Squadron HQ and Regimental HQ was not working properly and so the CO had decided to visit this leading Squadron alone on foot, all the way from Susteren, a distance of about 5 miles.[2] He was quite exhausted and very overheated. Space was made for him under the Squadron Leader's tank, and he was given a strong whisky. He was wearing a long, white German army sheepskin coat which had been acquired from a German depot in Nijmegen. When he was settled he said, 'Derek, I have just had a very nasty experience.' He then told us that whilst walking along the axis from Susteren, he had been joined by a column of infantry coming in from the right of the track. He was about to say to one of them, 'My boy, where are you going?' when he noticed that they were wearing German steel helmets. He refrained from

making the comment and walked on with them. After a short distance they turned off the track to the left. He had to make a quick decision as to whether to go with them, into captivity, or to continue on his lonely journey, and possibly be challenged and shot in the back. Not wishing to walk into captivity, he decided upon the latter course of action. This was the cause of his distressful condition. He spent the night under our tank and returned to RHQ the next morning.

After a bitterly cold night, C Squadron moved out of its harbour area with the infantry to secure the north-west side of Koningsbosch. For the second day in a row, they were to encounter several well-sited German self-propelled guns, resulting in squadron commander Major Cotter's tank being knocked out. This tank kill resulted in the deaths of Sergeant Frank Bradley and Trooper Stanley Read. Lieutenant Downer and Sergeant Carr's tanks were also hit, but thankfully, there were no casualties. The terrain was open and dominated by anti-tank guns, so no further advance was possible. Therefore, after receiving a bloody nose from their German opposition, C Squadron retired back to the previous night's harbour area.

In the first two days of Operation Blackcock, the Germans had claimed eleven of the regiment's tanks. Captain Julius Neave felt compelled to give credit to the opposition: 'The Boche use of self-propelleds [self-propelled anti-tank guns] is simply expert and one can't help admiring him.'

Under cover of darkness B Squadron now moved up, led by Major Stancomb, to join the King's Own Scottish Borderers, who had entered the regiment's objective for 19 January – Waldfeucht. Accompanied by infantry of the Glasgow Highlanders, they were able to pass through Aan de School under the cover of freezing fog and reach Koningsbosch, where they paused for half the night. Three inches of freshly fallen snow lay on the ground and soon they advanced into open countryside, in this eerie, wintery scene. As they crept over the German border and progressed to Waldfeucht, their presence had not gone unnoticed and a heavy mortar stonk began to rain down on the tanks, joined by anti-tank fire from their left flank. The squadron 2ic, Captain Robert Neave, was unlucky to receive a direct hit on his tank from an anti-tank gun in the dark. At dawn, each tank troop now fanned out with their respective infantry companies, heading to different quarters of the town to carry out their tasks. Unfortunately, Lieutenant Moulding, commanding 2nd troop, ran his tank over a complete box of British Hawkins anti-tank grenades, rendering his tank immobile; the remainder of his troop's tanks therefore joined 3rd and 4th troops.

Lieutenant Aitchison's 1st Troop was tasked with entering the western end of the town, but as it did so, three enemy tanks emerged from the mist. The

Glasgow Highlanders were able to brew up two of the enemy tanks with their 6-pounder anti-tank guns, but not before Lieutenant Aitchison's tank was knocked out, along with two other of his troop's tanks. Corporal Weston's tank was able to deal with the 3rd German tank. The troop commander was forced to retire to Squadron HQ on foot, but with the satisfaction of witnessing his enemy's tank destroyed at 50 yards' range.

Commanded by Lieutenant Franks, 3rd Troop took up positions in the town square. Unknown to them, German infantry had infiltrated the town and were at very close quarters in the buildings surrounding them, also supported by two tanks. Suddenly, all hell broke loose and during bitter fighting, one of the German tanks brewed up a Sherman. The remaining 3rd Troop tanks were now attacked by infantry, firing Panzerfausts from top-floor windows. Some of the surviving Hussars managed to make good their escape back to friendly lines on foot, but others were subsequently captured.

Meanwhile, 4th Troop under Lieutenant W.G. Denney had moved to the perimeter of the town square, to the north-east. At this stage, the Germans were desperately trying to recapture Waldfeucht from the King's Own Scottish Borderers and at 0900 hrs put in their main attack from the north-east, with 4th Troop directly in their path. Desperate fighting ensued and again the regiment's tanks were attacked at close range with Panzerfausts, knocking out two Shermans and damaging another. One crew commander, who had fought very bravely, was killed by a sniper firing from one of the surrounding buildings. Realising that the position had become untenable, Major Stancomb ordered the remaining two tanks to fall back, and they were then faced with a mad dash back through the town square, with all guns blazing, under a hail of enemy small arms fire and Panzerfausts. However, Lady Luck was shining on them, and they managed to extricate themselves without further loss.

Although the Germans managed to make significant gains in the town, they were unable to dislodge the Hussars entirely and through the afternoon, the remaining B Squadron's tanks were able to force the enemy infantry back. Fortunately, owing to the narrowness of the streets, some of the larger German tanks had been unable to enter the town itself. One of the Squadron's Sherman Fireflies had also successfully destroyed two of the German tanks with its powerful 17-pounder gun. B Squadron HQ under Major Stancomb and his 2ic, Captain Robert Neave, now advanced with the remaining tanks from the other troops in support, and following an afternoon of confused and frantic fighting, had by evening managed to reclaim the town square. Realising that their attack had failed, the Germans gradually withdrew and quitted the town. By midnight, the Allied units had consolidated Waldfeucht and although shelling continued through the night, no further counterattack was attempted by the

Germans. B Squadron was left to count the cost of a day that had claimed the lives of Sergeants Christopher Sheehan and Ernest Kenley, plus Troopers James Gardner and Frederick Sitch.

Consolidation of the Waldfeucht area and clearing up continued throughout 22 January. Concerned that there could still be enemy tanks and self-propelled guns lurking in the area, A Squadron was sent forward to the town under cover of darkness that night, to relieve B Squadron. They arrived without incident but while taking up defensive positions, an unusual occurrence presented itself, described in the A Squadron Diary:

> Captain Taylor excitedly came on the air and reported 'Enemy contact – I have collided with a Tiger [tank] at the crossroads behind you – HELP – Out!' Whilst contemplating what best to do about this request, the Squadron Leader received a Sitrep saying, 'Tiger has disengaged and withdrawn to the east.' End of contact, to the great relief of all parties! Captain Taylor's problem was that in his Artillery Observer's tank he only had a dummy gun, which was ineffectually pointing at the Tiger. No doubt frightening its crew. On the other hand, the Tiger could not engage him, because its gun was too long and could only traverse up against his turret.

So began several quiet days for the regiment, based around Koningsbosch. Waldfeucht was littered with destroyed B Squadron tanks and the largely peasant population in this rural part of Germany emerged from the remains of their town, having ignored instructions to evacuate before the fighting began. It was noted that they were in no way hostile toward the Hussars.

On 31 January, the Hussars were entertained by an ENSA[3] concert party called 'In Harmony', which was a pleasant interlude before the next large task ahead, Operation Veritable. On 1 February, an O Group was held for the squadron leaders on Veritable and the following day the tanks were loaded onto transporters to commence their journey back west through Bourg-Léopold, staging the night at Mol. Setting off from Mol at 0915 hrs on the 3rd, the remainder of the journey would take almost twenty-four hours, as the Hussars travelled all through the night in driving rain, finally arriving on the morning of 4 February at Berg en Dal, east of Nijmegen. After such a tough journey, it was a huge disappointment to discover that the billets that had been laid on to accommodate the regiment were both inadequate for their numbers, plus in very poor condition and entirely unsuitable. Fortunately, the Nottinghamshire Yeomanry were able to step in and invited C Squadron to share their area in Berg en Dal. RHQ and A Squadron found alternative billets in Nijmegen and B Squadron went to Beek.

Operation Veritable – the Reichswald Forest

The plan for Operation Veritable was to eliminate the enemy between the Rhine and Meuse rivers, with a southerly movement, to link up with the US 9th Army, attacking from the south. It would also pave the way for Allied forces to cross the Rhine, the last big natural barrier in Hitler's defences. The 8th Armoured Brigade would support the five divisions that would attack through the Reichswald Forest (the 15th (Scottish) Infantry Division, the 43rd (Wessex) Infantry Division, the 53rd (Welsh) Infantry Division, and the 2nd and 3rd Canadian Infantry Divisions). Ahead stood the twin spires of the towns of Goch and Cleve, but first the Reichswald Forest (8 miles deep and 5 miles wide) had to be breached. The attacks made by British and Canadian forces at the northern end of Germany's Siegfried Line defences prompted a reaction by Hitler, who sent forces north to meet them, weakening his defences to the south and once again easing the resistance met by advancing American units. The planners had prepared for frozen ground, enabling tanks and other vehicles to move easily on the largely unsurfaced, narrow forest tracks. However, the nature of the operation completely changed when a sudden thaw ensued, and in addition to terrain having been flooded by the Germans, this slowed down the whole effort.

For the opening day of Veritable on 8 February, the regiment would support Canadian units. A Squadron was placed under the command of the 9th Canadian Infantry Brigade of the 3rd Canadian Infantry Division, commanded by their brigadier, John 'Rocky' Rockingham, a veteran of the Dieppe Raid. He was by all accounts 'a very nice chap'! B Squadron would support the 7th Canadian Infantry Brigade, also of the 3rd Division, whilst C Squadron was to support the 5th Canadian Infantry Brigade of the 2nd Division. In anticipation of the Allied attack, the Germans breached several dams, to flood the road between Wyler and Cleve, plus much of the terrain to the north of the road. Because of this situation, plus generally waterlogged terrain and many ditches, tank movement would once again be largely limited to roads. Operation Veritable commenced during the night of 7/8 February with the familiar softening up tactics of the RAF and US Air Force bombing the towns of Cleve, Goch and Emmerich. At 0500 hrs the following morning, an enormous artillery barrage continued the process, involving up to 1,000 artillery pieces, each with 1,000 rounds to expend. Captain Julius Neave recorded: 'Cleve and Goch took a fair hammering.'

The 9th Canadian Infantry Brigade would advance with two battalions leading, with a third held in reserve to exploit the success of the others. In addition, 1st and 3rd troops of A Squadron would support the Glengarry Highlanders to the right, with 2nd and 4th troops supporting the Highland Light Infantry of Canada on the left. To add to the artillery barrage, all of A Squadron's 75mm tank guns (including Squadron HQ) were to fire 200 rounds each onto German positions.

The Regina Rifle Regiment, supported by B Squadron, managed to advance through the flooded terrain towards the village of Zyfflich. One troop of tanks managed to navigate the flooded terrain to support the infantry into the village, with another troop providing supporting fire from a position west of the Wyler Dam. During the evening and into darkness, 400 Germans were captured.

C Squadron's move to their start line resulted in five of their tanks becoming bogged in the appalling mud in the area, but the remainder of the squadron, under Captain Tetley, were in position by 1000 hrs. In a similar fashion to A Squadron, they also carried out a direct shoot on the village of Wyler until 1230 hrs. The infantry of the 5th Canadian Infantry Brigade were to engage in heavy fighting through the afternoon, but eventually captured the village, by 1600 hrs. The only casualty of the regiment that day was Trooper Sanders being wounded by 'friendly' artillery fire. C Squadron was released at 1700 hrs and was able to return to billets near Nijmegen. Thus ended the first day of the operation.

Corporal Patrick Hennessey recalled the conditions upon entering the Reichswald (Imperial Forest):

> As the rock-hard ground had already begun to thaw, coupled with the movement of men and vehicles and the results of artillery and mortar fire, the tracks in the forest were transformed into a sea of mud. It was very hard going.

Cosy Comfort remembered his impressions of the Reichswald:

> The Reichswald Forest – mud, trees, tracks and more mud. We passed Canadian Shermans with gaping holes, some brewed up, but with their guns pointing at all angles – weird! Only 88s could have collected that prize! Poor bastards – all those poor bastards!

No action took place on the 9th for the regiment, but three of B Squadron's tanks had to be evacuated and abandoned in Zyfflich, owing to the collapse of the dyke road. The Germans had breached dams to the north and with flood water engulfing the surrounding area, the three tanks became perched on top of a newly formed island.

The next day, C Squadron came under the command of the 43rd Infantry Division's Reconnaissance Regiment and set out before dawn headed for Nütterden, to the south-west of Cleve. The road was in very poor condition and carrying an enormous weight of traffic. It was midday before C Squadron reached the village. Meanwhile, Major Wormald had set out with Brigadier Rockingham in a Buffalo amphibious armoured personnel carrier, to carry out a reconnaissance of 9th Canadian Infantry Brigade's planned advance. It was clear that A Squadron's tanks could not operate in the flooded terrain to adequately support the infantry, so were released in the early afternoon and the squadron was able to enjoy some free time and went to the cinema in Nijmegen. Otherwise, the regiment remained on four hours' notice to move.

On the morning of 12 February, C Squadron's tanks were patrolling with vehicles from the 43rd Reconnaissance Regiment to the north-east of the Reichswald Forest. The 2nd and 4th troops had set off early, through Materborn and were patrolling south down the road towards Goch. Owing to their exposed position on the road, they were to encounter German 88mm guns firing at long range, which managed to knock out Sergeant Scamp's Sherman Firefly and two other tanks from 2nd Troop, as well as three vehicles of the Reconnaissance unit. Gunner, Trooper Doug Kay, would survive the attack. However, his commander, Sergeant Fred Scamp, with whom he'd served since they landed on D-Day, was killed, along with Trooper Robert Wilcox. Captain Tetley withdrew the remainder of the force back through Materborn and it was decided that a much larger operation would be required to seize this area.

Here the regiment would come under the command of the 130th Infantry Brigade, of the 43rd Division, and once preparations were made, the regiment's tanks moved from Nijmegen on the 14th to harbour between the villages of Materborn and Bedburg, to where C Squadron was waiting for them, billeted in Bedburg Sanatorium. After setting off at first light, the journey of 15 miles was arduous over difficult terrain and roads in poor condition, but the regiment was once more complete by early afternoon. A Squadron would support the 7th Hampshires, B Squadron the 4th Dorsets and C Squadron the 5th Dorsets. German troops of the 7th Parachute Division, 116th Panzer Division and Panzergrenadiers of the 5th Panzer Division were believed to be in the area. The paratroops in particular were gaining a reputation for fighting in a fanatical fashion, in defence of the Fatherland.

The initial plan was altered as 129th Brigade had been unable to capture their objectives the previous day. This attack would now resume with 4th Dorsets leading out its brigade, with B Squadron in support. A Squadron would follow behind with their infantry. As B Squadron moved through 129th Brigade's lines, Captain Noel Denny joined B Squadron as a forward liaison officer for A Squadron and was joined by his squadron commander, who wanted to gain a better understanding of the country over which his tanks would advance. Their arrival at B Squadron HQ was greeted by the arrival of a stonk of heavy shelling, making for an extremely unhealthy environment. Moving in a south-easterly direction and using the Cleve–Uedum road as their right boundary, during the morning B Squadron would meet stiff opposition from German troops of the 156th Panzergrenadier Regiment (of the 116th Panzer Division) occupying Cleve Forest on their right flank – a unit that had escaped the Falaise pocket a few months earlier. Lieutenant Flood, 4th Troop's commander, would have his tank destroyed by a self-propelled gun, and he would be the only survivor of his crew. His driver, Trooper James Horsman, had only recently transferred to the regiment from the 42nd Royal Tank Regiment and would leave a young widow, Hilda, back home in Castleford, Yorkshire.⁴

Another tank was hit by a bazooka and its driver also killed, but otherwise the rest of the crew were unharmed. A further two tanks were hit by self-propelled guns, but with no casualties to the crews; they were able to recover these last three tanks.

Having witnessed the fire coming from the right flank, as A Squadron prepared to move through B Squadron's position to assume the lead, Major Wormald had noted he would require this area to be screened off with artillery smoke. However, in a similar fashion to events a month earlier on the road to Waldfeucht, a thick fog descended, making this unnecessary. With visibility reduced to around 50 yards, the tanks were safe from attack from self-propelled guns, but now the fog presented problems with command and control, along with navigation. Upon the arrival of 7th Hants, they sent their leading company forward with 3rd Troop in support, towards their objective of an escarpment to the north-east of Goch. Very soon, the infantry had veered off its correct axis, so 4th Troop were sent forward to try to locate the leading company. Having realised his mistake, however, the company commander did manage to regain his correct axis of advance but was soon pinned down by enemy machine-gun fire and shelling. Having failed to locate the leading company, 4th Troop found themselves in the area of the 4th Dorsets, who were digging in, and so remained there in a counterattack role.

Meanwhile, 2nd Troop, under Lieutenant Spencer, was sent forward to assist the leading company to continue the advance. On the way, Sergeant Ron Hepper spotted an enemy 88mm self-propelled gun through the fog, which his tank successfully destroyed. His tank also managed to disperse some enemy infantry armed with bazookas, who were trying to infiltrate the Hussars' advance. A second infantry company was also brought forward, but they too became pinned down.

Having almost reached their objective in the fog, 3rd Troop were now ahead of the rest of the attack. Without a preceding artillery bombardment to announce the attack and with the benefit of the low visibility, they had been able to advance a mile beyond B Squadron's position. The A Squadron Diary records:

> They would have been employing the maximum 'Suppressive Fire with Movement' tactic, for which all tanks then carried the maximum amount of additional Browning ammunition, including crates of the stuff on the back of their tanks. In the landscape in which we were now operating the enemy defensive positions were likely to be either in the woods or in and around the isolated farm building complexes, which dotted the countryside. These latter areas usually had barns, the lofts of which were filled with hay and straw. It was on this day that we learned that MG [machine gun] Tracer bullets would ignite the contents of the lofts with the results that the enemy would be 'flushed out' of the complexes and that the resulting natural smoke screens could prevent enemy SPs [self-propelled guns] from engaging us.

With the leading two infantry companies unable to advance, a third reserve company was sent on a right flanking movement, following the tanks of Lieutenant Knowles's 1st Troop. However, sporadic machine-gun and mortar fire prevented the infantry from keeping up with the tanks, so having reached the north-east corner of Cleve Forest, Lieutenant Knowles sent back Sergeant Jerry Bell on foot, to make contact with their 'Feet', as their infantry were known. Having located the infantry company, Sergeant Bell persuaded one of its officers to accompany him back to 1st Troop's position, but at some stage during the return journey, the officer lost contact and failed to materialise to speak with Lieutenant Knowles. Sergeant Bell returned to his vehicle, somewhat out of breath, before a little further ahead, his tank became immobilised in an enemy trench system. Lieutenant Knowles's tank managed to get beyond the trench system with the help of some of the infantry company who had caught up, but his tank was soon brewed up by a bazooka, killing his driver, Trooper Victor Forrest, with another member of the crew receiving burns. Another senior NCO in the Troop, Sergeant Yeomans, also had his tank immobilised, when a high-explosive shell destroyed his tank's track sprocket.

Using the radio from Sergeant Bell's static tank, Lieutenant Knowles requested permission to withdraw and having lost three of his troop's tanks, the Hussars of 1st Troop retreated from the area. The reserve infantry company were then able to advance through the ground captured by the leading companies and having now pushed on and linked up with 3rd Troop's tanks, managed to achieve the original objective of the leading company in the dark, with the tanks returning fire on any enemy positions that tried to engage them. C Squadron was planned to have seized a crossroads near Louisendorf with 5 Dorsets, but this was subsequently postponed until the following morning.

As B Squadron was able to rest at Bedburg Sanatorium, 5 Dorsets commenced their attack with C Squadron at 0900 hrs on 16 February with two infantry companies 'up'; their advance would run parallel to the forest on their right, with their objectives some 2,000 yards to their south. It was another gloomy morning with persistent fog. The 4th Troop were to support A Company on the left with 3rd Troop supporting C Company to the right, and 1st Troop remained with B Company in reserve. Meanwhile, A Squadron was commencing its morning's activities with 7 Hants, which had already captured one farm complex. A Squadron HQ halted on the road and decided to have breakfast, but as they were doing so, were suddenly disturbed by a hail of machine-gun fire, hitting the back of Captain Noel Denny's tank and forcing them to hastily move off the road. Out of the gloom appeared a troop of Sherman tanks, which turned out to be Lieutenant Downer's 4th Troop from C Squadron, which had drifted off their intended axis in the fog. Major Wormald recorded:

> Fortunately, there were no major casualties. Minor casualties were Captain Denny's crew's bedding, his stock of whisky, the Squadron Leader's breakfast and his cooker, over which the 'enemy' had driven their tanks. The 'enemy' halted when they realised that they had made a mistake. The Squadron Leader had a word or two to say to Lt. Downer! He also conveyed his views to the C Squadron Leader.

The 4th Troop's crews, now aware of where they actually were, headed back out into the fog with their tail between their collective legs, to resume their attack with A Company.

Back with the C Squadron operation, 3rd Troop and C Company met little opposition and arrived at their objective without difficulty. In contrast, 4th Troop and A Company would meet stiff opposition from actual enemy in the form of both German infantry and self-propelled guns. Incredibly, Lieutenant Downer suffered his tank being hit by first a self-propelled gun, then a bazooka, yet the tank remained in fighting condition and there were thankfully no casualties. Enemy stonking of the area was reported by the troopers as the heaviest they'd experienced since Normandy and rather less fortunate was Sergeant Carr in a scout car, who received wounds to his face from a mortar round. The 4th Troop's tanks gave a very good account of themselves, though, and they too finally managed to achieve their objective by midday.

The 1st Troop moved up to support them, which proved well timed when the Germans attempted to counterattack 4th Troop's position, but the two C Squadron troops were successful in repulsing the enemy, with Lieutenant Downer redeeming himself by destroying a self-propelled gun. After their losses suffered on 12 February, 2nd Troop had now been able to reform with new vehicles and were sent forward to relieve 4th Troop, which after a hard morning's fighting, gratefully came back into reserve. Lieutenant Downer had experienced quite an exciting morning, in one way or another, but was yet to speak to his squadron commander about the morning's 'friendly' fire incident!

Despite the unwelcome interruption by Lieutenant Downer's Troop, A Squadron had continued their advance with 7 Hants. Visibility had improved to about 150 yards, which made navigation a little easier, but gave enough protection from attack, as the area was said to be 'infested' with enemy self-propelled guns. With his breakfast now squashed into the road behind him, Major Wormald personally led 4th Troop forward to link up with 2nd Troop, to ensure they didn't deviate from their axis in the fog. Two companies from the Hampshires tried to advance, supported by both 2nd and 4th troops' tanks, but the intense shelling kept the infantry pinned to the ground much of the time, so progress was limited, despite Major Wormald trying to keep the momentum going through the use of a loudhailer. The Hampshires did manage to capture another farm, but they too were glad when the 4th/7th Dragoon Guards came forward, supporting the 214th Infantry Brigade. With A Squadron able to provide suppressive fire into the woods to their right, the 4th/7th Dragoon Guards were able to advance and achieve the day's objectives. A Squadron then rallied with the infantry's battalion HQ and had their ammunition replenished by the support echelons, to enable them to act in a counterattack role. The intense shelling of the area had continued throughout, causing a number of casualties amongst the infantry companies. The A Squadron Diary records: 'The shelling this day was very heavy indeed and the Battalion suffered many casualties. Nebelwerfers were also fired at our positions.'

It was now clear to the Hussars that the Germans were intent on defending their homeland with all means available to them. These opening days of

Operation Veritable were just a foretaste of what was to follow. The Regimental Diary recorded: 'These were tough and dark days for the regiment.'

However, the escarpment overlooking the town of Goch was now in British hands and the regiment's squadrons were able to withdraw gradually out of the line.

The next few days provided the 13th/18th with an opportunity to refit the tanks, wash and rest. Lieutenant Richardson recorded some memories of the regimental headquarters in Bedburg-Hau and these 'quiet' days out of the line:

> RHQ was rather noisy at this time for it was right in the centre of the gun lines, 25 pounders in front, and the mediums behind, for hours on end the whole world would seem filled with continuous, deafening crash of those guns. There was also a battery of rocket projectors firing a carpet of missiles covering a large area. This went off with an incredible roar and was directed on the Forest of Cleve, a square wood forming the right boundary of our line of advance, and from which the attacking troops had been subjected to intense Spandau fire.

Lieutenant Richardson was able to enjoy the rare opportunity to wash properly and was well fed:

> I geared up a bath for myself in the kitchen of our house – the first I'd had since the 14th January, it was wonderful. A feature at this time which surprised me was the frequency and the enormous size of the meals which one's crew kept producing. This was of course Germany and although the slaughtering of animals was officially not permitted large numbers of chickens, ducks, and quite a few pigs and sheep unaccountably died a violent death. We seemingly had some good butchers, and the average British soldier is a reasonable cook – a fact which their wives would probably never believe – so a succession of poultry, roast pork and lamb appeared at regular intervals throughout the day. We did not go short of food, and it was a very welcome change from the rather monotonous Compo rations.

Some excitement occurred when the Luftwaffe sent sorties of ME 262 jet fighters to probe the Allied lines, described here by Lieutenant Richardson:

> On the 20th and 21st there was much activity by German jet-propelled aircraft, flying extremely high and fast they appeared mainly engaged in reconnaissance, but occasionally swooped down and dropped anti-personnel bombs. As usual an enormous amount of flak was shot at these intruders

which, as always, was far behind the fast-moving planes. As a German aircraft, and especially a jet, was an uncommon sight by then, people used to dash out of their cellars and houses to watch them and their attendant display of rather abortive British fireworks. It was during one of these jet sorties that one, rather braver than the rest, came hedge hopping in at zero feet, catching everyone completely by surprise. He dropped two anti-personnel bombs, one of which landed outside the door of RHQ and the other on a jeep belonging to HQ 9th Canadian Brigade. The Orderly Room Sergeant had a finger removed by the first, and the second caused a fire in the jeep and amongst a stock of about 100 jerricans full of petrol. What made the situation rather more exciting was the fact that there was a large pile of 75mm ammunition next to the jerricans. Everyone had taken cover when the bombs dropped, but they now began to emerge. I quickly organised a party to move the ammunition and as many of the jerricans as possible and went myself to move the two jeeps which we parked next to the burning one. I got the first one away alright, but had difficulty in starting the second, whilst I was struggling with the choke and accelerator the petrol tank of the jeep on fire burst and showered petrol over the one I was in, the hood and the nearside tyres caught alight and things started to get rather warm so I had to abandon the driving seat. However, by that time someone had organised a scout car with a tow rope and we pulled it clear and were able to put out the fire before the jeep became a dead loss. All the ammunition and most of the jerricans were recovered. The total damage done was: one finger, one jeep burned out, one jeep damaged, about ten jerricans of petrol burnt and a hole in the windscreen of the second-in-command's jeep which is there to this day. After this episode people weren't so keen on dashing out to look at jet planes.

A Squadron moved into the town of Cleve, but as the Squadron Diary records: 'We found covered accommodation for most of the Troops, but the town had been fairly well "liberated".'

The men of 8th Armoured Brigade were, at least, able to get cleaned up at the newly opened 'Fox's Mask Baths' in Cleve.

C Squadron was visited and inspected by Brigadier Prior-Palmer on 21 February, before a squadron leaders' O Group was held on the 22nd along with officers of the 160th (Welsh) Brigade, in preparation for Operation Leek. With the town of Goch now in British hands, the next stage was to dominate the ground between Goch and the town of Weeze to the south. The plan was for 160th Brigade's infantry to advance on Weeze, two battalions 'up', supported by the regiment. A Squadron would support the 2nd Battalion of the

Monmouthshire Regiment (2 Mons) on the right, B Squadron would support the 6th Battalion of the Royal Welsh Fusiliers (6 RWF) on the left, with the 4th Battalion of the Welch Regiment (4 Welch)[5] and C Squadron in reserve.

The regiment set off from the Cleve area, bound for Goch on 23 February, but the usual preparations for a large operation saw the roads between Materborn and Goch very congested. Fortunately, the weather was poor, otherwise the Luftwaffe could have caused havoc among the long lines of vehicles. Finally, Goch was reached around dusk and each squadron joined their respective infantry battalion.

It was believed that the terrain to the south was defended by the 7th and 8th German Parachute divisions, who held the woods about 1,200 yards to the south of Goch in strength. Minefields and anti-tank ditches were also expected. At 0530 hrs, an artillery barrage commenced, ranged on the woods to the south of Goch, with a mixture of smoke and high-explosive shells, to protect the exposed right flank of the 2 Mons and A Squadron. The initial plan was for a rapid advance by two sections of Recce Troop, under the command of Lieutenant Charles, to capture a crossing over a large anti-tank ditch to the north of Weeze before it was blown, then hold it until the infantry battalions and supporting tanks arrived. This would be supported by a Scout Platoon of the King's Royal Rifle Corps and 8th Armoured Brigade's Motor Battalion. However, this entailed a flat-out dash over a distance of 5,000 yards. Fortunately, this plan was abandoned as many felt that the dash forward would prove suicidal.

Having set off at 0300 hrs to make a 'silent' approach, so as not to bring down Nebelwerfer fire and alert the Germans as where best to deploy their anti-tank defences, the regiment's tanks crossed their start line south of Goch at 0600 hrs on 24 February. B Squadron with the Fusiliers made good progress towards their first objective of buildings in Host. Although suffering two tanks knocked out by self-propelled guns, another two driving over mines and a 17-pounder Firefly taken out of action by heavy machine-gun fire, they were fortunate to have no fatalities, just three men wounded. They were successful in capturing around 150 prisoners and it was estimated that the Germans in that sector had lost a similar number dead. B Squadron could advance no further, however, owing to the 7th Parachute Division offering stiff resistance to A Squadron as they advanced to capture the wooded area. In addition to small arms fire and bazookas, they would encounter mines, self-propelled guns, Nebelwerfer mortars and heavy calibre artillery.

Once over the start line, Lieutenant Spencer's 2nd Troop of A Squadron were advancing towards a row of farmhouses and had in fact entered a minefield. Sergeant Ron Hepper's tank drove over a mine, immobilising his tank. Witnessing what had happened, Sergeant Bill Hammond's tank advised him to bail out, as he was now vulnerable to anti-tank fire. Experienced though he was, Sergeant Hepper replied that his guns were still in operation and he would continue to support the advance a little longer. With gaps now beginning to appear in the smoke laid down by the artillery, a group of German paratroopers appeared from behind the buildings carrying bazookas. Trooper Joe Collins, in Bill Hammond's tank, remembered a huge explosion, which was Ron Hepper's tank being hit by an armour-piercing round and brewing up. This explosion was to kill both Sergeant Ron Hepper and his gunner, Trooper Tom Cowen. The remainder of the crew were unharmed and bailed out of their vehicle. Following the loss of Ron Hepper's tank, the Sherman now leading the troop also ran over a mine just a few yards from the German positions and another tank was brewed up by a bazooka. As two tanks from the reserve 1st Troop were sent forward to support 2nd Troop, Lieutenant Spencer's tank was then struck by two bazooka rounds, but despite this managed to continue engaging the enemy positions, to enable the survivors of the other disabled tanks to dismount and take cover behind their vehicles. Another armour-piercing shot now knocked out Lieutenant Spencer's tank, killing his driver, but not realising that he was dead, the Lieutenant tried to drag his driver from the stricken tank. In so doing, he was twice blown off the tank by explosions before he realised that his driver was dead and that he could do nothing for him.

Sergeant Hammond's tank gun was loaded with an armour-piercing round, but this was fired in the direction of the German paratroops in an attempt to put them to ground. They next fired their 2-inch smoke mortar and managed to lay down a smokescreen between the tanks and the buildings, before dashing round behind the knocked-out tanks, collecting survivors. Hammond's tank delivered the unhorsed crewmembers into the care of the infantry, before rejoining the fray and continuing to fire into the German positions, until they ran out of ammunition. Soon the infantry had managed to move up and capture the buildings, enabling Hammond's tank to withdraw.

Sergeant Ron Hepper had been awarded the Military Medal for his gallantry shown on D-Day and was a great loss to the regiment. He had served with the 3&8s since mechanisation, having joined from the Royal Tank Regiment Reserve.

For his actions on this day, Lieutenant Derek Spencer would be awarded the Military Cross.

In the centre, 4th Troop, A Squadron were to enjoy an easier day and were able to capture their local objective without tank losses, although Sergeant Morris would later have his tank immobilised by an artillery shell.

The 3rd Troop, A Squadron, on the left, were to encounter a large enemy trench system; the area peppered with bomb craters. Here both Sergeant Charlie Rattle and Corporal Reggie Binns's tanks became immobilised but were able to still provide fire support to their infantry company and Lieutenant Garlick's tank, as they moved forward to capture their objective. Lieutenant Hunter, in the last remaining tank in reserve from 1st Troop, was ordered forward to join Lieutenant Garlick, but on his way forward became bogged down in an anti-tank ditch. Lieutenant Garlick reported much enemy movement to his front and front left, and with a counterattack expected, the squadron commander and the attached artillery officer, Captain Taylor, moved forward to survey the scene. With several artillery units at his disposal, Captain Taylor called in a heavy stonking of the enemy positions and consequently no counterattack materialised.

The day was still not over, though, and Lieutenant Richardson recorded details of what still lay ahead for A Squadron:

> Their axis lay through a large wood, the fight to gain it had been bad enough, but once there they were subjected to the most devastating 'stonking' that had been seen since Normandy. Most of the shells burst in the tree tops; this has a far worse effect than a ground burst, because a trench is no protection, the blast and splinters going straight in. The poor Monmouthshires were suffering terribly, and A Squadron had lost a number of tanks.

While standing behind his tank in the wood, discussing the situation with an infantry company commander, Major Wormald remembered looking up to see:

> a large 'prune' descending upon him from the sky. He shouted 'DOWN' and spontaneously, ducked. There was then a large explosion not very far behind his tank. During the day three tanks were disabled in this way (Captain Taylor's, Sergeant Holdsworth's and Sergeant Morris's). Captain Walker was hit in the leg by shrapnel whilst he was walking from Battalion HQ, in a cellar, to his tank.

Lieutenant Richardson was sent to relieve Captain Walker:

> Later in the afternoon I was ordered to go and relieve Captain John Walker, second Captain of A Squadron, who was manning a wireless set at the 2 Mons HQ in the southern outskirts of GOCH. He had been wounded in the leg that morning and so far had had no attention. I went down in a scout car and found John in a cellar with the CO of the Monmouthshires. He was very white and obviously in pain. He went back in my scout car.

Now sat in a cellar with the Monmouthshires' colonel, Richardson recalled:

There in that cellar I was brought face to face with an aspect of war which was new to me, the aspect of a leader whose unit was taking a terrible hammering. Tired through weeks of hard and bitter fighting in the knee-deep mud of the Reichswald; tired after bringing his men up to their positions during the previous night; tired after fighting his battle since dawn that day; he sat there, dirty faced, unshaven, eyes red-rimmed and bloodshot. He was out of touch with his Companies on his own low-powered infantry wireless set, live communication constantly being knocked out by enemy shell fire, his only communication being via the supporting tanks of A Squadron through my set. Knowing that his men had won their battle and gained their objectives he sat and listened to the news that they were still being knocked to pieces down there in that wood by the murderous shell fire. There was nothing he could do – no going forward, or coming back, nothing, they just had to sit and take it.

Despite everything thrown at them, the 2nd Monmouthshires and A Squadron would succeed in capturing the wood and took 120 prisoners in the process. Major Wormald recorded: 'There were many more less mobile enemy on the objective!'

Losses had been high on both sides!

In the evening, C Squadron would pass through with 4 Welch and were able to capture the next wood further to the south without opposition, the enemy seemingly having abandoned the area. A Squadron were able to retire at 2100 hrs and returned to Goch, to begin the process of refitting tanks and obtaining replacements for those lost. C Squadron remained in the second wood captured, until relieved on the evening of the 25th, but B Squadron remained at Host in a counterattack role for several days.

A few days later, Lieutenant Richardson passed through the wood captured by A Squadron on the 24th and remembered: 'There was not a single tree in it that had a branch on it, let alone leaves, it looked like a forest of battered telegraph poles.'

To echo this, Paratroop officer Martin Pöppel, who had escaped Normandy and was now one of those facing the Allied advance, stated: 'The Reichswald Forest was shelled to pieces, shattered, only stumps were left.'

Lieutenant Richardson was soon to leave RHQ, since, as he recorded:

On the evening of the 26th the Colonel told me that because C Squadron were down to one troop officer, he was able to grant a request I had made on joining the Regiment, namely that I should be given a troop in a sabre

Squadron. Lt Charles was coming with me, and we were to report at 0900hrs the next morning.

Having joined his sabre squadron on 27 February, Lieutenant Richardson was very quickly sent out into the field when that night he was given forty-five minutes' warning for his troop to move, in support of the 6 RWF, who were supporting the 2 EYR – old friends of the 3&8s from D-Day. The East Yorks had been counterattacked by the enemy and driven back across a bridge over a tributary of the Niers River, east of Weeze. The action was fluid and confusing, with rounds cracking overhead, or hitting his tank's hull. Upon surveying a farm, he noted:

> Dead men were everywhere, in no definite order so no one could have said that the Germans had held one side of the farm and we the other, but all mixed up, inside and outside the farm buildings, evidence of the chaotic hand to hand struggle which must have taken place – the smell of death and corruption hung everywhere.

At one stage, a squadron of Spitfires proceeded to bomb and strafe a wood, far too close to his position for comfort. All the coloured recognition smoke that could be found was quickly let off, but it was some time before the aircraft disengaged from their attack.

Later, a white flag appeared from behind a potato clump and a German soldier emerged, so Lieutenant Richardson dismounted to get an identification for their intelligence officer. It transpired that they were facing men of the 8th Parachute Division and the German soldier asked if they could help his wounded comrades. A stretcher party was being organised, when a burst of enemy machine-gun fire from a wood ensured that this plan was called off. Lieutenant Richardson continues the story:

> Some time later a couple of red cross flags started waving from the end of the wood, firing again ceased and three German medical orderlies, two of them carrying a stretcher, came out and walked over to the potato clumps and disappeared behind. I got someone in the infantry who could speak German to improvise a megaphone out of a sheet of tin and shout to them that they were to bring the wounded into our lines and under no circumstances to take them back to their own. This to our surprise was answered by sharp bursts of fire from two machine pistols from behind the clumps. A number of our infantry who had their heads up having a look were wounded. I was livid at the injustice of this act and shelled the area as

hard as I could. No further movement was seen after that. A few days later I again passed this point and noted with satisfaction that there were two dead bogus medical orderlies – both armed – behind that potato clump.

Without doubt, the fighting in the Reichswald was bitter, causing Captain Julius Neave to record this note in his diary:

Unquestionably the Boche is fighting for every inch of ground and there is no doubt that once again the British and Canadians have drawn the entire German reserves onto themselves, in order to allow the Yanks to push straight through. It was extremely effective at Caen, so why not do it again is what the Pundits must say, but in effect it means we suffer frightful casualties and get none of the glamour or a break-through!

Back in Goch, Major Wormald assembled his men of A Squadron so that crews could be reallocated. He approached Joe Collins and instructed him, 'You, Collins, will take over a tank with a new crew.' Collins, with the ace card up his sleeve, replied, 'Not me Sir! How can I command a tank of Troopers when I am the same rank as them?' The major told him, 'From today you're a Corporal so go and get your stripe up!'

Refitting continued for several days before, on 5 March, RHQ moved with A & C squadrons beyond Kevelaer to the southeast of Weeze, to Veert on the western edge of Geldern. B Squadron finally left Host and moved to Kevelaer. On the morning of the 6th,

Corporal Joe Collins.

A Squadron were tasked with supporting units of the 160th Brigade once more, half the squadron supporting 2 Mons, with the other half supporting 4 Welch. They were to push north-east of Geldern, in the direction of Issum, then Alpen, with a view to dominating an escarpment overlooking the Rhine valley and the town of Wesel beyond. It was assumed that opposition would be light, since there was no artillery fire plan in place and A Squadron and the infantry moved off, on time, at 0400 hrs. Some enemy troops were encountered a mile before they even reached their start line, but this nuisance was dealt with and did not cause any deviation from the plan. As dawn broke, the Hussars entered an environment ideal for the siting of self-propelled guns, with large woods and farm buildings to their left and a forest on the right, which in places was up to 1,000 yards from the road.

Among 1st and 2nd troops supporting 2 Mons, one tank had drawn up close to a building. Squadron HQ tried to reach the tank over the radio to recommend that they move on, but it seemed that the commander had dismounted to speak to an infantry officer and the operator appeared to be on the B 'Troop' Net, so the warnings went unheeded. Suddenly there was the unmistakable sound of an armour-piercing shot, destroying the tank and killing the operator inside. It transpired that the man who lost his life had beforehand stated that he feared for his life on this day but was told not to be so pessimistic. A similar example of this sense of doom was described by Corporal Patrick Hennessey:

> I was talking to Jack Maxwell. Normally, he was full of fun and optimism, but not on that day. He was very serious and depressed, and though I tried to jolly him along, he would have none of it. He told me that he had packed up his personal kit and had left it and some letters with the Quartermaster. 'I've been bloody lucky up to now,' he said, 'but I have the feeling that I am not coming back from this lot.' That day, we had a number of skirmishes, but it was by no means a hard fighting day. When we harboured for the night, I learned that Maxwell's tank had been hit. Apparently, the shot had come in at the driver's visor, and Jack had been killed outright. This incident caused much speculation as I was not the only one to whom Jack had spoken of his premonition. Could it be that he knew for certain that the end had come, or was it merely coincidence? There was no doubting his sincerity when he spoke of it and one had heard of similar cases of men forecasting that they would not come back, particularly in aircrew. What is certain is that the longer one survives in battle, seeing one's comrades falling day by day, the more one begins to wonder how much longer the luck can last. It is not a thing to dwell on, but I am sure that every fighting soldier has had the feeling.[6]

Despite the use of artillery smoke to try to protect the flanks, A Squadron were to lose three tanks to self-propelled guns during the morning's advance and were engaged from the front, side and rear. There was also small arms fire to contend with, along with enemy artillery, and casualties were beginning to mount. By midday, about halfway to their objective, 1st and 2nd troops with 2 Mons could advance no further, with the infantry companies having captured and holding several local objectives along the way. As their advance ran out of steam, the other half of the squadron was ordered to enter the forest to the right. Owing to the density of the forest and the soft mud, it was only possible for the tanks to operate on forest tracks, but at least the trees offered more protection than the exposed road. However, it was not long before tanks of 3rd Troop were engaged by an anti-tank weapon in the forest. Lance Corporal Sid Beesley describes the encounter:

> Both Sergeant Charlie Rattle and Corporal Reggie Binns were wounded. By this time I was a L/Corporal and was following behind them as Crew Commander of a 17 pdr tank in pretty thick pine woods. We were moving in single file, I think, because of the thickness of the wood. I heard the crack of gunfire and saw chaps bailing out in front of me and at that very moment my tank just sank into a trench system and ended up well and truly stuck at about a 45 degree angle. So, my crew and I went forward to help the wounded. I remember Shuttleworth, Charlie's driver, had a facial wound but could walk. Charlie was minus a boot and had an injury to his heel but could hop along a bit. Reggie Binns had collected some shrapnel in his chest, but this was not serious. A German Medical Officer and a soldier carrying a black box with a large Red Cross came across a field and joined us. I drew my revolver, but the officer spoke perfect English and told me that he only wanted to find a building or shelter in which to set up a Medical Post to treat all soldiers, no matter where they came from. Charlie and I accepted this, and our now enlarged group went slowly on until we came to a farmhouse. On arrival there the MO stripped off his jacket and while he was washing his hands shouted 'Essen', I think it was, and the lady of the house held a piece of black looking bread for him to eat. From then on, he was the organiser and in control in that house which quickly filled up with wounded, mostly Welshmen. After I had seen him attend to Charlie, the doctor told him that it was only a flesh wound; but I think myself it turned out to be a bit more serious than that – I left with my crew to walk further back. Within a short distance we heard a Welsh voice shouting for help. I could not see him, but I found him in a hollow with a shattered thigh. He had a tourniquet on and told me that his mate had put it on and had gone off to organise a stretcher. He also told me that it was a minefield and to be careful – so I was. I eventually found an Officer and four Welsh lads who knew about this chap and were waiting for a mine detector to arrive. They also told me that it had been a bad day and that they had suffered a great many casualties. My crew had, by now, gone further back so I found my own way back to A1 Echelon where Duffy Hind (the Regimental Sergeant Major) came to meet me and gave me a drink of rum and looked after me for a while. On reflection, I remember the MO saying, as we walked along together, 'I am sure the war is lost for

us now. We have not eaten for two days.' He must have decided to give up. Whatever it was, he made a great impression on me. He was obviously a leader and a fine figure of a man, and I wished him well.

As 4 Welch advanced, their companies were also required to hold certain strategic points along the way, with some tanks committed in support. The final assault would be to the north-east tongue of the forest, where it met the Geldern–Wesel road on the escarpment. The number of infantry available for the final assault had dwindled to very few, as their casualties had mounted too, and with only two tanks of 4th Troop available, the Squadron Commander elected to move forward himself to help form a composite troop. As he moved forward, he passed Sergeant Rattle and the rest of his dismounted party: 'Sergeant Rattle was in good form. Smiling, he raised a bandaged hand and shouted, "Blighty for me". (He had in fact lost two joints of a forefinger – but was also limping badly.'

The final assault was successful, but Major Wormald spoke to his commanding officer over the radio and explained their exposed position; only one sergeant and six other infantrymen of 4 Welch had reached the final objective. As the escarpment was of strategic importance to both sides, a counterattack seemed inevitable, and they would struggle to repulse it. The colonel promised to see what he could do, but it was a further four hours before a Carrier platoon of 4 Welch arrived to help defend the area. This small force was able to hold the position, until relieved in the morning by 1st and 2nd troops of C Squadron, with accompanying infantry.

The day had taken nine of A Squadron's tanks out of action, three men were dead (Troopers Walter Sutherland, William Cumbes and John Cummings) and eight men were wounded, not to mention the terrific casualties suffered by the Welsh infantry. Major Wormald recorded it as a 'bloody awful day' and was scathing in his assessment:

> The Brigade's plan for the day was probably based upon the usual over optimistic and inaccurate intelligence reports about the enemy withdrawals. It was certainly undertaken without any reconnaissance of the ground over which we were to attack and without any pre-arranged Artillery support.

Once relieved, A Squadron moved into regimental reserve in Issum to rest and refit.

The following day, B Squadron had moved forward to Issum and three troops were immediately committed to relieve the C Squadron troops and support 6 RWF to the south-east of Alpen. They were to ensure that the area of the escarpment was secure by evening. C Squadron now came under the command of the 156th (Scottish Rifles) Brigade, of the 52nd (Lowland) Infantry Division; two troops with the 4th/5th Battalion Royal Scots Fusiliers (4/5 RSF) and two troops with the 6th Battalion Cameronians (6 Cams). On the afternoon of 8 March, 4/5 RSF and 6 Cams attacked Alpen, but owing to the wooded terrain through which they were operating, C Squadron were unable to provide the optimal weight of supporting fire.

Lieutenant Richardson commented:

> This could hardly be called a success as we were firing indirect from the wood on the top of the escarpment overlooking the town, and had no means of observing or correcting our fire. However, the attack itself got home.

The next day, C Squadron supported the 7th Cameronians for an attack on a factory at Alpen, which resulted in the enemy firing Panzerfausts directly at the assaulting infantry, such was the level of desperation of the fighting at this stage. However, the attack was entirely successful, and the squadron remained with the infantry at that location overnight. Friday, 9 March also heralded the sight of American forces moving along the Rhine valley from the south and with the Guards' Armoured Division approaching from the north, the regiment would soon be able to withdraw.

Lieutenant Richardson recalled:

> During the afternoon I watched an American attack coming in from our right. It was preceded by a terrific barrage and appeared to be going splendidly. The attack was backed up by a squadron of Thunderbolts; they were painted silver with red engine cowlings, and they made a fine sight as they dived almost vertically on to their targets.

Once relieved on the 10th by the 34th Armoured Brigade, they would retire to Issum and once more, the regiment was complete, before moving through Geldern and Weeze to Goch, arriving at 1100 hrs on 12 March. Here the regiment would rest, refit, and prepare for crossing the Rhine. At midday, the regimental band arrived from England and set up to entertain the Hussars.

Cosy Comfort remembered the afternoon's events:

> Out of Line, the Regimental Band appeared by magic and played in the sun. A queue formed by the cookhouse tent. 'Don't think I'll bother yet – wait a bit.' Boche planes – two perhaps – swooped – bombs and carnage. In that minute half of Recce Troop went – 7 dead and 28 wounded! Edisbury and my driver, young Morris, both died in my arms. Edisbury just looked

up at me, coughed, and went! Sergeant Busby never got over that day and he'd served the Regiment all his life; India, Dunkirk and now Germany.

Cosy's driver, Trooper Tom Morris from Richmond, Surrey, was just 19 years of age at the time of his death.

Corporal Frank Edisbury was 34 and left a wife, Margaret, back in Northenden, near Manchester.

With nothing further he could do for either Morris or Edisbury, Cosy went to the aid of another Hussar who had lost a leg, securing a tourniquet to stem the bleeding. Some fifty years later, Cosy received a phone call at midnight. 'Who's that calling at this time of night?' It was a call from Australia… 'Is that Peter Comfort? You saved my life!' It transpired that the man he'd helped back at Goch was Trooper Hatt and all those years later, he'd found out who had helped him and had at last tracked Peter down to thank him.

Corporal Frank Edisbury.

Since Goch housed a concentration of troops at that time, it became an obvious target for the Luftwaffe. The 3&8s were attacked by two ME 262 jets, causing a horrific number of casualties, and aside of the fatalities, many were severe cases. If that were not bad enough, in the evening a heavy calibre artillery shell collapsed a cellar occupied by members of B Squadron, killing one and wounding another four Hussars. The regiment had suffered its worst day for casualties since D-Day yet hadn't even been engaged in battle. Major General Miller recorded these events in his history of the 13th/18th as: 'A very dark day for the Regiment.'

Those lost were Corporal Frank Edisbury, along with Troopers Robert Carmichael, Reginald Fletcher, Nicholas Mitsialis, Francis Broadhurst, Thomas Morris, Charles Searle and Frank Wood.

By contrast, 13 March 1945 heralded an entirely different experience for one of the regiment's sons. After being shot in the head by a sniper during Operation Goodwood, back in July the previous year, Bob Charmbury had been confined to a wheelchair and had lost the use of his left arm. Through grit, determination and the help of his father-in-law, Christopher Reeder, Bob had managed to learn to walk unaided. He had been invited to receive the award of his Military Medal at Buckingham Palace, from King George VI himself. Bob

Bob Charmbury, outside Buckingham Palace to receive his Military Medal.

was not only able to manage the train journey south from Skipton to London but also posed upright outside the palace with his proud wife, Muriel, his mother Louise and his mother-in-law Alice. He then went inside and stood before the king to receive his medal.

The following days were comparatively peaceful for the Hussars as they prepared for Operation Plunder – the crossing of the Rhine. On the evening of 20 March, the colonel and his officers entertained Major General Gwilym Ivor Thomas of the 43rd (Wessex) Division (known to his men by the nicknames of 'Butcher Thomas' or 'von Thoma') and their own Brigadier Prior-Palmer.

The next day, the whole regiment paraded through Goch, accompanied by the regimental band on their way to a lecture from their colonel on the upcoming operation. On the return march, the brigadier took the salute, as his Hussars passed.

Chapter 10

Advance to Bremen

Prisoners, prisoners, thousands upon thousands, unshaven vacant faces.

As Operation Plunder loomed, thoughts turned to a speedy end to the war once the Allies were able to operate east of the Rhine; it was the final, natural obstacle in their path. The Hussars' friends from D-Day, the 3rd Infantry Division, had been led to believe that they would lead the assault crossing of the river and commence fighting on the east side. Unfortunately, this decision was later reversed, and they were instead tasked with securing the west bank opposite the town of Rees. They were to evacuate civilians from the area and secure all road junctions and bridges, so that no unauthorised people could interfere with the operation. The crossing would take place between the towns of Rees and Wesel and the Allies amassed over 4,000 artillery pieces on the west bank, while over 250,000 tons of supplies were moved up. To mask this activity from prying German eyes, special generators were set up to create a huge smokescreen, which had been laid since 16 March. An artillery bombardment was arranged for the evening of the 23rd to keep the Germans occupied while the 153rd and 154th brigades of the 51st (Highland) Infantry Division left the assembly area prepared by the 3rd Division and made their crossing of the river in amphibious Buffalo vehicles, north of Rees (Operation Turnscrew). They would be supported in the crossing by the Staffordshire Yeomanry in DD Sherman tanks, who were temporarily under the command of the 8th Armoured Brigade; of course, they had left this brigade back in Normandy, to return to England to be trained for this very day.

The 75mm Shermans of the 13th/18th had moved up earlier in the day to positions overlooking the river and enjoyed the sight of RAF Tempests and Typhoons zooming overhead to harass German forces across the river. The Hussars were to add further weight to the artillery bombardment, by means of a shoot, described as 'pepper potting'. After concealing their tanks behind camouflage netting, they commenced firing at 1900 hrs; most of the shells fired were high explosive, which would burst upon contact, but some solid shot and delay-fuse shells were included for good measure. It was hot, furious work and the gunners and loaders were stripped to the waist, as they fired as quickly as they could, not stopping until the order to cease fire was given at 2300 hrs. Cosy Comfort remembered: 'Our Regiment hull down, huge piles of Ammo – what a bombardment.'

Lieutenant Richardson, in C Squadron, recorded that his tank had managed to fire 286 shells during the shoot and the ground around the tanks was littered with the empty, brass shell casings. The Regimental Diary recorded: 'All the Pepper Potting was on targets to the NE and NW of Rees. This went off very successfully according to all reports.'

Indeed, the 51st Division and the Staffordshire Yeomanry had successfully established a bridgehead on the far side of the river.

To deepen the Allied bridgehead and to silence any German artillery targeting the area, Operation Varsity began the next morning, and the Hussars watched in awe as 16,000 airborne troops were inserted on the other side of the Rhine. It was all reminiscent of the airborne display on the evening of D-Day, when the sky had become black with gliders and their towplanes heading for the Orne bridgehead. Captain Julius Neave recorded the sight in his diary for 24 March:

DD Shermans of the Staffordshire Yeomanry collapsing their canvas screens after crossing the Rhine. (*Courtesy of The Tank Museum, Bovington – Image 0338-D4*)

Watched the Airborne show at about 1000 hrs. They arrived plum on time and the air was literally black for two hours. The scene of flight upon flight of Dakotas first and Halifaxes towing gliders following, was quite beyond description.

After much waiting around, starting at 1800 hrs, both A & B squadrons commenced their crossing of the river on Class 50/60 rafts at the 'Gravesend Ferry'.

C Squadron would have to wait until 0400 hrs the next morning for their turn at the 'Tilbury Ferry', completing their crossing by 1000 hrs on the 25th. RHQ spent most of the 24th to the 26th as spectators before they too could join the rest of the regiment on the evening of the 26th, by way of the 'Gravesend Ferry'.

Captain Julius Neave wrote in his diary for the 26th: 'We watched the Typhoons strafing up the Boche, which was the most impressive sight. I haven't seen so many operating at once and they certainly give the place absolute stick time and time again.'

Corporal Patrick Hennessey recorded that by the evening of the 26th, the Royal Engineers had successfully constructed twelve bridges across the river. The Rhine had been well and truly breached!

Once across the river, both A and B squadrons were soon sent into battle, supporting the 130th Infantry Brigade in an attack on Millingen, to expand

Vehicles loading onto a Class 50/60 raft. (*Courtesy of The Tank Museum, Bovington – Image 0340-B5*)

the bridgehead around Rees to the north-west. They would attack along the axis of the main railway line to the south-east of Millingen. The attack was successful, 200 prisoners were captured and by midnight, they had linked up with the 51st (Highland) Division on their right.

The next day, 27 March, C Squadron 13th/18th joined forces with C Squadron of the 4th/7th Dragoon Guards in support of old friends from Mont Pinçon, the 129th Brigade. C Squadron 13th/18th would support 5 Wilts on the left of the advance, with C Squadron 4th/7th supporting 4 Wilts on the right. They were to seize the ground to the north of Millingen, to reach a half-constructed autobahn, some 2,000 yards beyond the town. Passing through the battered town at 0500 hrs, with some buildings still in flames, a quick O Group was undertaken with the infantry, followed by a hurried breakfast, to enable the Hussars to reach the start line on time at 0900 hrs. The first objective for Lieutenant Richardson's 2nd Troop, along with their company of 5 Wilts, was a hamlet of houses approximately 600 yards from the start line. However, after advancing behind an artillery barrage, they soon found their way barred by an anti-tank ditch, forcing a detour to the right of some 400 yards across open ground. Corporal Lamont was first to run the gauntlet, his tank racing at top speed to reach a farm. Hearts were in mouths for a few moments, but his tank thankfully drew no fire. Each tank then took its turn to race across to the farm. One enemy soldier did emerge from the farm buildings armed with a Panzerfaust, but upon realising that he was somewhat out-gunned, threw it to the ground and surrendered. Meanwhile the infantry had captured the hamlet, along with several prisoners. These comprised a mixed force with some soldiers from the 104th Panzer Grenadier Regiment (21st Panzer Division) and others from the 6th Parachute Division; both units had served in Normandy. Then 2nd Troop moved up to join them and quickly consolidated the position, ready for Lieutenant Charles's 4th Troop to move through towards the autobahn. However, their supporting artillery barrage began to land around the hamlet, catching the infantry in the open with their half-constructed slit trenches and forcing any dismounted tank commanders to dive rapidly for their vehicles. Lieutenant Richardson describes the situation:

> I frantically sent word back by wireless and the barrage was lifted, but too late for the enemy had played his well-known trick of shelling the area of our barrage so that our advancing troops would walk into it. It was extremely unpleasant, and also for a time, I was still under the impression that it was our own barrage and continued to scream down the mike for it to be lifted. However, after 5 minutes I was sarcastically told that if I

had it lifted any farther it would be falling on BERLIN!! So, it was an enemy stonk after all.

This barrage held up 4th Troop for a time, but they then advanced towards the autobahn, where they were met with machine-gun and mortar fire. Sergeant Haygarth's tank managed to reach the autobahn, but none of the infantry could get within 200 yards of it, so being rather isolated, it was forced to retire. C Squadron's 2ic, Captain Tetley, came forward to 4th Troop's position, but the moment he arrived, a mortar round struck his turret, directly in front of him. It was a miracle that he wasn't decapitated by the blast, but a large piece of shrapnel smashed his jaw and was embedded in the roof of his mouth. Partially blinded and completely deaf, he was carried to the rear.

A stalemate had been reached in the battle, so at 1300 hrs, 5 Wilts were ordered to retire to at least 400 yards south of the autobahn, to be a safe distance from the fire plan arranged to shoot in infantry of the 214th Infantry Brigade, supported by the 4th/7th Dragoon Guards. They were successful in crossing the autobahn but lost several tanks and men in the process. Having completed their part of the attack, C Squadron 13th/18th withdrew, and the regiment harboured for the night in Millingen.

The following morning, both A & B squadrons, supporting 7 Hants and 4 Dorsets respectively, advanced west as far as the Issel River, to the south of Anholt. An artillery bombardment had been requested, targeted at likely enemy positions, and would consist of high-explosive shells and smoke, to provide a smokescreen on the exposed, left flank of the advance. Halfway forward, the smoke suddenly ceased, and tanks of A Squadron were immediately engaged by an anti-tank gun, brewing up two. The Hussars quickly responded by firing tracer rounds into farm buildings and barns to set them ablaze, and again deployed their own smoke mortars to cover their movements. The damage was done, however, and all five crewmen in one tank were dead, including the previously mentioned Trooper Jack Maxwell, who had predicted his own demise. Major Wormald was furious that the smokescreen had been lifted and complained to Brigadier Coad of the 130th Brigade; it transpired that the instruction had come directly from the brigadier himself, since he no longer considered the smoke necessary. The major responded that he considered him entirely responsible for the unnecessary deaths of his men.

Although A Squadron's advance was held up for a time through this incident, the day's objectives were achieved, ready for C Squadron to carry forward the leading company of 5 Dorsets, in the early hours of the 29th. Then 1st and 2nd troops of C Squadron moved the infantry to the village of Megchelen and harboured there, while the Dorsets moved off to make an assault crossing of the river, to secure a bridgehead on the far side, enabling sappers of the Royal Engineers to construct a bridge over the river, which was completed by dawn. The two troops of C Squadron crossed the bridge, to allow an attacking force to pass through to assault the town of Anholt, and 2nd Troop of C Squadron located a wooded bank facing north, where they could adopt a hull down position. Corporal Lamont's tank was soon trading rounds with a German 75mm PAK, sited in woods some 600 yards to their front, and it managed to destroy the gun with three rounds. A Squadron with 7 Hants and B Squadron with 4 Dorsets crossed the bridge and passed through to commence their attack on Anholt at 0930 hrs. Their assault was successful, and the town was in their hands by 1100 hrs.

Lieutenant Richardson, back with 2nd Troop, C Squadron, remembered the following incident:

> At about midday after a quiet period there were three loud reports in quick succession. At first we thought that it was one of our own 17 pdrs firing from behind, but actually it was the astounding noise an 88mm solid shell makes when passing low overhead. We were not left long in doubt of this as there was another vicious crack, followed instantaneously by a shattering crack and a shower of sparks and our Sherman bulldozer which was parked about 100 yds down the road burst into flames. Fortunately, there were no crew inside but Trooper Beecham, the driver, who was standing on the back had a lucky escape. It was puzzling as to where this 88mm was firing from as we appeared to be well behind cover. After making several observations we decided that it must be firing blind from behind the woods to the north, as the shells were dropping at quite a steep angle. The gun probably had the road registered and hearing track movement had started shelling. A thick column of black smoke was soon rising from the burning tank and indicating to the Boche gunner that he had scored a hit. We were accordingly subjected to a period of heavy 'stonking' both HE [high explosive] and AP [armour piercing].

At this time one man per troop was granted two weeks' leave, so in 2nd Troop, A Squadron, each name was written down on a slip of paper, placed in a beret and the lucky winner's name was drawn from the hat. Corporal Joe Collins's name was drawn, and excited at the prospect of returning to 'Blighty' for his first leave in eleven months, he prepared to travel back to Calais by 3-ton truck, before the long train journey north to Paisley. He was to hand over command of his tank to Lance Corporal Frank Tapley, who had been slightly wounded on D-Day and sent back to England. Upon returning to the regiment some three weeks later, the lorry Tapley was on overturned, breaking his arm. Finally, Tapley had his opportunity to get some battle experience as a crew commander. Joe Collins jokingly told Tapley that he was a jinx and that he was to take good care of his crew in his absence, as they had lived and fought together for the last few weeks with no problems. Tapley reassured him, with a slap on the shoulder, saying, 'Don't worry Jock, they will still be here when you come back.'

After what felt like the shortest fourteen days of his life, Joe arrived back at Dover by train and bumped into the next batch of lucky leave recipients, who had just arrived from Calais. Joe enquired how things had been going and whether there had been any losses in A Squadron.

'Four tanks between 1st, 2nd and 4th Troops,' came the reply.

'Who was the tank of 2nd Troop,' he asked with mounting apprehension.

'It was Corporal Tapley who was crew commander.'

'Any of the crew killed?'

'The lot, including Tapley.'

Naturally this news came as a hammer blow to Joe, and the journey back to the regiment felt like an eternity, as he ruminated about his dead crew and tried to come to terms with the fact that he'd been at home relaxing, when they'd all lost their lives. Once reunited with his troop, Sergeant Bill Hammond explained what had happened: how Tapley's tank had been one of the two knocked out by a self-propelled gun on the 28th, when the smokescreen lifted. Joe was immediately put in command of a new crew, with a new tank, and got back to the task at hand.

Sadly, these A Squadron deaths could have been easily avoided, and even more painfully, they would also be the last fatal casualties of the war in A Squadron. Those who lost their lives on 28 March were Lance Corporal Frank Tapley, Troopers James Baxendale, Thomas Forbes, John Mason, Jack Maxwell and Cyril Symons.

As an aside, whilst on leave, Joe Collins had his lost wallet returned to him. It transpired that a Royal Naval rating from Saltcoats in Ayrshire had been a member of a party tasked with clearing the beach of debris after D-Day and had happened upon Joe's discarded uniform, from when he'd changed into dry clothes after his swim ashore. In his clothing, the rating discovered Joe's wallet, containing a photo of his wife, Rose, and his mother's address. While on leave himself, the sailor took the trouble of travelling to Paisley to return the wallet to Joe's mother.

On 30 March, an O Group indicated that German resistance was beginning to slacken, and that the Guards' Armoured Division had broken out of the bridgehead. Now 8th Armoured Brigade, supporting the 43rd Infantry Division, were to break out on the Guards' left, with Canadian armour operating to their left.

The advance north was planned to be swift with most of the infantry travelling in personnel carriers, but the leading company of each battalion to be carried by the tanks. The regiment was to support the 214th Infantry Brigade and the afternoon of the 30th was spent with the tank commanders trying to organise the collection of new maps that they had been issued.

On the morning of the 31st, the breakout commenced, codenamed Operation Forrard-on, with C Squadron leading the regiment with the 1st Battalion of the Worcestershire Regiment (1 Worcs). They had now crossed back into Holland, but with 4th Troop leading, several bridge demolitions slowed their progress and by midday they had only managed to advance around 6 miles north of Anholt. Consequently, the advance was ended for the day and the regiment harboured in the area of Sinderen. At least the Hussars were glad to be among the cheerful and hospitable Dutch people once more, rather than glum and dispirited German townsfolk. An O Group that evening confirmed the order of march to be the same for the next day, with 4th Troop, C Squadron at the front, carrying the leading company of infantry on their tanks. They were to advance north with all speed through Varssveld, then Lichtenvoorde to capture intact a bridge over the Twenthe Canal, to the south-west of Goor. After an 0600 hrs start, progress was going reasonably well, until some opposition was met at Borculo. While trying to scout around this, the lead tank of Lieutenant Uttley's troop found itself upside down in a river, when a bridge collapsed under its weight. The crew managed to escape the tank, except for the loader/operator, Trooper McDonald, who was up to his neck in water inside the upturned tank and in danger of drowning. It was several hours before the enemy could be silenced and two AVRE vehicles were able to attend to the stricken tank from the far bank of the river, moving the vehicle into a position whereby McDonald could be rescued. Despite his dire predicament, he emerged unhurt, but rather cold, soggy and shaken.

C Squadron forged on and had reached Diepenheim as dusk was falling, close to the objective of the canal crossing. Lieutenant Smith's 3rd Troop headed off rapidly towards the bridge and upon turning a corner just a short distance from the objective, Lance Sergeant Bristow's tank in the lead was struck by a bazooka, killing the tank's gunner. Despite being on fire, the tank continued towards the bridge and was just 15 yards away, when their ammunition began to explode, forcing the remainder of the crew to bail out. As they did so, the Germans blew up the bridge. The troop commander's tank was next to be attacked by a bazooka, but his crew were all able to dismount safely and took cover in a ditch. Despite German troops being in the area in force, they managed to extricate themselves and having gone ahead of the supporting infantry, Lieutenant Smith now met up with their leading platoon. He led both the 3&8s' dismounted troopers and the infantry platoon to the rear and would later be awarded the Military Cross for his actions on this day. Lance Sergeant Bristow and his loader/operator had both been wounded when dismounting their burning tank and were assumed 'missing'. It later transpired that they had been taken prisoner but were liberated two weeks afterwards by the Canadians.

Despite covering 40 miles during the day and with a very gallant attempt to seize the bridge, the members of the regiment were naturally very disappointed to only snatch defeat from the jaws of victory. If that were not bad enough, Lieutenant Richardson remembered:

> We harboured for the night in a nice green looking field which turned out to be half a bog and nearly all my troop got stuck, it took half the night to get them out, and to make matters worse it started raining.

The regiment remained to the south of the canal in the Diepenheim and Neede area until 3 April, when they moved east to a concentration area, south of Hengelo, arriving in the evening. The Regimental Diary records: 'The plan at this time was to continue the advance doing left flank protection to the Guards Armd Div on our right with the final objective of Hambourg.'

It also recorded: 'Major D B Wormald DSO MC given immediate award of bar to his MC.' In short, Major Wormald had now been awarded no less than three gallantry awards.

The Guards had been held up around Lingen, back over the border, and it wasn't until 7 April that the regiment was able to advance along congested roads with the 214th Brigade, back into Germany, via Nordhorn, then Lingen, arriving at 1600 hrs. Progress from here was slow, with numerous reports from prisoners and civilians alike, that the woods ahead were positively bristling with self-propelled guns and bazookas. Two crossroads lay ahead, and it was decided that A Squadron, carrying men of the 7 SLI on their tanks, supported by the King's Royal Rifle Corps, should make a charge up the road. This would be preceded by a ten-minute artillery barrage ranged on the two crossroads. A Squadron then raced up the road, all guns blazing on either side into the woods, laying down suppressive fire as they advanced. This modern-day version of a cavalry charge proved very effective, and the squadron had soon crossed the first crossroads and in twenty minutes had seized the second crossroads, some 3 miles ahead. A Squadron remained on the crossroads for the night, as the remainder of the regiment harboured some 2 miles further back down the road.

In the morning, A Squadron resumed their advance with 7 SLI and B Squadron moved up to support them with 5 DCLI. The weather was unseasonably hot for April and with the weight of vehicles on the roads, gritty dust stung the faces of the tank drivers and commanders, with some of the dust finding its way into their goggles too.

A Squadron and 7 SLI captured Bawinkel with little difficulty and reported only twenty enemy in the town. They then pressed on, clearing the left side of the advance, with B Squadron and 5 DCLI clearing the right side, as far as the town of Haselünne. It was reported that Haselünne contained a strong garrison of German troops, and the bridge over the Hase River had been blown, so in order to bypass the town, 7 SLI conducted an assault crossing of the river to the west of the town at Bückelte, supported by A Squadron from the south bank. With a bridgehead established on the north bank, Royal Engineers were able to construct a bridge across the Hase overnight. The regiment had harboured in the area of Bawinkel and would be joined by A Squadron on 9 April. They would remain here for the next couple of days, providing a welcome opportunity to rest and carry out maintenance on the tanks. In the meantime, Haselünne had been captured and a second bridge built over the Hase River.

Cosy Comfort poses for the camera in shirtsleeves, in the unseasonably warm weather.

On 12 April, the regiment moved to Haselünne to join 214 Brigade in preparation for the next operation in the area of Löningen to the north-east. On the 13th, the sabre squadrons met up with their respective battalions: A with 7 SLI, B with 5 DCLI and C with 1 Worcs. The plan was that 130th Infantry Brigade would seize the next town beyond Löningen, Cloppenburg, and support the building of a bridge there, if this was necessary. Then 214th Brigade with the 3&8s would pass through Cloppenburg to seize the next town to the north-east, Ahlhorn. The battle for Cloppenburg continued into the night. The next morning, C Squadron led the way towards the objective of a crossroads at Ahlhorn, but large craters on the road caused some delays as either these had to be bypassed or bulldozers needed to be called forward to repair the road. The sides of the road were thickly wooded and it was ideal for an enemy ambush, so the tanks fired their machine guns into the undergrowth as they advanced.

While held up by one crater in the road, which required the attention of a bulldozer, Lieutenant Richardson describes the next events:

> While it was working several enemy came down the road on bicycles apparently quite unconcerned, we held our fire until the leading cyclist turned into a group of buildings, we then opened up. Utter confusion reigned and they scattered in all directions. The crater was soon filled and we went on. Shortly afterwards a German staff car appeared over the crest about 2000 yds ahead of us. This also evidently failed to spot us and motored on forwards. My gunner got it in his sights and I called out the ranges as it got nearer. It started to slow down near the buildings so I gave the order to fire. This first shell hit the car smack on the radiator and destroyed it completely. A pity because it was a nice car.

As 2nd Troop had almost exhausted their ammunition, Lieutenant Uttley's 1st Troop took over the lead, to allow Lieutenant Richardson's tanks to retire and replenish their ammunition. Having reached the hamlet of Neulethe, about 2,500 yards short of Ahlhorn, Lieutenant Uttley discovered that the bridge there was blown, but having dismounted and checked the area on foot, he located another bridge some 200 yards to the south, which the enemy had neglected to destroy. He was therefore able to cross to the far side with a Company of 1 Worcs and entered buildings, where a short battle commenced. Uttley's tank was attacked with a bazooka from the rear, but fortunately not put out of action. Then 1 Worcs sent up a second infantry company, which was quickly able to end the engagement, and the infantry consolidated the surrounding area. The plan was now for Royal Engineers to construct a Bailey bridge over the river, to enable 2nd and 3rd troops, C Squadron, to attack Ahlhorn at first light with 1 Worcs. This was the situation until 0300 hrs, when the Germans counterattacked the positions of 1 Worcs with a force estimated at two companies, supported by two Jadgpanther self-propelled guns, with their 88mm main armaments.

The Germans caught both the infantry and engineers by surprise, driving the engineers off the bridge they were trying to build. The fighting was intense until one of 1st Troop's tanks managed to fire a couple of shots at one of the German vehicles. Although the rounds bounced off the front in a shower of sparks, the shells sufficiently worried the German commander enough to order his vehicle to withdraw. C Squadron's 2nd Troop was also sent forward at this point, and they took over covering the ground to the front and right, supporting A Company of 1 Worcs, with 1st Troop covering the front and left, supporting

D Company. The 2nd Troop had been fired upon during their approach to the hamlet by a Panther tank sited on the crest of a hill 600 yards away and being unable to traverse their guns to engage it, owing to the close proximity of trees alongside the track, they raced ahead, out of harm's way. Several 17-pounder Fireflies were also moving up to support the hamlet, but one was to prove less fortunate, when the Panther scored a hit, although fortunately no one was killed. By the time 2nd Troop had adopted firing positions in the hamlet, the Panther had withdrawn. A short truce followed, whereby British medical orderlies were able to bring in the wounded of both sides. The German infantry company to the front of 2nd Troop were then invited to surrender, but it seemed that they would prefer to die for the Führer. However, thirty minutes later, having given the matter some more consideration, they agreed to surrender and forty German soldiers filed in, to be taken prisoner by 2nd Troop. In the afternoon, the two C Squadron troops and their infantry companies did extend the perimeter of their positions back up to the wooded area to their front, without opposition. In readiness for another counterattack, they began placing mines along the surrounding tracks. As they were doing this, the other German company from the earlier counterattack emerged from the wet fields where they had lain hidden all day to surrender, along with their officers.

Later that day, an operation was planned for 1400 hrs to capture woods and a crossroads to the north-west of Ahlhorn. B Squardon would commence a 'pepper pot' barrage onto the woods, fifteen minutes before H Hour. A Squadron would only help bring the infantry of 7 SLI forward, but couldn't directly support the infantry in their assault, owing to the marshy fields approaching the woods. The 7 SLI waded through a stream and made their way across the marshy ground into the woods and although they met some opposition, were able to clear the area without too much difficulty. Next, the remainder of 1 Worcs, supported by the uncommitted C Squadron troops, moved up to seize the first crossroads beyond the woods and were able to do so without opposition, linking up with 7 SLI on their left. The third phase was for A Squadron and 7 SLI to leapfrog ahead to the next crossroads, which was captured after a short engagement, resulting in ninety enemy prisoners being captured.

Early on 16 April, 1st and 2nd troops of C Squadron joined the rest of the squadron and supported 1 Worcs through the woods to the north of the Cloppenburg/Ahlhorn road – the same woods cleared by 7 SLI the day before, but they had only cleared the first 500 yards and enemy troops were suspected of being further north, preparing to counterattack. Then 1 Worcs moved through the woods with four companies 'up', each supported by a C Squadron troop. A few German stragglers were mopped up in the process, but otherwise they reached the far side of the wood by midday, without difficulty. The 2nd Troop moved on a little further with A Company of 1 Worcs, along with an infantry mortar platoon in their carriers. After discovering a smouldering Canadian Sherman, the infantry carriers pushed north, before planning to turn east and rejoin the battalion. However, the leading carrier had gone no further than 50 yards when there was a huge explosion as it detonated a mine; there was no sign of its driver, and the gunner and commander were both injured. Lieutenant Richardson recalled the event:

> I grabbed a first aid box and ran forward, I had almost reached the group around the wounded men when there was another deafening explosion – the carrier platoon Sgt had very foolishly tried to lift a half exposed mine which was lying on the track, as usual it was booby trapped, and he blew himself to pieces. This caused a 'flap' and everyone became extremely jittery, there were also three more casualties, another rifleman had been severely hurt, the carrier platoon officer had had most of the skin blown off his face and although not seriously hurt was a shocking sight, streaming with blood and half blinded. Major Hall also had a splinter of steel in his eye, which although it luckily missed the pupil was extremely painful.

Major Peter Hall of A Company, 1 Worcs, took the decision to end the patrol at this stage, since they'd clearly entered a minefield, but since the detonations hadn't drawn any enemy fire, he was sure that any enemy had already withdrawn from the area.

The next day, B Squadron moved into the town of Ahlhorn with infantry of 9 DCLI and quickly consolidated the town without opposition. In the evening of the 17th, orders were received that the regiment would now leave the 43rd Infantry Division and would instead support the 51st (Highland) Division. At dawn, the regiment moved off for an uneventful move east from Ahlhorn, passing through Wildeshausen, finally arriving that morning at Wohlde. Here they would have two days to rest and carry out maintenance duties.

On 20 April, as the other squadrons rested, B Squadron supported an attack by the 152nd Brigade on Delmenhorst, to the south-west of Bremen. The enemy had withdrawn to the northern suburbs and after an initial easy start to the operation, the infantry suddenly found themselves engaged in a fierce battle and B Squadron lost one tank, resulting in several casualties.

B Squadron remained in Delmenhorst on the 21st, but by the afternoon of 23 April, the regiment once again came under the command of the 43rd Division and moved across the Weser River to Walle, in the north of Bremen. The infantry was to clear up the east side of Bremen as far as the Bremen–Hamburg autobahn and as B Squadron were supporting 5 Dorsets to clear the road leading to Ahausen, they met some opposition. They captured 100 prisoners of war, but not before Lieutenant Edward Moulding's tank was attacked by a self-propelled gun; he would subsequently die of his wounds.

Meanwhile, C Squadron, supporting 5 DCLI, had been making slow progress all day owing to boggy ground. By late afternoon, the tanks were advancing towards some farm buildings from where the Reconnaissance Regiment of 43rd Division had suffered two vehicles knocked out by bazookas earlier in the day. Lieutenant Richardson describes what happened next, as 2nd Troop approached the buildings:

> 2nd Troop was giving covering fire with smoke onto the last objective, a large farm when an ancient man of about 80 summers dashed out of the farm and came hobbling towards us, apparently undeterred by the smoke shells which must have been passing very close to his head. We stopped firing immediately and watched in amazement. The ancient eventually arrived at my tank and shouted 'Minen! Minen!' pointing a few yards in front. I hastily dismounted and sure enough the whole track was sewn with mines for about ten yards in front of my tank right up to the farm. I blessed that old man then. The first and last time I've ever felt well towards a German!

Having been held in reserve the previous day, on the 24th A Squadron supported 4 Dorsets in an attack on Hellwege, to the east of Bremen. The operation was carried out successfully and two enemy self-propelled guns were destroyed, without loss to the Hussars. The attack on Bremen itself commenced well with the 52nd (Lowland) Division attacking from the east with the 4th Armoured Brigade and the 3rd Infantry Division attacking from the south. However, Captain Julius Neave recorded in his diary:

> We heard the shattering news tonight that Derek Wormald is to be posted to India forthwith as second-in-command of a regiment. Derek, who has been with the Regiment all his service, had commanded 'A' Squadron for two years and won the D.S.O. and two M.C.s since the war. He has been detailed personally by the Commander-in-Chief, so we can do nothing about it. It's a great blow to the Regiment as Derek's reputation is legendary and he is the best Squadron Leader out here.

The next morning, 130th Infantry Brigade took over from 157th (Highland Light Infantry) Brigade and was supported in attacks into the east of Bremen by all three sabre squadrons of the regiment, but little opposition was met and, according to Captain Julius Neave, 500 prisoners of war were captured, along with over a dozen 88mm guns intact. Still in support of the 43rd Division pressing further into Bremen, Lieutenant Richardson described C Squadron's approach into the eastern suburb of Blockdiek:

> We crossed the start line at 0100 hrs and advanced into the pitch darkness. It was trepidatious work, at each street crossing we expected a blast from a Panzerfaust or an 88mm, also all the tram wires had been brought down by air raids and hung at turret level, one had to keep a sharp lookout to avoid being decapitated. However, we met no opposition and reached our objective just as dawn was breaking. This was our first experience of a German city which had been subjected to heavy RAF attack and the sight which met our eyes as the sky lightened is well-nigh indescribable. We were in what had been a large area of well to do flats – had been because now 75% of the buildings were reduced to heaps of rubble and the remainder to gutted shells. The air was putrid with the smell of burst drains, and the unmistakable stench of death. Numbers of corpses lay in the streets and goodness knows how many were buried under the rubble. It was like a city of death, not a sound was heard and not a soul was seen except for our own troops who crouched in position behind the rubble.

At one stage, fanatical SS troops held up the advancing infantry of the 43rd Division at the Bürgerpark, despite the burgomaster having agreed to surrender the town. They were, however, silenced by midnight and the survivors surrendered.

A rather grisly episode was documented in Captain Neave's diary:

> In the evening we went round rather ghoulishly to a most remarkable sight … the chief Nazi (the Gauleiter of Bremen) and his wife both shot dead, suicide, in their chairs upstairs in the office of the HQ S.A. Bremen![1] It was worth seeing and just like a play. Apparently, a Doctor's sizing-up of the situation is that first they drank a bottle of brandy and then she shot him and then herself! It was nevertheless rather beastly, but a sign of the times!

Captain Neave then went on to describe how much silk and alcohol was being liberated from the town.

On 27 April, A Squadron remained east in Osterholtz, while B and C squadrons patrolled the town, but by the afternoon all resistance in Bremen had vanished and the remainder of the regiment concentrated in Bremen itself. It was now time to say goodbye to the very capable and well-respected commanding officer of A Squadron, Major Derek Wormald, DSO, MC & BAR. He recorded in his diary:

I had returned to England just in time for my 29th birthday (28/4). I had four weeks leave before I flew to India to Command the 25th Dragoons which was to be the (Sherman) DD Regiment to be employed in the assault and recapture of Malaysia.

In his history of the regiment, Major General Miller had this to say of the major:

> Major Wormald left the regiment to take command of the 25th Dragoons in India. He had commanded 'A' Squadron with particular distinction for 2.5 years and served in it his whole soldiering career. He was awarded the MC and Bar and the DSO.

Captain Akers-Douglas would now be promoted to replace Major Wormald in command of A Squadron.

Although an end to the war in Europe seemed imminent, some resistance from the Wehrmacht was still expected and now O Groups were held for operations to the north of Bremen to seize Bremerhaven and Cuxhaven on the coast. On 29 April, the regiment concentrated in Osterholtz, along with the 214th Brigade, then made slow progress in the afternoon to Quelkhorn, to the north-east of Bremen. Opposition was light, with the occasional Nebelwerfer stonk, but the bigger enemy was the poor condition of the roads and the surrounding terrain, which caused many of the tanks to get badly bogged. Once again, on the 30th, the ground was the principal enemy, with collapsing verges causing hold-ups as the regiment pushed further east with the infantry. Captain Julius Neave recorded:

Major Derek Wormald, DSO, MC & BAR.

> After late to bed was up early to get on the air to continue the frigging around and to find more and more tanks bogged – we have now had 17 bogged and unbogged and still have about 9 to get out. The enemy shows little stomach for proper resistance – why, goodness knows, they bother to fight at all.

By the afternoon, the squadrons were dismissed, and the regiment was released from 214th Brigade and concentrated back at Quelkhorn. On 1 May, Captain Julius Neave noted in his diary:

> The war news is good enough though speculation as to the peace offers still runs high. However, the 'end of exercise' atmosphere on our front continues.
>
> The news that Hitler is dead came at 10:30 tonight as we had just tuned in the wireless – dramatically four minutes after the Germans had announced it – is it true I wonder? It is futile to continue now, but futility has been about the form for some weeks now!

After a couple of days of inactivity, the 3&8s were placed under the command of 129th Brigade and it was proposed that they would marry up at Tarmstedt to the north-east of Bremen, then operate with infantry from Glinstedt in a north-westerly axis towards Bremerhaven. However, after what Captain Neave described as 'a certain amount of "stand up, sit down" this morning', news came that the German forces in that sector had all surrendered and the operation was cancelled. Captain Neave had also documented that Hamburg had surrendered: '100,000 surrendered to the 2nd Army yesterday – The End is near!'

He was not wrong in his assessment, since, as Neave recorded on 4 May, an operator on the command radio net interrupted the officers during the evening:

> He said, 'Excuse me Sir, but there's been a news flash – the German Army is surrendering on our front tomorrow morning.' We managed to take the news calmly and carried on with our 'O' Gp. However, the phone rang in the middle and a message from 43 Division read:-
> 'No tactical movements without further orders. No harassing fire will be laid. No move from present locations. BBC news flash confirmed German Army facing us will surrender from 08:00 hrs tomorrow morning!'

All was quiet for the next couple of days, with the Regimental Diary simply recording, 'Nothing to Report' for 6 May.

On 7 May, at the Supreme Headquarters Allied Expeditionary Force in Reims, General Dwight Eisenhower accepted the unconditional surrender of all German forces from General Alfred Jodl. The Hussars would learn of this news via a BBC broadcast that evening. The war in Europe was over!

Tuesday, 8 May – Victory in Europe Day. The regiment, with the 52nd (Lowland) Division, moved north of Bremen towards Bremerhaven to organise the surrender of the German 480th Infantry Division and 15th Panzer Grenadier

Division. Captain Neave did comment that the German commanders were cooperative and did their best to ensure that everything ran smoothly.

Cosy Comfort recalled meeting his former enemy, face to face: 'Prisoners, prisoners, thousands upon thousands, unshaven vacant faces, horses, odd-looking carts; a fallen, hopeless Army.'

Captain Julius Neave wrote: 'At 15:00 hrs, Churchill, in a short announcement, told us about the unconditional surrender and at 21:00 hrs the King spoke.'

Peace at last and Cosy Comfort recalled his first night following the Wehrmacht's surrender: 'The first night's sleeping not in or under the tank, but beside it! Looking up at the stars and hearing a lone plane and not being scared; Peace!'

Chapter 11

British Army on the Rhine

HQ Squadron riot squad called out to deal with the situation.

The total number of killed and missing during the eleven months' campaign had been 11 Officers and 131 Other Ranks; 23 Officers and 213 Other Ranks had been wounded. Honours and awards included 4 Distinguished Service Orders, 1 Bar to the Military Cross, 12 Military Crosses, 1 Member of the Order of the British Empire, 3 British Empire Medals, 20 Military Medals and 22 Mentions in Despatches.[1]

The week following VE Day was quiet, as more German units were disarmed and processed. In the main the surrendering German soldiers seemed pleased that their war was over, and that they had survived to see the end of it. They presented no significant problems to the Hussars, and it might be argued that they were rather relieved to surrender to the British, rather than the Russians, and this fact may have even hastened the decision of some units to surrender.

Then, on 16 May, an O Group detailed the regiment's planned move to the town of Hannover on the 19th, to the south-east of Bremen. The Yalta Conference, held in February 1945, led by Britain's Prime Minister Winston Churchill, US President Franklin D. Roosevelt and Russian Marshal Joseph Stalin, had laid down the plans for the end of the war. It was agreed which territories would become the responsibility of which nation and although US forces had finished the war in Hannover, this area would now become part of the British sector, so the 8th Armoured Brigade was to take over from the US 84th Infantry Division.

A reconnaissance party was sent to Hannover on 17 May, followed by advance parties from each of the regiment's squadrons on the 18th. The 19th heralded the move of the remainder of the regiment to Hannover, led by Recce Troop, with the Shermans and other vehicles following back across the Weser River, to be loaded onto transporters. On the journey to Hannover they would pass elements of the 15th Panzer Grenadier Division, a unit they had met in battle on several occasions. Some German soldiers waved at the Hussars as they passed and the gesture was reciprocated, since at the end of the day, they were all soldiers.

Upon arrival, the 3&8s had to quickly adjust to their new role of the administration of a large town, which despite the destruction it had suffered, still housed approximately 300,000 people. Hannover was about 75 per cent destroyed, its roads cratered, its bridges demolished, the rail network crippled and its telephone exchange out of action. The US troops had already begun the task of clearing the roads and they were helpful in indicating the most habitable areas of the town, where accommodation might be found for the men.

Major Eric Cox, of 8th Armoured Brigade's Signals Squadron, was not only tasked with restoring the town's telephone network, but also with finding undamaged dwellings in which to house the 200 men of the brigade's headquarters. The Americans had highlighted some up-market properties in the west of the town and Major Cox identified a three-storey block of flats. Having located the burgomaster, the residents were given forty-eight hours to evacuate the premises. He remembered: 'It was obediently done but seeing the many old and young people leaving with their meagre possessions on hand-drawn carts made us feel inhuman.'

One of the first challenges facing the 3&8s was the large number of displaced persons (DPs) roaming the area. These were slave labour, largely from Eastern Europe, who had been forced to serve the Third Reich. Their German guards had abandoned the camps in the Hannover area that had housed these people and they now looked to the Hussars to be fed. Although they naturally wished to return to their homelands, such as Poland, Hungary and Romania, these countries now lay in the Russian-held sector, so the DPs were to return to their camps for the time being, under guard of the 3&8s and the other regiments of the 8th Armoured Brigade. The Regimental Diary recorded one incident in June: '1,000 Poles due to move from Accu Plant Camp on the 9th started breaking out of Camp. HQ Squadron riot squad called out to deal with the situation.'

Another issue presented itself in the fact that many German soldiers and local officials had dressed themselves as civilians and attempted to hide themselves amongst the DPs, to try to evade examination, detention and possibly death. Therefore, the Control Commission was established, staffed by both military officers and British civilians to carefully screen and process all DPs, although inevitably some Germans did manage to escape punishment for their crimes. However, some individuals were rooted out, as the Regimental Diary states:

> Ludwig Gopel was arrested as being a suspected member of the SS Div Leibstandarte. His papers were false and in the name of Sermholz. On interrogation he admitted to being Gopel and a member of the above-mentioned Division.

On 12 June, Lieutenant Colonel the Earl of Feversham returned to the UK to resume his political career and the regiment welcomed back Lieutenant Colonel Vincent Dunkerly, DSO as its commanding officer. The following day, Captain Julius Neave was promoted to major and assumed command of HQ Squadron. Lieutenant H.S.R. Watson was promoted to captain and took over the role of adjutant.

German discipline had enabled their demobilisation to be almost completed before the first Hussar was able to return to England to end his military service. The first man to be released from the regiment began his journey home on 27 June 1945 – a year to the day since Trooper William Henry 'Dutch' Hollands lost his life back in Normandy. Those who were not professional soldiers would now be discharged depending on age

Bill Mawson with one of the regiment's horses in Germany.

The Guard of Honour – Cosy Comfort is in the centre of the photo, in the rear rank below the mantlet of the Sherman Firefly.

and length of service. Each soldier would be paid what might be considered a meagre sum of only a few hundred pounds for junior ranks. They were issued a set of civilian clothes, known as a 'Demob Suit', which was topped off with a felt Trilby hat, an item that very few men chose to wear. In theory, those returning from war were entitled to be re-employed by their former employers, provided of course that their previous companies were still in business.

Recreational activities were soon organised, to keep the Hussars occupied when not on duty, including various sports and even a riding school for those who could already ride or wished to learn. The local Herrenhausen Theatre was reopened and provided opera and concerts.

On 3 August, His Royal Highness the Prince Regent of Iraq visited the regiment, accompanied by the commanding officer of 30 Corps, Lieutenant General B.G. Horrocks, and their own Brigadier Prior-Palmer. In the Herrenhausen district of Hannover, the prince took the salute as the regiment paraded past, with tanks of the various squadrons following a march past of dismounted Hussars. Cosy Comfort was a member of the Guard of Honour, directly opposite the saluting dias.

Information was received that drafts of men were required for the South East Asia Command (SEAC) to continue the war against the Japanese. Therefore, it was with much relief, after the dropping of the Hiroshima and Nagasaki atom bombs, that at midnight on 14 August, it was declared that Japan had surrendered. Following that news, 17 and 18 August were observed as a 'Victory over Japan' holiday, with a thanksgiving service conducted on the 19th.

Major A. Rugge-Price leads B Squadron past the Prince Regent of Iraq.

B Squadron's Major A. Rugge-Price escorting Brigadier G.E. Prior-Palmer to his car.

Upon arrival in Hannover, a strict 'No Fraternisation' rule was imposed, forbidding all friendly relationships with German civilians. The rule did not apply to displaced persons, however, so from early days a number of friendships and romances blossomed between some Hussars and DPs. After restrictions had

The German children of Münterstraße. Jutta Oppermann is third from the right at the back.

been gradually relaxed, the same began to occur with the German population and Hussars and the young Fräuleins were permitted to mix.

Doug Kay befriended a group of German children living in Münsterstraße, in Hannover, and one young girl, Jutta Oppermann, began a lifetime of exchanging letters with him.

A more significant change had been communicated in late September, in that the regiment would leave the 8th Armoured Brigade to become the divisional cavalry regiment of the British 5th Infantry Division. As they had done back in Normandy when they replaced their much-loved Seahorse shoulder patches with the Fox's Mask, now they would take down the 8th Armoured Brigade patch to be replaced with a white letter 'Y' on a black background. Reminiscent of Normandy, Major Julius Neave wrote in his diary: 'All ranks were very sorry when the day came to take down the Fox's Mask from their shoulders.'

The regiment had trained and fought under the command of Brigadier George Erroll Prior-Palmer, DSO for more than three years, and on 12 October, he took the final salute in Hannover as the regiment paraded past.

This change also heralded a change of location for the 3&8s, and on 18 October 1945, the majority of the regiment moved to Vienenburg area in the Goslar district, close to the Harz mountains, following their advance parties, C Squadron moving further south to Bad Harzburg. The first peacetime Balaclava Day for several years was celebrated with the usual sporting fixtures and evening dances. After having to postpone their last Christmas, the regiment

Doug Kay (centre) with two crewmates outside their civilian accommodation in Münsterstraße, Hannover.

The 'Y' shoulder patch of the British 5th Infantry Division.

Major A.G. Ackers-Douglas of A Squadron salutes the brigadier.

was treated to a half-day holiday on 24 December and two full days relaxing on Christmas Day and Boxing Day.

Also in October, the first batch of twenty tank transporters left Hannover, taking away the regiment's wartime vehicles to Hamburg. The 3&8s would be issued with the M24 'Chaffee' Light Tank,[2] plus armoured cars, and would operate for the latter stages of their time in Germany in these vehicles.

Squadron Sergeant Major A.C. Vickery of A Squadron in a scout car.

The M24 Chaffee Light Tank. (*Courtesy of The Tank Museum, Bovington – Image 2829-C6*)

Fast forward to 8 June 1946, when the British Commonwealth and Allied victory over Nazi Germany and Japan were celebrated in London at the Victory Parade. King George VI took the salute in Whitehall, accompanied by Queen Mary, other members of the British royal family and Winston Churchill, among other world political leaders. A detachment was selected to represent the

Doug Kay in the driver's seat of a Chaffee in the snow.

The 13th/18th contingent to the bottom right of the picture, as they march through Whitehall as part of the Royal Armoured Corps column during the Victory Parade. Doug Kay is to the right of the image, his new corporal stripes visible, beyond the sergeant in the foreground.

13th/18th Royal Hussars (QMO), to march within the Royal Armoured Corps column. The 3&8 detachment was under the command of Captain W.G. Denney, MC, and included both Sergeant Bill Hammond and Corporal Doug Kay, following his promotion.

In July 1946, the regiment moved to modern barracks in Wolfenbüttel, south of Brunswick, where it would remain until orders were received to return to Aldershot in October 1947. After a short period of reorganisation, the regiment sailed in February 1948 for North Africa, bound for Benghazi in Libya, as an Armoured Car Regiment. With most of the wartime conscripts and volunteers now demobilised and replaced with fresh faces, a few 'Old Sweats' still remained, including Sergeant Bill Hammond and Sergeant Jerry Bell, MM, who'd been with the regiment since its mounted days on the North-West Frontier in India.

Corporal Doug Kay (right) with two fellow 3&8s on the day of the Victory Parade.

The Last Post

Each 6 June and 11 November, Joe Collins remembered those who did not come home. Having to make the decision to leave Harry Hughes to his fate on D-Day was one of the hardest things he ever had to do; it haunted him for his whole life. Being just a few feet away when Dutch Hollands had been killed by shrapnel, Joe fully appreciated how easily it might have been him who had lost his life that day. With the memory of other friends who did not return home in his mind, Joe would also think back to his own crew, who had all perished in Germany.

In 1994, a large group of 3&8 veterans returned to Normandy for the fiftieth anniversary of D-Day, including Peter Comfort, Joe Collins, Bill Mawson and Doug Kay. Joe Collins kept his promise to return and pay his respects at the grave of Trooper William Henry 'Dutch' Hollands.

> They went with songs to the battle, they were young,
> Straight of limb, true of eye, steady and aglow.
> They were staunch to the end against odds uncounted,
> They fell with their faces to the foe.
>
> They shall grow not old, as we that are left grow old:
> Age shall not weary them, nor the years condemn.
> At the going down of the sun and in the morning
> We will remember them.
>
> From 'For the Fallen', by Robert Laurence Binyon

We'll Meet Again

Of those Hussars fortunate enough to survive the ravages of war, a return to civilian life beckoned. Let's discover what became of some of the men we've met in this story.

Lionel 'Bob' Charmbury

Although originally from the West Country, after receiving his Military Medal from the king, Bob Charmbury settled in Skipton with his wife Muriel, whom he'd met while stationed there in 1942. Owing to the tight security surrounding D-Day, he was required to obtain a permit in May 1944 to leave the Gosport area to return to Skipton to marry Muriel. Gil Masters was also granted leave to return to marry Olive, and both couples were married on the same day in Skipton. Bob and Muriel would go on to raise a family of three children – two boys and one girl.

Bob was not alone in returning to Skipton after the war and became a member of the 13th/18th Old Comrades.

Old Comrades, 13th/18th Royal Hussars (QMO), Skipton. Left to right: Messrs T. Whelan, G. Masters, J. Higham, F. Watson (Chairman), C. Rattle, MM, C. Preston (Secretary and Treasurer), L. Charmbury, MM, P. Ridley, S. Potts, G. Bateman. (*Courtesy of Charge!, the museum of the Light Dragoons*)

Joe Collins

Before heading off to war, Joe married his sweetheart Rose in 1942, and their eldest son, Joe Jnr, was born while Joe was away on basic training. Once released from military service, in 1947 Joe and Rose found a home in Denmark Street, Possilpark; just in time, as it happened, since later that year they welcomed their second child into their family. Their new daughter was named Maureen, after Bill 'Happy' Hammond's own daughter. Joe began work in the tyre business, specialising in vulcanisation, and did well, being able to move his growing family to the new housing district of Ruchazie, Glasgow, in 1953. Joe had joined a company by the name of The Rapid Tyre Service and as a confident, natural salesman rose in seniority and it wasn't long before he was headhunted by Dunlop.

In the early 1960s, Joe's family had grown to include eight children: six boys and two girls. This prompted another house move to a detached property in Garrowhill, on the outskirts of Glasgow. At this time, Joe was persuaded to join a friend, Bill Tracey, in a new venture, WM Tracey Ltd, based in Johnstone. As managing director of their tyre division, Joe remained with the company until his retirement, bringing his son Phil into the business too. Joe and Rose also moved to a new bungalow in Paisley.

Joe loved football, even representing his squadron while in the Army, and was a staunch Celtic man and could be found at Celtic Park for every home match. The family caravan was another distraction, and many trips were taken

Joe and Rose Collins.

around the UK and into Europe. With a son raising his own family in Canada, Joe and Rose would also fly out to Calgary, where Joe was known to don the cowboy gear to attend their famous stampede.

Upon retirement, Joe's daughter Maureen signed him up with the Normandy Veterans Association. Joe jumped in with both feet, attending meetings, raising funds and in particular was involved in the creation of the regiment's monument on Mont Pinçon. While in his eighties, his children clubbed together to pay for a tank-driving experience day and Joe quickly impressed the instructors with his prowess at the controls. They had never had a Normandy veteran show up to drive one of their tanks before, so he became something of a celebrity and demonstrated that after sixty years, he hadn't lost his touch!

Tears were shed when in later life Joe was reunited with his old friend Bill 'Happy' Hammond, who had returned to the UK from New Zealand; they would meet in London or Normandy, whenever an opportunity presented itself. Shortly after attending the funeral of Bill Hammond, Joe passed away in October 2007, leaving behind Rose and their eight children and twenty-one grandchildren to remember his impact.[1]

Doug Kay

Doug was one of the few Hussars selected to represent the regiment in the London Victory Parade in June 1946. Doug married Phyllis upon his return to Darlington from Germany in 1947 and they would be blessed with a son and two daughters. Clearly missing the camaraderie of the war years, Doug was to join the Parachute Regiment, in the Territorial Army. Doug was employed in several driving jobs, before becoming a sales rep for Mander's Paints, and proudly drove around in his turquoise Austin A40 company car.

In the 1990s, on one of his many trips back over to Normandy, Doug was introduced to German veteran Willy Hornach, who had been an infantry soldier defending Sword Beach in 1944. Doug shook his hand with the words, 'Bloody hell, how did I miss you?' They would become good friends during their later years.

Doug was an active member of the Normandy Veterans' Association and his efforts there were rewarded by the presentation of the Légion d'honneur, France's highest award both military and civil, by French President Jacques Chirac. In later life, Doug had switched careers and worked as a surveyor in the south for Crawley Council. He attended many services and military events with his new partner, Sylvia, Doug often acting as a standard-bearer for the Royal British Legion.

It was pointed out to Doug that a Chinese toy company, Dragon, had produced a model of his Sherman Firefly – Number 71 – *Carole*. This prompted him to contact the company and informed them that he was the gunner of that very tank on D-Day. The Dragon company were thrilled to learn this, and promptly rebranded their product with Doug's image and the new name of the 'Douglas Kay Firefly'. There was a model kit of *Carole* to build, plus a display version of the tank.

Dragon then produced an Action Man-sized collectors' figure of Doug, complete with battledress, 27th Armoured Brigade shoulder patch and tank suit to wear over the top. Next, inexplicably, Doug found his image used for a set of commemorative D-Day postage stamps for the island of Grenada, alongside

Doug Kay and his partner Sylvia at the Tower of London.

the stamp of none other than Field Marshall Bernard Montgomery; he never did find out how that came to pass.

Doug kept in regular contact with Peter Comfort via telephone and they would exchange betting tips. Doug would pass away within three weeks of Peter, in April 2019, and standard-bearers of the Royal British Legion attended his funeral. Even Jutta Oppermann from Hanover sent a note of condolence upon Doug's passing, when she was 85-years-young:

> The little girl from 1945 wants to send you the last letter for her friend in England.

Johnny Hardie

Johnny Hardie's war service had taken him to France with the BEF, Dunkirk, DD training and the assault on Sword Beach on D-Day, where he was fortunate to survive his tank being blown onto its side by a mine. He was awarded the Military Medal for his gallant actions that preceded his tank being mined. After D-Day, Johnny would be required to fight on without his two best friends, Corporals Ernie Booker and Bill Wilson; they called themselves the Three Musketeers. Ernie lost his life on D-Day and Bill was wounded in the face while fighting on the beach, and although able to continue for a while, he was evacuated back to England the following day.

Lance Sergeant Johnny Hardie, Corporal Bill Wilson and Corporal Ernie Booker.

After having been wounded himself in August 1944, evacuated out of France, and then rejoining the regiment during the occupation of Germany, Johnny returned to Haslingden, Lancashire, and became a coal merchant in Hardie Brothers (Haslingden) Limited. While out delivering coal, he took a shine to one of his customers, Edith, and they were married in 1955. Together they would raise a family of three boys and two girls.

Later, one of Johnny's brothers took over the coal business. Johnny went into the haulage trade and was self-employed, transporting raw materials between the textile mills still operating in Lancashire and Yorkshire in the 1960s and 70s.

Johnny Hardie with his (pregnant) wife Edith and daughter Carole in 1958.

Johnny had a great interest and knowledge of flowers and plants – probably something he picked up from his father, who was a market gardener. He also enjoyed writing poetry, and a Christmas card from Johnny was likely to contain a verse. Johnny Hardie passed away in December 1989.

Bill Mawson

Following demobilisation, Bill went to work for the Commercial Union insurance company, where he remained until retirement, settling in Edenbridge, Kent. His service with the Hussars gave him a love of horses and it was through horse riding that he was to meet Kate, and they were married in 1949. Two daughters were to follow, to complete their family unit. Besides horses, Bill's other passion was for trains and trams, about which he possessed an encyclopaedic knowledge, and built a model train line in his shed in

Bill Mawson, proudly wearing his regimental blazer badge and tie.

the garden. Bill spent a good deal of time at the Bluebell Railway, his closest preserved steam railway, of which he was an enthusiastic and life-long supporter. Once a Hussar, always a Hussar, and Bill's sitting room was crammed with books about the regiment, tanks and the war, and probably rivalled many museums with the wealth of information it contained. Shortly before his death, the French government awarded Bill the Légion d'honneur. Bill passed away shortly before his ninety-fifth birthday in 2018.

Jerry Bell

Although Jerry Bell opted to remain with the Hussars for a time after the war, travelling with them to Libya, upon his return he informed his wife Enid that he'd tossed his medals into sea on the voyage home. Upon returning to the village of Bugbrooke, Jerry struggled to settle down into civilian life and was found stood at the bus stop one day. Enid challenged him as to what he was doing and Jerry simply replied with, 'I'm sorry, I can't do this any more,' and with that he left his wife and young daughter, Barbara. Enid was to remarry in 1956, changing her married name from Bell to Pell in the process, and Barbara soon had a younger brother and sister. They were to learn that Jerry had joined the Merchant Navy, but only discovered

Sergeant Jerry Bell, MM, after the war with his Military Medal and campaign medal ribbons.

this when someone knocked on the door one day to discuss his pension, following his death, as he'd recorded Enid as his next of kin. Jerry had told Enid that during the European campaign, he had suffered three of the tanks he'd commanded knocked out by enemy fire. There's a good chance that young lads in his charge were killed or wounded in the process, yet Jerry escaped all three tanks. It is impossible to know whether Jerry was suffering the effects of survivor's guilt, or PTSD, as such conditions weren't readily acknowledged at the time. Perhaps he was just a restless soul and felt trapped in a quiet corner of Northamptonshire. Regardless, the fairy-tale wedding to Enid in 1941 was not destined to last and they remained estranged for the rest of their lives.

Bill Hammond

After serving with the Royal Artillery in the Territorial Army, Bill joined the 3&8s at Shorncliffe, in time to go with them to France in the BEF. Having returned through Dunkirk, Bill was married in 1940, before leaving for France once more for D-Day. He lost his tank to the sea on Sword Beach, plus two of his crew, and was quickly provided with a new tank and two new crewmembers (one of whom was Trooper William Henry Hollands). Bill's tank was one of the first to charge to the summit of Mont Pinçon, to capture that feature. He was later Mentioned in Dispatches during the fighting in the Reichswald Forest.

Bill was selected to represent the regiment in the Victory Parade in London in June 1946. After serving with the 3&8s in Libya, he returned to serve once more in Germany with the British Army on the Rhine but transferred to the 3rd (The King's Own) Hussars in 1948. He spent a time back in the UK with the 2nd Royal Tank Regiment, for compassionate reasons, before returning to the 3rd Hussars in Germany. When the amalgamation loomed between the 3rd and 7th Hussars, at the rank of warrant officer 2nd class and a squadron sergeant major, Bill opted for retirement in 1958. He emigrated to New Zealand that year with his wife and two daughters and worked as a taxi driver, a school caretaker, a swimming pool manager and a foreman at a Ford Motors assembly

Chelsea Pensioner Bill Hammond with Peter 'Cosy' Comfort at the Cavalry Parade, Hyde Park.

plant. However, once widowed, Bill applied to the Royal Hospital Chelsea and was accepted to become a Chelsea Pensioner, so returned to the UK in 2004. Bill Hammond passed away in September 2007, just six weeks before the death of his former comrade and friend, Joe Collins.

Peter 'Cosy' Comfort

Following the loss of his mother and elder brother during the war years, plus being wounded himself in Normandy, Peter was released from the Army while the regiment was stationed at Wolfenbüttel. His father, Percy, ran the ironmongery shop in Deal High Street and Peter took over the business and became a well-known character in the town. One of his biggest regrets was agreeing to move premises from the High Street to Queen Street in Deal, where he was to discover that the footfall was much reduced and his profits along with it. Peter married Rosemary and they were blessed with a son and daughter and settled in the nearby village of Ripple. Peter's love of horses from being a cavalryman remained with him and he was a keen member of two local hunts – the West Street Hunt and East Kent Hunt. Cornwall was a popular family holiday destination and Peter loved to make the trip in his gold Ford Zephyr, with all manner of purchased items strapped to the roof on the return journey.[2]

On a whim, after attending a steam rally, Peter decided to purchase a traction engine, although he admittedly knew nothing about them. Fortunately, he had the land and outbuildings to accommodate such a large vehicle and he soon got to grips with his 1909 Marshall Engine, *Boadicea*, and proudly showed her off at local steam rallies.

Although not a fan of the city, Peter always made a point of attending the Cavalry Parade in Hyde Park and would attend other regimental gatherings and parades, such as the Guidon Parade in Tidworth in 1987, attended by the regiment's colonel-in-chief, Diana, Princess of Wales.[3] He also returned to Wolfenbüttel in

Cosy Comfort with his 1909 Marshall Steam Engine, *Boadicea*.

1992 for the Regimental Association reunion weekend and drumhead service in the year that the regiment would be amalgamated into The Light Dragoons.

In 2014, Peter attended several services in Normandy on the seventieth anniversary of D-Day, along with the British royal family and several political heads of state. In the evening of 6 June, he felt compelled to attend the British 3rd Infantry Division Service behind the beach at La Brèche d'Hermanville, where he'd landed on D-Day with B Squadron. Before the service began, he sat on a bench, just taking in his surroundings

and remembering. At the age of 90, it would be the last time that he would ever visit Normandy. In his nineties, Peter was awarded the Order of the Légion d'honneur by the French government. Peter passed away in April 2019 and was laid to rest just a few yards from the final resting place of Field Marshal John Denton Pinkstone French, 1st Earl of Ypres, a senior commander in the First World War and a prominent person in Kent. Peter's funeral at the church of Saint Mary the Virgin in Ripple was attended by representatives from Home Headquarters of The Light Dragoons from Newcastle upon Tyne.

Fury

Who is he then? I've never heard of him.

My wife Fiona called me into our living room. 'It's Peter for you,' she said, handing me the telephone. Even though they spoke on the phone from time to time, even Fiona wasn't allowed to call him Cosy! He was very particular about that.

'Hi, Cosy!'

'Guess what I've been up to today?' he blurted out.

'I don't know, Cosy – what have you been up to then?'

'I've been working with a film crew, who are making a film about Sherman tanks. HQ in Newcastle contacted me and asked whether I'd be interested in helping them. I said I'd sleep on it, but the next day I agreed, so today they sent a car to collect me and I was driven to an airfield, where they had a couple of tanks parked up. The actors hadn't arrived, but the film crew wanted to know what happened on D-Day and what followed, so I had a captive audience for about an hour. Then the actors turned up. Have you ever heard of an actor called Brad Pitt?'

'Yes, of course, Cosy.'

'Who is he, then? I've never heard of him. My son Stephen says he's God!'

'Yes, he's probably the most famous male actor on the planet. He's probably like Errol Flynn in your day.'

'Oh!' said Cosy. 'Well, when I was introduced to him, I shook his hand and said, "I'm very pleased to meet you Mr Pitt – I'm afraid I haven't seen any of your movies – the last movie I went to see was *Bridge on the River Kwai* in 1957!" Everyone fell about laughing!'

'I'm not surprised. I can't imagine that he meets many people who don't know who he is.'

'Anyway, he was a very nice chap and was very professional and wanted to know all the details. At one point, we were stood beside one of the Shermans and he asked me to show him the workings of the tank's turret. I said, "You must be bloody joking! I'm 90 – I can't get up there now!" But Brad led me around the other side of the tank and they'd had a chippy build a staircase, so

I could walk up and explain the turret to Brad. I'd taken along a mug with the 13th/18th cap badge on it, which I gave to Brad as a gift. When I left, he was sat there in a director's chair, having a cup of tea from his 3&8 mug!'

I concluded the conversation by saying, 'Well, famous though Brad Pitt is, just remember that he'll only be pretending to do what you had to do for real, so keep that in perspective.'

A couple of weeks later, I received a note from Cosy in the post, along with a couple of photos he'd had taken on his camera of him with Brad Pitt.

Before long, the photos of Cosy and Brad had gone viral. Cosy told me that an unscrupulous chemist shop in Deal had recognised who was in the photos when processing his film, had made a duplicate set of prints without his consent and chose to share them with the press. Friends and colleagues were calling me at work, to ask me if that was my friend with Brad Pitt. When I got home from work that evening, I called Cosy's number. His wife Rosemary answered and passed the phone to Cosy. I began with, 'Hello, is that the international megastar Peter Comfort I'm speaking to?'

His initial response cannot be repeated here, but he then told me, 'This bloody phone hasn't stopped ringing all day. I've got the BBC coming round tomorrow – they want to interview me in the garden!'

I said, 'Hardly surprising – you're all over the internet. I've had colleagues calling me from the US to ask if the photos were of my friend.' Initially, Cosy didn't seem particularly happy about all the fuss, but over time I believe that he came to quite enjoy the attention.

Fast forward one year and I was delighted to learn from Cosy that he'd been invited to attend the movie premiere of *Fury*, the 'film about Sherman tanks', as Brad Pitt's personal guest on the red carpet. At this point, I will hand over to Cosy's granddaughter, Annabel.

A Night to Remember

Peter 'Cosy' Comfort attends the premiere of Fury *in Leicester Square, written by his granddaughter Annabel Steadman (née Church), who accompanied him*

When the invitation arrived for Peter (or Popa, as I have always called him) to attend the premiere of *Fury* alongside Brad Pitt everyone in the family was a little unsure about it. In the previous year or so Brad Pitt mania had rushed through the Comfort household like a storm, leaving Nanny (Rosemary Comfort) rather fed up with the whole thing. I remember very clearly going down to Ripple to visit them and managing to speak to Popa on his own while Nanny was glued to the Formula 1 racing in the kitchen. Popa and I started to talk about the premiere. He was keener to go than I'd realised from family phone calls. He had a genuine respect and fondness for Brad Pitt that I hadn't fully comprehended.

'It would be rude not to go, if he's asked me,' he said, starting to come around to the idea.

'You can stay with me in London,' I remember offering. 'It's not far from mine.' I lived in Islington at the time.

'All right, Annie. I'll go – on one condition.'

'What's that?'

'You be my escort. I want my young granddaughter on my arm. And I want to wear my medals.'

On Sunday, 19 October 2014, Popa arrived in a taxi to my flat in Islington around the middle of the afternoon. I'd never seen him in a big city in all my twenty-two years – or in a tux! My boyfriend, Joseph (now husband), helped him with his bow tie. 'Never could get the hang of these!' We had a roof terrace at the time and we went out to take photos.

The taxi arrived, organised by the film company. Popa hung his disposable camera around his neck, and collected the 13th/18th Hussars pen in a presentation box that he wanted to give to Brad as a gift. I'd tried to talk him out of it, saying it might be better to send it or give it to him later on. But he was insistent. As we drove towards central London, streetlights starting to come on as it became dark, I remember Popa staring out the window in disbelief, shaking his head.

'All these people,' he said. 'It's not for me. Not for me at all.' He seemed completely bewildered that anyone would choose to live in the city. I knew he was nervous as the car rounded the corner to Leicester Square, the crowd coming into view. He took my hand.

The car pulled up at the end of the red carpet, the crowds behind railings on either side. The noise was incredible. It hit you like a wave. I was worried at that point that Popa wasn't going to get out of the car; even I was nervous and I'd half-known what it might be like, having watched film premieres on YouTube. But of course he got out. Thanked the driver like they were old friends – remembered his name, picked up his stick and emerged into the din of Leicester Square, clutching the pen he'd brought to give Brad, touching his medals nervously.

We linked our arms. He couldn't believe it. The people, the noise. And then we realised why it was quite so loud. Brad Pitt was ahead of us on the red carpet. People screaming, trying to reach for him, cheering, shouting.

'Oh there's my friend,' Popa said, as though we were meeting him in a café rather than on a red carpet for a film premiere.

I was subtly moved out of the way of the camera shots (quite right!) as Brad came to greet Popa. He gave him an enormous smile, a huge hug. Popa was absolutely chuffed by it all.

'This is my job, Cosy,' I think Brad said.

'Is it like this for you all the time, then?'

Brad said something like. 'Sometimes, yeah.'

'You poor bugger,' Popa said, laughing and shaking his head. 'You couldn't pay me enough to put up with all this.'

Popa then held out the gift he'd brought for Brad. I was worried Brad's security team wouldn't allow it, but Brad took it and was absolutely touched. The film teams moved the two of them onwards, the pair talking like old friends.

The wall of press was next. I've honestly never seen so many cameras together in my life. The flashes, the shouting – 'Peter!' 'Cosy!' 'Look over here!' He took it all in his stride.

Then Brad was ushered into the cinema building, and then so were Popa and I. It was all a lot calmer inside. A relief after the shouting of the photographers. Peter was shaking a little but he was grinning.

'I gave him the pen – I think he liked it,' he told me. 'It's my regiment's pen. He'll like that.'

The film started. I was a little worried that it might be triggering for Popa. Would he be faced with images he'd tried to forget? Of men dying in tanks? Of war?

At one point in the film, two tanks circle each other in a one-on-one fight. Some odd noises were coming from Popa, I thought he might be crying. I turned to look at him. And—

He was laughing. 'It's a good film,' he whispered. 'But this bit isn't realistic at all! Look what the tanks are doing!'

After the film, we were invited to the after party, which I think was at the Bloomsbury Hotel off Great Russell Street. I'd been very non-committal about whether or not we should go, thinking Popa would be exhausted after all the red carpeting and the long film. Oh no. My grandfather loved a party, and as soon as we arrived in a swish lounge, he settled himself on a fancy armchair and took it all in. I swear he was the most popular guest there, holding court as all kinds of different actors and film industry people came to say hello. Eventually, when we'd had enough to drink and had our fill of fun, a car came to pick us up to take us home.

What a night to remember. I was so pleased Popa decided to take up the invitation and feel so lucky he wanted to take me with him. I'll never forget it as long as I live.

* * *

New Year's Day, 2015. I picked up the phone and called Cosy, to wish him a happy New Year. When he answered, he said to me, 'You're the second call I've had today, Andy. The last one said, "Putting you through now Sir" and it was Brad Pitt, to wish me a happy New Year! Also, I saw one of his movies earlier – *Troy*. Blimey, how many thousands of people were in that?' Then after a short pause he said, 'I wonder how many of them got a call today from Brad Pitt?'

Notes

Chapter 1
1. On 26 November 1940, it was converted into the 27th Armoured Brigade.
2. Operation Dynamo.

Chapter 2
1. Peter Comfort's younger brother, Dennis, would sadly die of acute appendicitis at a young age, leaving Peter as the only survivor of three brothers.

Chapter 5
1. Today, both officers and other ranks receive the Military Cross.

Chapter 6
1. DD Tank details for the respective landing beaches were as follows:
   Utah – Us 70th Tank Battalion – 30 tanks launched at 3,000 yards; 1 foundered.
   Omaha – US 743rd Tank Battalion and US 741st Tank Battalion.
   743 – not launched – all beached direct from LCTs.
   741 – 29 tanks launched at 6,000 yards; 27 foundered, 2 swam in, 3 beached from LCT.
   Gold – Nottinghamshire Yeomanry and 4th/7th Dragoon Guards – not launched – all beached from LCTs.
   Juno – 6th Canadian Armoured Regiment and 10th Canadian Armoured Regiment.
   6th Canadian – A Sqn launched 10 tanks at 1,500–2,000 yards – 7 touched down on beach, 6 landed by LCTs.
   B Sqn – launched 19 tanks at 4,000 yards, of which 14 reached shore.
   10th Canadian – not launched – all beached from LCTs.
   Sword – 13th/18th – 40 tanks embarked; 6 failed to launch, 34 launched at 5,000 yards, 3 sank during swim, 31 reached shore.
2. Ordinary Seaman Peter Hutchins moved to New Zealand after the war. In 1994, for the fiftieth anniversary of D-Day, he travelled to England, met Bill Mawson and was able to thank him personally at his Edenbridge home. The story of their reunion was published in the *Daily Mirror*.
3. The 15th/19th The King's Royal Hussars amalgamated with the 13th/18th Royal Hussars (QMO) in 1992 to form The Light Dragoons.
4. Quote taken from *Fighting Iron: The 1st Battalion South Lancashire Regiment from D-Day to VE-Day* by Dominic Butler.
5. Although I have not located an account to confirm this, it seems likely that the tanks lost from B Squadron would have been commanded by Lance Sergeant Joseph Gillibrand and Corporal Ernest Booker, both killed on 6 June.
6. The Crab flail tanks did arrive, but not until after the gap through the minefield had already been created by Lieutenant Heal RE.

Chapter 7

1. There is a typing error in the Regimental Diary, which records '7th and 11th Airborne Bns', but there was no 11th Battalion within the 6th Airborne Division at that time. However, the 5th Parachute Brigade contained both the 7th and 13th Parachute battalions. The error was reproduced in Major General Miller's history of the regiment; presumably, the Regimental Diary was the source. Thank you to photographer Robin Savage for helping to confirm the correct details.
2. The grandson of Trooper John Cunliffe's brother Len, also named John Cunliffe, later joined the 13th/18th in 1976 and served with the regiment in Northern Ireland.
3. The German forces were derisively known as the 'Boche' by British troops – a throwback to the First World War. This contemptuous slang word is an abbreviated form of the French portmanteau '*alboche*', derived from the French words '*Allemand*' (German) and '*caboche*' ('blockhead' or 'cabbage').
4. The family home in Kensington was destroyed during the blitz, prompting the relocation to Fulham.
5. It is estimated that the civilian deaths in Caen totalled 800 after the first forty-eight hours following the invasion. The bombing of Caen by the RAF in preparation for Operation Charnwood would kill a further 350, with two direct hits on civilian shelters, bringing the total to an estimated 1,150.
6. Captain Lyon-Clark would be replaced as Technical Adjutant by newly promoted Captain John McMichael.
7. Thirty-three-year-old Sergeant Robert O'Brien from Kinsale, County Cork, who left behind a wife, Mary.
8. Panzerfaust – literally, 'Tank Fist'.
9. Quote from Richard Harris of the 1st Battalion, The Suffolk Regiment – from Mark Forsdike's book *Fighting Through to Hitler's Germany*.
10. Johnny Hardie rejoined the regiment in Germany on 29 June 1945.

Chapter 8

1. Estimates quoted on Wikipedia.
2. The Bailey bridge, named after its inventor, Donald Bailey, was a prefabricated truss bridge. Its components were light enough to be assembled without cranes or specialist machinery yet were strong enough to carry tanks. The simple design enabled the bridge to be erected quickly.
3. Troopers William Cockerham, Harry Evans and Gerard Wilton.
4. The Regimental Diary records that it was a 17-pounder round that killed Lieutenant Jennison.
5. The Commonwealth War Graves Commission records the death of Trooper Joseph William Robinson as 9 September 1944. However, the 13th/18th Royal Hussars Journal from autumn 1945 records his death as 10 September, in their Roll of Honour.
6. 'The Lilywhites' is a nickname of the regiment that refers to the white plume that is worn on their full dress ceremonial uniform.
7. Major Cotter's C Squadron Diary records that the regiment was beaten in the football final by the Essex Yeomanry. In this situation, the Regimental Diary trumps the C Squadron Diary.
8. Balaclava Day was an annual holiday in the regiment's calendar, to mark the crucial battle during the Crimean War, which included the Charge of the Light Brigade (25 October 1854), in which the 13th Hussars participated on the right of the line.

Chapter 9

1. The Battle of the Bulge, which spanned the period 16 December 1944 to 25 January 1945.
2. It would appear likely that the colonel decided to leave his tank at Susteren and walk on, since the Regimental Diary records the following for the early hours of 20 January, Geleen being twice the distance from Koningsbosch than Susteren: 'The Regt less 'A' & C Sqns returned for the night to Geleen, arriving at 0300 hrs. Very cold, snow, sleet, hail, rain.'
3. Entertainments National Service Association – an organisation set up to provide entertainment for British Armed Forces personnel during the Second World War.
4. Trooper Horsman's grandson, Doug Horsman, would later serve in the regiment during the 1980s and was named after his grandfather (James Douglas Scott Horsman).
5. Welch being an archaic form of 'Welsh'.
6. Trooper Jack Maxwell lost his life on 28 March 1945.

Chapter 10

1. The SA being the Sturmabteilung, which was a paramilitary organisation associated with the Nazi Party. The SA was integral to the rise of Adolf Hitler and the Nazi Party, violently enforcing party norms and attempting to influence elections.

Chapter 11

1. Information from *A Brief History of the 13th/18th Royal Hussars (Queen Mary's Own) – The Lilywhites*.
2. The M24 Light Tank obtained its nickname from US General Adna R. Chaffee Jr., who helped develop the use of tanks within the US military.

We'll Meet Again

1. In February 2010, three of Joe Collins's sons, Tony, Phil and James, travelled down from Scotland to The Tank Museum at Bovington. There they met the author, his wife Fiona and sons Adam and Glenn by the last surviving DD Sherman tank in the world. Sixty-five years after Henry Hollands's death on that fateful day of 27 June 1944, his niece got the opportunity to meet Joe Collins's sons; stories and photographs were then exchanged over a cup of tea in the museum's café.
2. One trip home from Cornwall saw Peter transporting a grandfather clock in a large wooden crate, plus a live goose in a crate on the roof of his car. Having stopped for refreshments in West Sussex, the honking goose soon drew a crowd, and a police officer came to investigate the commotion. He asked Peter what was in the large crate, and he told the policeman that his mother-in-law had unexpectedly passed away on holiday and that he was transporting her body back to Kent. He was quickly sent on his way!
3. The Guidon is the regimental flag, encompassing its history and traditions. Originally used as a rallying point in battle, the Guidon carries the regiment's battle honours, stretching back through all the campaigns in which it has served.

Acknowledgements

Although it may be my name on the cover, in truth the production of this book has been a collaborative effort of a large number of people. I hope that I have not missed anybody out, but if I have, please forgive me and know that I am eternally thankful for all the support and advice that I have received.

Firstly, my gratitude goes to my wonderful bride, Fiona, and sons Adam and Glenn, who have patiently followed me around Normandy, plus many military events, museums, and cemeteries.

It was important to me that the project had the blessing of Home Headquarters of the Light Dragoons and I would like to thank the following for their support over the years: Captain (Retd) Gary Locker, Captain (Retd) Christopher 'Dicky' Bird, Major (Retd) Mel Tazey, MBE, Captain (Retd) Mick Reed, MBE, and Roberta 'Bobbi' Goldwater at Charge!, the museum of the Light Dragoons.

I cannot thank Bruce Crompton enough for his unwavering support and willingness to write the foreword for this book. Bruce, you have demonstrated hospitality and generosity that far exceeded my expectations, and our nation's military museums are fortunate indeed to have you championing their cause. Not forgetting Sue and Lois, also – thank you.

The Tank Museum at Bovington has been an important partner, providing copies of regimental diaries, personal memoirs, voice recordings and photographs. I should like to express my thanks to Valerie Bedford, Marjolijn Verbrugge, Stuart Wheeler and Sheldon Rogers.

The Imperial War Museums have been most helpful in providing photographs for the book. My thanks go to Sophie Fisher in the IWM media team. The Commonwealth War Graves Commission has been an important resource too, providing accurate details of those lost in battle.

How can I ever forget my dear, departed 3&8 D-Day veteran friends – Peter 'Cosy' Comfort, Bill Mawson and Doug Kay? You all welcomed this intrusive character into your lives, and I feel truly blessed that I was granted the privilege to get to know you all. Thank you for your friendship and for sharing your stories and photographs with me, with the odd pub lunch thrown in for good measure!

To my good friend, Major General Robin Anderton-Brown. Thank you for your candid feedback and advice, which certainly helped produce a better book than would have otherwise been the case. I have hugely benefitted from your insightful battlefield tours, in the company of Howard and Richie Atkin, and cycling up Mont Pinçon and Mont-Ormel certainly gives one a great appreciation of the terrain over which the battles were fought.

I am indebted to Major John Flexman for going to the trouble of reading the first draft of the manuscript and providing many helpful comments and suggestions.

To the many 3&8 family friends I have made, plus former veterans of the regiment, I thank you all for contributing information and photographs of your family members. Barbara Bell, Carole Pringle, Penny and Angus McKay, Rosemary and Stephen Comfort, Tony Collins, Con Collins, Jan Curtis, Jayne Donohue, John Pugh, Ian Edisbury, Frank Underhay, Jon Richards, Sylvia Elliott, Karen and JP Theobold, Hugh Craft, Onne Visser, Major Eric Cox and Pat Cox, Doug Horsman, Gary Watson, John Cunliffe, John Wooldridge Snr, Russell Kirk and Andrew Groves.

I reserve a special mention for my good friend, John Charmbury, and his dear wife, Pat. Our trips to Normandy together have been very rewarding and great fun, and I can think of no one better with whom to share a meal of steak and frites with a cold beer!

Thank you to Annabel Steadman for agreeing to write a piece for the book, despite being under a demanding deadline from her own publisher. Thank you to my talented sister, Jeanette Cole, for helping with the artwork for the book, and to Michael Cole for his suggestions.

I received excellent direction from authors Mark Forsdike, Phil Wakeford, Paul Chrystal and Dilip Sarkar about their experiences with compiling a book and getting it published; I am grateful to you all.

Stephanie Robotham – my friend, mentor and boss for many years. I lost count of how many times you told me to write the book. Well, I finally did!

To Kyler Nishimura, who at a young age has already forgotten more about tanks than I will ever know. Your knowledge of tank warfare is truly encyclopaedic, and I appreciate the books that you passed on to me.

Huge thanks to the Pen & Sword team for agreeing to commission the book, and for patiently working through the process of publication with me as a greenhorn. I am grateful to Charles Hewitt and Henry Wilson for placing their faith in me, and to Matt Jones and Jon Wilkinson for preparing the finished book and jacket design. Lastly, I must highlight the enormous contribution of my editor, Linne Matthews, who has methodically chipped away the rough edges of my manuscript to produce something that I hope you have enjoyed reading.

Bibliography

A Brief History of the 13th/18th Royal Hussars 'The Lilywhites' (pamphlet).
Ambrose, Stephen E., *Pegasus Bridge – D-Day: The Daring British Airborne Raid*, Simon & Schuster UK, 2003.
Beevor, Anthony, *D-Day: The Battle for Normandy*, Penguin Books, 2010.
Bowman, Martin W., *Remembering D-Day*, HarperCollins, London, 2004.
Brookes, Jack (John), *A Conscript Goes to War – In A Tank*, Tracprez Publications, Derby, 1999.
Buckingham, William F., *Arnhem: The Complete Story of Operation Market Garden 17–25 September 1944*, Amberley Publishing, Stroud, 2019.
Butler, Dominic, *Fighting Iron: 1st South Lancashire Regiment from D-Day to VE-Day*, Lancashire Infantry Museum, Preston, 2021.
Cotter, Major Sir Delaval, *13th/18th Royal Hussars C Squadron Diary*.
Cox, Eric, *Nine Lives to Berlin with a Tank Brigade, 1939 to 1946*, Fentland Books, Durham, 2001.
Cruickshank, Charles, *Deception in World War II*, Oxford University Press, Oxford, 1981.
Daglish, Ian, *Operation Goodwood*, Pen & Sword Books, Barnsley, 2004.
Elstob, Peter, *Battle of the Reichswald*, Ballantine Books, New York, 1970.
Fletcher, David, *Sherman Firefly*, Osprey Publishing, Oxford, 2008.
Fletcher, David, *Swimming Shermans: Sherman DD amphibious tank of World War II*, Osprey Publishing, Oxford, 2006.
Ford, Ken, *Caen 1944: Montgomery's break-out attempt*, Osprey Publishing, Oxford, 2004.
Ford, Ken, *Dieppe 1942: Prelude to D-Day*, Praeger Publishers, 2004.
Ford, Ken, *Falaise 1944: Death of an army*, Osprey Publishing, Oxford, 2005.
Forsdike, Mark, *Fighting Through to Hitler's Germany: Personal accounts of the men of 1 Suffolk 1944–45*, Pen & Sword Books, Barnsley, 2020.
Gardner, Ian and Day, Roger, *Tonight We Die as Men*, Osprey Publishing, Oxford, 2009.
Guderian, Heinz Günther, *From Normandy to the Ruhr: With the 116th Panzer Division in World War II*, Aegis Consulting Group, 2001.
Hart, Stephen A., *Panther Medium Tank 1942–45*, Osprey Publishing, Oxford, 2003.
Hart, Stephen A., *Sherman Firefly vs Tiger: Normandy 1944*, Osprey Publishing, Oxford, 2007.
Haupt, Werner, *German Anti-Tank Guns: 37mm - 50mm - 75mm - 88mm PAK, 1935–1945: Without Self-Propelled Mountings*, Schiffer Publishing, 1997.
Hennessey, Patrick, *Young Man in a Tank*, privately published, Camberley, 1994.
Hills, Stuart, *By Tank into Normandy*, Weidenfeld & Nicolson, Leatherhead, 2003.
History of the 4th Bn. The Somerset Light Infantry (Prince Albert's) In the Campaign in North-West Europe June, 1944 – May, 1945, Anthony Rowe Ltd., Eastbourne.
Hunt, Eric, *Mont Pinçon*, Pen & Sword Books, Barnsley, 2003.
Jarvis, Robert B., *Chariots of the Lake*, The Heritage Workshop Centre, Lowestoft, 2003.
Kilvert-Jones, Tim, *Sword Beach*, Pen & Sword Books, Barnsley, 2003.
Levine, Joshua, *Operation Fortitude: The Story of the Spies and the Spy Operation that Saved D-Day*, Lyons Press, 2011.

Lindberg, Leo, *Captured Tanks WW2 – Captured & converted French vehicles in German service*, Amazon, 2021.
Memoirs of 3&8 veterans: Gil Masters, Peter Comfort, Joe Collins, George Treloar and Bill Mawson.
Miller, Major General C.H., *History of the 13th/18th Royal Hussars (Queen Mary's Own) – 1922–1947*, Oliver Burridge & Co., London, 1949.
Neave, Julius, *The War Diary of Julius Neave*, privately published, 1994.
Parr, Barry, *"What d'ya do in the war, Dad?"*, Trafford Publishing, Oxford, 2007.
Pöppel, Martin, *Heaven and Hell: The War Diary of a German Paratrooper*, Spellmount Publishers, Staplehurst, 1988.
Porter, David, *German Tanks of World War II*, Amber Books, London, 2021.
Saunders, Tim, *Operation Epsom*, Pen & Sword Books, Barnsley, 2003.
Shilleto, Carl, *Pegasus Bridge/Merville Battery*, Pen & Sword Books, Barnsley, 1999.
Spielberger, Walter J., *Panther & Its Variants*, Schiffer Publishing, Atglen, Pennsylvania, 1993.
The 13th/18th Royal Hussars (QMO) Journal, Vol. 7, No. 1, Hanover, 1945.
The Wiltshire Regiment in the Second World War – 4th Battalion, The RGBW Wardrobe and Museum Trust, Salisbury, 2006.
The Wiltshire Regiment in the Second World War – 5th Battalion, The RGBW Wardrobe and Museum Trust, Salisbury, 2006.
Trigg, Jonathan, *D-Day Through German Eyes: How the Wehrmacht Lost France*, Amberley Publishing, Stroud, 2020.
Various Commanding Officers, *13th/18th Royal Hussars Regimental Diary (1939–1945)*, courtesy of The Tank Museum, Bovington.
von Rosen, Richard Freiherr, *Panzer Ace: The Memoirs of an Iron Cross Panzer Commander from Barbarossa to Normandy*, Greenhill Books (Pen & Sword Books), Barnsley, 2018.
Welchman, Gordon, *The Hut Six Story: Breaking the Enigma Codes*, M.&M. Baldwin, 1997.
Wormald, Major Derek, *13th/18th Royal Hussars A Squadron Diary*.
Zaloga, Steven J., *M3 & M5 Stuart Light Tank 1940–45*, Osprey Publishing, Oxford, 1999.

Index

105mm Howitzer, 37
17-pounder gun, 44, 63, 72, 77, 91, 103, 109, 134, 139, 150, 173, 207
2-pounder gun, 8, 12
37mm PAK, 73
50mm PAK, 73
75mm gun, 55, 72, 115, 134, 136
75mm PAK, 37, 73–4, 113, 120, 167
81mm mortar, 76
88mm Flak, 74, 92, 122
88mm PAK, 57, 60, 83, 91, 102, 106, 108–109, 143, 145, 167, 172, 176

Aan de School, 138
Aarschot, 118
Abwehr, 35
Ahausen, 175
Airspeed Horsa glider, 49, 65, 163–4
Aitchison, Lieutenant S.C. de L., 138–9
Akers-Douglas, Captain A.G., 5, 83–4, 86, 177
Albert Canal, 118–19
Aldershot, 39, 188
Aldham, Lieutenant J.H., MC, 23, 41, 56–7
Alexander, Major General H., DSO, MC, 4–5
Allan, Trooper, 135
Alpen, 155, 158–9
Amayé-sur-Seulles, 97–8
Amiens, 114
Amphibious Tank Escape Apparatus (ATEA), 22
Anderson, Lieutenant T.A.S., 65
Anholt, 166–7, 169
Annan, 29
Antwerp, 126
Ardennes Forest, 132
Argentan, 109, 112–13
Arnhem, 120, 122–5

Arras, 2–3, 114, 117
Atkinson, Trooper J., 65
Atlantic Wall, 14, 37–8, 59
Avranches, 110
AVRE (Assault Vehicle Royal Engineers), 28, 53, 56, 91, 136
Avro Lancaster, 51, 82, 88

B-17 Flying Fortress, 89
B-24 Liberator, 59
B-26 Marauder, 89
Bad Harzburg, 185
Bailey bridge 112–13, 172
Bailleul, 112
Balaclava Day, 26, 127, 185
Ball, Trooper, 24
Bangalore torpedoes, 63
Bannard, Freda, 9
Bannard, Trooper S.W.J., 9, 93–4
Bannerville, 91
Barnard, Trooper T.E., 136
Battle of Britain, 7
Bauchem, 128–30
Bawinkel, 171
Baxendale, Trooper J.W.N., 168
Bayeux, 95
Bayeux Memorial, 57, 70
Bayeux War Cemetery, 93
Becker, Alfred, 36–7, 73–4
Bedburg-Hau, 143, 146, 148
Beek, 140
Beesley, Lance Corporal S., 18, 157
Bell, Enid (née Nightingale), 8–9, 39, 197
Bell, Sergeant J.D., MM, 8, 39, 54, 59, 88, 93, 145–6, 188, 197
Belson, Trooper A.J., 119
Benghazi, 188
Bénouville, 49, 60, 66–7, 88
Berg en Dal, 140

Beringen, 118–19
Berthoud, Major, 116
Beverloo, 119–20
Binns, Corporal R., mm, 151, 157
Birgden, 133
Black Watch, 73
Blake, Sergeant R., 70
Bletchley Park, 5, 35, 96, 110
Blitzkrieg, 3
Blockdiek, 176
Bocage, 87, 96
Bone, Trooper H., 119
Booker, Corporal E., 65, 195, 206
Borculo, 169
Bouquemaison, 115, 117
Bourg-Léopold, 120, 140
Bourguébus Ridge, 87, 89
Bovington, 7, 12
Bradley, Lieutenant General O.N., 34, 110
Bradley, Sergeant F., 138
Bray-Dunes, 5
Bray-et-Lû, 114
Bremen, 74, 162, 174–8
Bremerhaven, 177–8
Brest, 2
Bréville, 69, 71–3
Bristow, Lance Sergeant J., 169–70
British Army Units:
  Airborne/Commandos:
    Divisions:
      1st Airborne Division, 120, 124
      6th Airborne Division, 49, 50, 69, 72
    Brigades:
      1st Special Service Brigade, 60
      3 Parachute Brigade, 69, 71
      6th Airlanding Brigade, 65
    Regiments:
      Oxfordshire and Buckinghamshire Light Infantry, 49
    Battalions/Commandos:
      No. 4 Commando, 14, 60
      7th (Light Infantry) Parachute Battalion, 69
      12th (Yorkshire) Parachute Battalion, 72–3
      13th (Lancashire) Parachute Battalion, 69
  Armour:
    Divisions:
      7th Armoured Division, 87
      9th Armoured Division, 7, 10–11, 16
      11th Armoured Division, 87, 89, 92, 112, 114
      79th Armoured Division, 16, 18, 26
      Guards Armoured Division, 87, 92–3, 114, 117, 121–4, 136, 159, 168–70
    Brigades:
      1st Armoured Reconnaissance Brigade, 2
      8th Armoured Brigade, 95, 113–14, 116–17, 120–2, 126, 132–3, 141, 149–50, 162, 168, 180–1, 185
      27th Armoured Brigade, 7, 26, 32, 85–9, 93, 95, 110, 194
    Regiments:
      144th Regiment Royal Armoured Corps, 94
      148th Regiment Royal Armoured Corps, 81
      15th/19th The King's Royal Hussars, 58
      24th Lancers, 95
      25th Dragoons, 177
      2nd Royal Tank Regiment, 144, 198
      3rd (The King's Own) Hussars, 198
      34th Armoured Brigade, 159
      42nd Royal Tank Regiment, 144
      4th/7th Dragoon Guards, 16, 24, 26, 32, 95, 105–106, 108, 114, 119, 147, 165–6
      7th Queen's Own Hussars, 198
      East Riding Yeomanry, 24, 26, 95
      Fife and Forfar Yeomanry, 92
      Grenadier Guards, 133
      Irish Guards, 121–2
      Sherwood Rangers Yeomanry/ Nottinghamshire Yeomanry, 133, 140
      Staffordshire Yeomanry, 32, 75, 95, 162–3
      The 43rd (Wessex) Reconnaissance Regiment, 142–3, 175
  Infantry:
    Divisions:
      1st Infantry Division, 4, 5

Index   215

3rd Infantry Division, 26, 29, 40, 48–9, 75, 86–7, 162, 175, 200
5th Infantry Division, 185
15th (Scottish) Infantry Division, 141
43rd (Wessex) Infantry Division, 101, 123, 128, 130, 141, 143, 161, 168, 174, 176
51st (Highland) Infantry Division, 74, 76, 87, 162–3, 165, 174
52nd (Lowland) Infantry Division, 159, 175, 178
53rd (Welsh) Infantry Division, 141
59th (Staffordshire) Infantry Division, 81

Brigades:
8th Infantry Brigade, 49, 88
56th Infantry Brigade, 97
69th Infantry Brigade, 97, 106
129th Infantry Brigade, 98, 100–101, 120, 128, 143, 165, 178
130th Infantry Brigade, 101, 124, 129, 143, 164, 166, 171, 175
151st Infantry Brigade, 106, 108
152nd Infantry Brigade, 76, 174
153rd Infantry Brigade, 74–6, 162
154th Infantry Brigade, 162
156th (Scottish Rifles) Brigade, 132, 159
157th (Highland Light Infantry) Brigade, 132, 175
160th (Welsh) Brigade, 149, 155
176th Infantry Brigade, 82
214th Infantry Brigade, 105, 147, 166, 169–71, 177–8
231st Infantry Brigade, 108

Regiments:
Glasgow Highlanders, 138–9
King's Own Scottish Borderers, 133, 138–9
King's Royal Rifle Corps, 122, 150, 170
The Royal Scots, 135–6

Battalions:
1st Battalion Gordon Highlanders, 75–6
1st Battalion South Lancashire Regiment, 49, 56, 59–60, 88–90
1st Battalion Suffolk Regiment, 49, 62–5, 88, 91

1st Battalion Worcestershire Regiment, 105, 169, 171–4
2nd Battalion East Yorkshire Regiment, 49, 60–1, 88, 154
2nd Battalion Monmouthshire Regiment, 150, 152–3, 155–6
4th Battalion Dorset Regiment, 123–4, 143–4, 166–7, 175
4th Battalion Somerset Light Infantry, 99–105, 128
4th Battalion Welch Regiment, 150, 153, 155, 158
4th Battalion Wiltshire Regiment, 99–105, 128, 165
4th/5th Battalion Royal Scots Fusiliers, 159
5th Battalion Cameron Highlanders, 76
5th Battalion Dorset Regiment, 129–30, 143, 146, 166, 174
5th Battalion Duke of Cornwall's Light Infantry, 105, 131, 171, 175
5th Battalion East Yorkshire Regiment, 97–8, 107–108
5th Battalion Wiltshire Regiment, 99–102, 104–105, 128, 131, 165–6
6th Battalion Cameronians, 159
6th Battalion Durham Light Infantry, 106, 109
6th Battalion North Staffordshire Regiment, 83–5
6th Battalion Royal Welsh Fusiliers, 150, 154, 158
7th Battalion Cameronians, 159
7th Battalion Green Howards, 97–8, 108
7th Battalion Hampshire Regiment, 101, 103, 146–7, 166–7
7th Battalion Royal Norfolk Regiment, 83–4
7th Battalion Somerset Light Infantry, 105, 170–1, 173
7th Battalion South Staffordshire Regiment, 83
7th/9th Royal Scottish Fusiliers, 137
8th Battalion Durham Light Infantry, 106, 113
9th Battalion Durham Light Infantry, 106, 108–109

12th Battalion King's Royal Rifle
    Corps, 122–3, 150, 170
Other:
  Regiments:
    5th Field Regiment Royal Artillery,
      83, 85
    15th Field Regiment Royal
      Artillery, 83
    17th Field Regiment Royal
      Artillery, 4
    147th Field Regiment Royal
      Artillery, 127
    54th Training Regiment (RAC), 10
    58th Training Regiment (RAC), 7
    76th (Highland) Field Regiment,
      Royal Artillery, 60–1
    Glider Pilot Regiment, 49
    Royal Army Service Corps, 10, 15
    Royal Electrical & Mechanical
      Engineers (REME), 126
    Royal Engineers, 5, 16, 28, 50, 56, 63,
      101, 103, 112–13, 164, 167, 171–2
    Special Air Service Regiment
      (SAS), 50
  Companies/Squadrons:
    246 Field Company, Royal
      Engineers, 63
    265 Forward Delivery Squadron, 66
    8th Armoured Brigade Signals
      Squadron, 116–17, 181
  Other formations:
    21st Army Group, 36
    Second Army, 95, 111, 120–1, 178
    12 Corps, 109
    30 Corps, 109, 120, 132, 134, 183
    43rd (Wessex) Reconnaissance
      Regiment, 142–3, 175
    Royal Armoured Corps (RAC), xi, 7, 8,
      10–12, 15–16, 23, 81, 94, 188
    Royal Tank Corps, 2
    Royal Corps of Signals, 42
    British Expeditionary Force (BEF), 1–3,
      5, 7–8, 42, 54, 58, 195, 198
Broadhurst, Trooper F.D., 160
Brookes, Trooper J., 120
Brown, Trooper F.J., 108
Browning machine gun, 72, 78, 89,
    133, 145

Brunssum, 128
Brussels, 3–4, 117–18, 120–1, 126–7, 132
Bückelte, 171
Buckingham Palace, 160–1
Bugbrooke, 7–8, 93, 197
Bull shoulder patch (79th Armoured
    Division), 16
Burbury, Lieutenant Colonel R.P.H., 56
Burgess, Lieutenant R.B., 65
Burghead Bay, 30
Burgoyne, Trooper R.W.C., 108

Cadogan, Trooper R., 55, 66
Caen, 81–3, 85–7, 93, 96, 155
Caen Canal, 49–50
Café Gondrée (Bénouville), 49
Cagny, 92–3
Cahagnes, 97
Calais, 14, 167–8
Canadian Army Units:
  Infantry:
    Divisions:
      2nd Canadian Division, 141
      3rd Canadian Division, 141
    Brigades:
      5th Canadian Infantry Brigade, 141–2
      7th Canadian Infantry Brigade, 141
      9th Canadian Infantry Brigade, 141,
        143, 149
    Regiments:
      Glengarry Highlanders, 141
      Highland Light Infantry of
        Canada, 141
      Regina Rifle Regiment, 142
    Other formations:
      1st Army, 111
      II Canadian Corps, 93
Canterbury, 10
Cap d'Antifer, 51
Carmichael, Trooper R., 160
Carr, Sergeant J., 138, 147
Causebrook, Sergeant S., 126
Cazelle (Cazelles), 84–5
Chamberlain, Prime Minister Neville, 2
Chambois, 111, 113
Channel Islands, 14
Chante-Pie, 100–101
Chariots of the Lake (Robert B. Jarvis), 24

Index   217

Charles, Lieutenant R.J., 150, 154, 165
Charmbury, Corporal L.R., MM, 47, 59, 75, 89, 93, 160–1, 190
Charmbury, Muriel, 161, 190
Chartres, 82
Château de la Londe, 83, 85
Château Saint-Côme, 73
Cheal, Trooper R., 4
Cherbourg, 14, 33
Chief of Staff to the Supreme Allied Commander (COSSAC), 33
Chippenham Park/Chippenham Camp, 10, 12
Chipping Campden, 16
Chirac, President Jacques, 193
Chrysler Gasoline 370Hp Engine, 24
Churchill, Prime Minister Winston, 16, 33–4, 179–80, 187
Churchill tank, 14, 28, 56
Clamesnil, 109–10
Class 50/60 raft, 164
Cleve (Kleve), 141–2, 144–5, 148–50
Cloppenburg, 171, 173
Coad, Brigadier B.A., DSO & BAR, 166
Coates, Lieutenant P.B., 104
Cockerham, Trooper W., 207
Cocoran, Trooper J.G., 107
Cod (WN20), 60
Coker, Lieutenant D.H.E., 60, 70
Colleville-sur-Orne/Colleville-Montgomery, 62, 64, 75
Collins, Lance Corporal J., 26, 55, 56, 66, 78, 151, 155, 167–8, 189, 191–2, 208
Collins, Rose, 168, 191–2
Colombelles, 77–8, 88
Combined Operations Headquarters, 33
Comfort, Lance Corporal P.R. (Cosy), 10–12, 15–16, 18, 22, 24–6, 28–9, 51, 54, 71, 74–5, 90, 93, 123, 132, 142, 159–60, 163, 171, 179, 182–3, 189, 195, 198–206, 208
Comfort, Rosemary, 199, 202–203
Commonwealth War Graves, 10, 56, 71, 75, 94, 207, 209
Condé-sur-Noireau, 109
Control Commission, 181
Cooper, Sergeant E., 77, 83
Cordy-Simpson, Major J.R., MC, 16, 57, 70, 119

Corfe, 7
Cornwell, Lieutenant M.S., 94
Cotentin Peninsula, 33, 38, 87, 92, 94, 96, 110
Cotter, Major Sir D.J.A., DSO, 16, 64, 83, 86, 104, 112, 120, 132, 138, 207
Coulombs, 95
Couvre Chef (Couvrechef), 84–5
Covenanter Cruiser Mk V tank, 8, 16, 19, 24
Coward, Lance Sergeant R.H., 5
Cowen, Trooper T., 151
Cox, Major E., 116–17, 181
Crab 'Flail' tank, 27, 49, 63, 84, 91, 128, 136, 206
Creighton, Lieutenant Commander Charles (RNVR), 52
Creully, 72
Crimea, 1, 207
Crocodile tank, 27–8, 84
Cubbitt, Lance Corporal, 119
Cumbes, Trooper W., 158
Cummings, Trooper J.W., 158
Cunliffe, Trooper J., 70, 207
Cuverville, 77, 88
Cuxhaven, 177

Daimler (WN12), 61, 63
Danvou, 100–101, 105
Davies, Corporal, 103
Davies, Major, 5
Davies, Trooper W., 70
Davis Submarine Escape Apparatus (DSEA), 22
D-Day Through German Eyes, 38
de Havilland Mosquito, 83
Delmenhorst, 174
Demob Suit, 183
Démouville, 78, 81, 88, 92
Dempsey, Lieutenant General Sir M.C., GBE, KCB, DSO, MC, DL, 120
Denny, Captain N.N.M., MC, 53, 65, 74, 102–104, 109, 113, 131–2, 143, 146
Denney, Lieutenant W.G., MC, 139, 188
Despatch rider, 4, 43
Diana, Princess of Wales, 199
Diepenheim, 169–70
Dieppe, 13–14, 16, 18, 28, 33, 60, 141

Diest, 118, 120
Displaced persons (DPs), 181, 184
Distinguished Conduct Medal (DCM), 43, 64
Distinguished Service Order (DSO), 72, 132, 170, 176–7, 180, 182, 185
Diver, Sergeant S.G., 62, 137
Dives River/Valley, 111
Dodson, Trooper A.E., 98
Douglas A-20 Havoc (Boston), 89
Douglas C-47 Skytrain (Dakota), 65, 164
Douglas, The Reverend J., 101
Doullens, 114
Douvres-la-Délivrande, x, 75, 80
Downer, Lieutenant J.D., 138, 146–7
Driel, 124–5
Druance stream, 99–100
DUKW, 62, 124
Duncome, Lieutenant Colonel Earl of Feversham C.W.S., DSO, 75, 84–6, 125, 132, 134, 137, 182
Dunkerly, Lieutenant Colonel V.A.B, DSO, 85–6, 102, 104, 106, 108, 114, 120, 125, 182
Dunkirk, 5–8, 43, 48, 54, 58, 63, 160, 195, 198
Duplex Drive (DD) Sherman Tank, 19–21, 30, 39–40, 46, 48, 52–3, 59, 67, 95, 162–3, 208
Duplex Drive (DD) Valentine Tank, 18–19, 27, 29

Eastern Front/Russian Front, 7, 13, 34, 37, 73, 82
Ecclefechan, 29
Echt, 135
Edisbury, Corporal F., 159–60
Eindhoven, 119, 121–3, 125, 132
Eisenhower, General Dwight D., 36, 38, 41, 47, 111, 178
Elliott, Lieutenant H.R.A., 98
Elliott, Sylvia, 193–4
Elst, 123
Emmerich, 141
English Channel, 7, 14, 33, 35–6, 46–7, 51, 82
Enigma, 35
Entertainments National Service Association (ENSA), 140, 208

Épron, 83–6
Erpen, 130
Escoville, 74–7, 88–9, 93
Escurès, 99
Evans, Trooper H., 207
Exercise Bumper, 9
Exercise Cupid, 32
Exercise Fabius IV, 40, 45
Exercise Linney Head, 132
Exercise Thet, 23

Fairbanks, Trooper B. (Fairy), 22
Falaise, 87, 92, 109–12, 144
FFI (Forces françaises de l'Intérieur), 114–15
FH 14/19 100mm howitzer, 62
Field Ambulance station, 90
Fire piquet, 22
First US Army Group (FUSAG), 34–5
Fletcher, Trooper R.W., 160
Floater (code-word), 52
Flobecq, 4
Flood, Lieutenant P.E., 144
Focke-Wulf 190 (FW109), 59, 125
Folkestone, 6–7
Forbes, Trooper T.J.M., 168
Force S (Royal Navy), 29, 47
Fordson 15cwt truck, 12
Forêt de Breteuil, 113
Forêt de Nieppe, 5
Forrest, Trooper V., 145
Fort George, 29–31, 39
Fourges, 113–14
Fox's Mask shoulder patch (8th Armoured Brigade), 95, 126, 185
Franks, Lieutenant A.H., 91, 105, 139
Fraser, Brigadier S.C.J., Lord Lovat, DSO, MC, TD, JP, DL, 14, 60
Frederick the Great, 14
French Army Units:
  Divisions:
    2nd Armoured Division, 111
    French, Field Marshal J.D.P., 1st Earl of Ypres, KP, GCB, OM, GCVO, KCMG, PC, 200
Fritton Lake, 18, 22
Fullbrook, Trooper W.G., 65

Gale, Captain G.C., 75, 85–6
Gale, General Sir R.N., GCB, KBE, DSO, MC, 72
Gangelt, 133
Garbo (Juan Pujol García), 35
Garlick, Lieutenant R.N.T., 73–4, 136, 152
Gascoigne, Trooper F.W., 65
Gasny, 113
Geilenkirchen, 128–9, 131–3
Geldern, 155, 158–9
Geleen, 137, 208
Gelrode, 118
German Army Units:
  Divisions:
  6th Parachute Division, 165
  7th Parachute Division, 143
  8th Parachute Division, 154
  346th Infantry Division, 69
  352nd Infantry Division, 38
  709th Infantry Division, 38
  716th Infantry Division, 38
  719th Infantry Division, 119
  10th SS Panzer Division, 82, 121, 123, 130
  116th Panzer Division, 143, 144
  12th SS Panzer Division Hitlerjugend, 81–2, 85
  15th Panzer Grenadier Division, 178, 180
  1st SS Panzer Division Liebstandarte SS Adolf Hitler, 82
  21st Panzer Division, 36, 49, 65, 67, 75, 77, 81, 165
  2nd Panzer Division, 82
  2nd SS Panzer Division Das Reich, 82
  5th Panzer Division, 143
  9th SS Panzer Division, 82, 121, 123
  Panzer Lehr Division, 81
  Regiments:
  104th Panzer Grenadier Regiment, 165
  125th Panzer Grenadier Regiment, 77
  156th Panzergrenadier Regiment, 144
  723rd Grenadier Regiment, 119
  736th Grenadier Regiment, 38, 54, 63, 65
  858th Grenadier Regiment, 69
  Battalions:
  642nd Ost Battalion, 38

  Other formations:
  7th Army (Wehrmacht), 109
  15th Army (Wehrmacht), 37
  I SS Panzer Corps, 88, 92
  II SS Panzer Corps, 124
  LXXXVI Army Corps, 88
  16th Luftwaffe Field Division, 89
German High Command, 13–15, 34–5, 93
Ghyvelde, 5
Giberville, 88
Gillibrand, Lance Sergeant J., 61, 64, 206
Gillrath 128, 130, 132
Gisors, 114
Glevering Hall, 18
Glinstedt, 178
Goch, 141, 143–4, 148–50, 152–3, 155, 159–61
Gold Beach, 38, 48, 206
Goodwin, Lieutenant Colonel R.E., DSO, 64
Goslar district, 185
Gosport, 26–7, 39, 41, 44, 190
Grave, Holland, 120, 128
Green, Trooper J.T., 65
Guy 15cwt truck, 12
Gyrocompass, 21

Hall, Major P.G.B, DSO, 174
Hambourg, 184
Hammond, Sergeant W., MiD, 54–5, 66, 78, 80–1, 101, 103, 117, 150–1, 168, 188, 191–2, 198–9
Handley Page Halifax, 82, 164
Hannah, Captain D.G., 57
Hannover (Hanover), 180–1, 183–6, 195
Hardie, Edith, 196
Hardie, Lance Sergeant J., MM, 57–8, 91, 106, 195–6, 207
Harding, Lieutenant J.M., 26
Hardy, Lieutenant B.T., MM, 42–4, 69–71
Harold, Lieutenant D., 55
Harrap, Lieutenant Colonel R.T.G., 16, 39–40, 67, 73, 75
Hartley, Arthur C., CBE, 35
Hase River, 171
Haselünne, 171
Hastenrath, 133
Hatt, Trooper W., 160

Hatterath, 130
Hawker, Major J., 5
Hawker Tempest, 162
Hawker Typhoon, 74, 77, 115, 121, 162, 164
Hawkins anti-tank grenades, 138
Haygarth, Sergeant, 166
Heal, Lieutenant Arthur, 63–4, 206
Hechtel, 121
Heinsberg, 135
Hellwege, 175
Hengelo, 170
Hennessey, Lance Corporal P., 12, 46, 51, 82, 96, 98, 102, 107, 115–17, 121, 126, 133–4, 142, 156, 164
Hepper, Sergeant R., MM, 145, 150–1
Hermanville War Cemetery, 56, 71
Hermanville-Sur-Mer, 56, 62, 66, 71, 75
Hérouvillette, 76, 88
Herrenhausen, 183
Hillman (WN17), 63–5
Hind, Corporal G.A., MM, 70
Hind, WO1 A.L. (Duffy), 17, 26, 30, 43, 113, 157
Hiroshima atom bomb, 183
Hitler, Führer Adolf, 2, 7, 14, 34, 36–8, 59, 81–2, 110–11, 141, 173, 178
Hitler Youth/Hitlerjugend, 82, 90
HMS *Rodney*, 83
HMS *Warspite*, 51
Hobart, Major General Sir (Hobo) P.C.S., KBE, CB, DSO, MC, 16–18, 27
Hobart's Funnies, 16, 27
Hockley, Trooper F.G., 65
Hoddam Castle, 28
Holdsworth, Sergeant W., 152
Hollands, Trooper (Dutch) W.H., x–xii, 23–4, 66, 79–81, 182, 189, 198, 208
Holmfirth, 17
Homoet, 125
Hornach, Willy, 193
Horrocks, Lieutenant General Sir B.G., KCB, KBE, DSO, MC, 25, 109, 120, 134, 183
Horsman, Trooper J.D.S., 144, 208
Host, 150, 153, 155
Hotchkiss H-39 tank, 37
Hotchkiss Plant, 37, 73
Howard, Major R.J.H., DSO, 49

Hubbard, Sergeant J., 5
Hughes, Trooper H., 55–6, 65, 189
Humphries, Trooper, 44
Hunter, Lieutenant P.D.V., MC, 78, 97, 107–108, 152
Hunter, Private James (Titch), DCM, 64
Hutchins, Ordinary Seaman P., 57, 206
Hutchinson, Lieutenant Colonel G.F., 61

Indirect Shoot/Pepper Pot Shoot, 129–30, 162–3, 173
Inverness, 29
Isle of Man TT Races, 42
Issel River, 166
Issum, 155, 158–9
Ivergny, 114–15

Jackson, Trooper, 119
Jagdgeschwader 26 (JG26), 59
Jagdpanther, 74, 172
Jennison, Lieutenant H.D., MC, 65, 102, 115, 207
Jodl, General A.J.F., 178
Jones, Lieutenant, 60
Junkers 88, 67
Juno Beach, 38, 47, 206

Kangaroo Armoured Personnel Carrier, 136
Kay, Phyllis, 192
Kay, Trooper J.D.K, 11, 44, 109, 126–7, 135, 143, 185, 187–9, 192–5
Kelvin sphere magnetic compass, 21
Kershaw, Lance Corporal L., 65
Kevelaer, 155
King George VI, 25, 41, 160–1, 179, 187, 190
Kippax, Trooper W., 22, 24
Knight's Cross of the Iron Cross, 92
Knowles, Lieutenant E.J., 145–6
Koningsbosch, 137–8, 140, 208
Krug, Oberst Ludwig, 38, 63, 65

La Bijude, 83–4, 86
La Brèche d'Hermanville, 49, 56–7, 60, 200
La Butte de la Hogue, 77, 89–90
La Délivrande War Cemetery, 10, 75, 80

Index

La Houssoye, 114
La Quesnee (Le Quesnoy), 105
La Roguerie, 102–103
La Senaudière, 95
La Varinière, 99–102, 104–105
La Verderie, 5
La Villette, 108–109
Lamont, Corporal, 165, 167
Landing Craft Personnel – Navigation (LCP(N)), 52
LCA (Landing Craft Assault), 56
LCT (AVRE), 53
LCT Mk III (Landing Craft (Tank)), 18, 26–9, 40, 46, 52–3, 56, 206
Le Mesnil Frémentel, 93
Le Plessis-Grimoult, 100, 104, 106
Le Pré Baron, 88–9
Le Roucamps stream, 100
Le Toque (La Toque), 102
Lee Enfield Rifle, 7
Légion d'honneur, 193, 197, 200
Lens, 117
Leroux family, 117
Lewis, Lance Corporal P.J., 93
Lichtenvoorde, 169
Light Dragoons Charitable Trust, xiii
Lilywhites, 123, 207–208
Lingen, 170
Linney Head, 12, 25
Lion-Sur-Mer, xi, 49, 54, 59–60
Little, Lance Corporal W., 83
Littlehampton, 40
Lockerbie, 29
Lockheed P-38 Lightning, 74
Lommel Ranges, 134
Longueval, 78
Louisendorf, 146
Louvain, 120
Lovell, Trooper C., 65
Lucheux, 114
Luc-Sur-Mer, 81–2
Luftwaffe, 4, 13, 15, 33–4, 59, 67, 89, 92, 122, 125, 132, 148, 150, 160
LVT-2 Buffalo, 143, 162
Lyon, Captain P.E.L., MC, 10, 72, 75, 85, 89, 97–8, 102
Lyon, Major E.L., 98
Lyon-Clark, Captain A.W.P., 17, 92, 207

M24 Chaffee Light Tank, 186–7, 208
Maastricht, 132
Maczek, Major General S., 111
Maquis, 96
Mason, Sergeant C.H., 68
Mason, Trooper J., 168
Mason, Trooper R.F., 137
Masters, Lance Corporal G., 70, 190
Masters, Olive, 190
Materborn, 143, 150
Mawson, Kate, 196
Mawson, Trooper M.E., 7–8, 23, 40–1, 51, 56–7, 66, 118, 182, 189, 196–7, 206
Maxwell, Trooper J.S., 156, 166, 178, 208
McDonald, Trooper, 169
Megchelen, 166
Mentioned in Dispatches (MiD), 198
Merville Gun Battery, 50
Messerschmitt Me 262, 148, 160
Meuse River, 120, 125, 128, 141
Midhope, 17
Military Cross (MC), 72, 115, 119, 131–2, 151, 170, 180, 206
Military Medal (MM), 43, 58, 64, 132, 151, 160–1, 180, 190, 195, 197
Miller, Major General C.H., CB, CBE, DSO, DL, 94, 160, 177, 207
Miller, Sergeant J., 137
Miller, Trooper E., 65
Millin, Private W., 60
Millingen, 164–6
Mills, Trooper L., 55–6
Milne, Major J.F., 101–102
Mitsialis, Trooper N., 160
Moissy, 111
Mol, 140
Mole, Brigadier G.H.L., DSO & BAR, MC, 100
Molenhoek, 128
Monchy-le-Preux, 117
Mont Pinçon, 96, 98–105, 107, 109, 165, 192, 198
Montgomery, Field Marshal, B.L., KG, GCB, DSO, PC, DL, 25, 31, 36, 62, 72, 81–2, 86–8, 132, 195
Mont-Ormel, 111
Mook, 128
Moray Firth, 30, 32, 39

Morgan, Lieutenant General Sir Frederick Edgworth, KCB, 33
Morris (WN16), 62–3
Morris, Sergeant H., MM, 151–2
Morris, Trooper T., 159–60
Mortain, 110
Mortley, Barbara, x, 66
Moulding, Lieutenant E., 138, 175
Moulton-Barrett, Lieutenant Colonel R.A., 9, 16, 39
Mountbatten, Lord Louis Francis Albert Victor Nicholas, 33
Moyse, Trooper K., 70
Mulberry Harbours, 82
Murchison, Sergeant D., 93
Murley, Trooper C., 75

Nagasaki atom bomb, 183
Neave, Captain J.A.S., MBE, 15, 17–18, 25, 30, 54, 65, 84, 86, 88, 93–5, 106, 112–15, 121–2, 128, 130–1, 136, 138, 141, 155, 163–4, 175–9, 182, 185
Neave, Lieutenant R.M.S, MC, 120, 132, 138–9
Nebelwerfer (Moaning Minnie), 68–9, 75, 78–9, 91, 100, 130, 147, 150, 177
Neder Rijn River, 124–5
Neede, 170
Neulethe, 172
Newmarket, 10, 15
Niederbusch, 128
Niers River, 154
Nijmegen, 120, 122–3, 125, 127, 137, 140, 142–3
Ninove, 117
Nissen hut, 22
Nordhorn, 170
Norris, Lieutenant R.E., 77
Norris, Sergeant C., 65
North American P-51 Mustang, 59
Nütterden, 142

O'Brien, Sergeant R.J., 207
Ogy, 4
Old Comrades, 13th/18th Royal Hussars (QMO), Skipton, 190
Omaha Beach, 38, 48, 59, 206
Oosterhoot, 125
Operation Blackcock, 138
Operation Bluecoat, 96, 128
Operation Bodyguard, 34, 50
Operation Charnwood, 81–2, 85, 207
Operation Clipper, 128
Operation Cobra, 87, 93, 110
Operation Fortitude, 34
Operation Glimmer, 51
Operation Goodwood, 86–7, 91–2, 109, 123, 160
Operation Jubilee, 14
Operation Leek, 149
Operation Lüttich, 110
Operation Market Garden, 110, 120, 136
Operation Neptune, 48, 50
Operation Overlord, 33, 38, 47–8, 59, 66, 81
Operation Perch, 81–2
Operation Phukkit, 123
Operation Plunder, 161–2
Operation Pluto (Pipe-lines Under The Ocean), 35
Operation Rutter, 13
Operation Sealion, 7
Operation Shears, 132
Operation Spring, 93, 95
Operation Taxable, 51
Operation Titanic, 50
Operation Turnscrew, 162
Operation Varsity, 163
Operation Veritable, 140–1, 148
Oppermann, Jutta, 184–5, 195
Oresmaux, 114
Orford Battle Area, 23
Orne River, 49, 65–7, 69, 72, 76, 78, 82, 85–8, 94–5, 112, 163
Osborne Bay, 26
Ost battalion, 37–8
Osterholtz, 176–7
Otway, Lieutenant Colonel T.B.H., DSO, 50
Ouistreham, x, 49, 60–1, 66
Owens, Trooper J.K., 64

P-47 Thunderbolt, 159
Paisley, 8, 167–8, 191
Panda Shoulder Patch (9th Armoured Division), 10–11

Panzerfaust, 96, 102, 139, 159, 165, 176, 207
Panzerjäger, 73
Panzerkampfwagen IV, 74–5, 82, 84
Panzerkampfwagen V (Panther), 74, 82, 107, 109, 112, 173
Panzerkampfwagen VI (Tiger), 66, 74, 89, 109, 112, 114, 128, 140
Panzerschreck, 83
Paris, 37, 73, 92, 109, 113
Pas de Calais, 33–5, 37, 51
Patton, Lieutenant General George S., 34, 110
Peace, Captain T.H., 101–102
Pearson, Lieutenant Colonel J.H.C., 101
Pell, Trooper A., 70
Pendlebury, Corporal K., 93–4
Pepinusbrug, 135
Perham Down, 10
Perry, Trooper J., 74
Petard mortar, 28
Petworth Park, 39, 41–2
PIAT anti-tank weapon, 49
Pickard, Trooper R.R., 65
Pink, Corporal F.T., 114
Pitt, Brad (actor), 201–205
Polish Army Units:
  Divisions:
  1st Armoured Division (Poland), 109, 111
  Brigades:
  1st (Polish) Independent Parachute Brigade, 124
Poperinge, 5
Pöppel, Martin, 74, 153
Porpoise (Ammunition Sledge), 45, 62
Potigny, 109
Prince, Corporal, 135
Prince Regent of Iraq, 183
Prior-Palmer, Brigadier G.B., CB, DSO, 22, 26, 75, 114, 134, 149, 161, 183–5
Pruth, 130
Putanges-le-Lac, 112

Queen Mary, 1, 7, 187
Queen Red Beach, 48–9, 51, 57, 60
Queen White Beach, 48–9, 56, 61
Quelkhorn, 177–8

Ramsay, Admiral Sir Bertram Home, KCB, KBE, MVO, 48
Ranville, 67, 69, 72–4, 76, 81
Ranville War Cemetery, 94
Rattle, Sergeant C., MM, 53, 84, 103, 151, 157–8, 190
Rattle Conference, 33
Read, Trooper S., 138
Rees, 162–3, 165
Reichswald Forest, 141–3, 153, 155, 198
Remembering D-Day, 58
Rheinmetall-Borsig AG, 73
Rhine River, 120–1, 141, 155, 159, 161–4
Rhino tank, 87
Richardson, Lieutenant J.H., 148, 152–4, 159, 163, 165, 167, 170, 172, 174–6
Risalpur, 1
Risborough Barracks, 2
Riva-Bella coastal battery (WN08), 66–7
Robinson, Lance Corporal J.G., 65
Robinson, Trooper J.W., 119, 207
Rockingham, Brigadier, J.M., DSO & BAR, 141, 143
Rodwell, Sergeant S., MM, 73
Roer Triangle, 135
Roermond, 135
Rommel, Generalfeldmarschall J.E.E., 16, 36, 38, 59, 95
Roosevelt, President Franklin D., 180
Royal Air Force formations:
  617 'Dambusters' Squadron, 51
  218 Squadron, 51
  RAF Bomber Command, 82
Royal Hospital Chelsea, 199
Rugge-Price, Major A.A.K., 16, 75, 85, 105, 120, 125, 183–4
Ruperts, 50

Saint-Clair-sur-Epte, 114
Saint-Jean-le-Blanc, 99–100
Saint-Lambert-sur-Dives, 111
Saint-Lô, 87
Saint-Pierre-la-Vieille, 106–108
Sainte-Honorine La Chardronette, 76, 81
Sainte-Honorine-la-Chardonne, 112
Sainte-Mère-Église, 49
Sanders, Trooper R., 142
Sannerville, 88, 91

Sayce, Trooper F., 70–1
Scamp, Sergeant F.E., 44, 109, 143
Scargill, Trooper, 119
Schinnen, 133
Schinveld, 135
Schofield, Trooper C., 57, 65
Seahorse shoulder patch/Pregnant Prawn (27th Armoured Brigade), 26, 95, 185
Searle, Trooper C., 160
Seine River, 109, 113
Sentilly, 112
Sevastopol, 1
SFH 414 French howitzer, 61
Shaw, Trooper F., 44
Shorncliffe 2, 198
Short, Lance Sergeant W.J., 83
Shuttleworth, Trooper C., 108
Sialkot, 1
Siegfried Line, 141
Sinderen, 169
Singleton, Corporal S., 65
Sittard, 135
Skipton, 15–18, 161, 190
Smith, Lieutenant E.E., 22
Smith, Lieutenant J.W., MC, 64, 169–70
Smith, Sergeant, 137
Smith, Trooper D.R., 93
Smith, Trooper H., 65
Sole (WN14), 60–1, 63
Somme River, 114
South East Asia Command (SEAC), 183
Southampton, 1–2
Southwick House, 47
Spaven, Trooper E., 91, 93
Special Air Service (SAS), 50
Spencer, Lieutenant D.F., MC, 145, 150–1
St Aubin d'Arquenay, 66–7
Stagg, Group Captain J.M., CB, OBE, FRSE, 47
Staha, 138
Stalin, Marshal Joseph, 180
Stancomb, Captain J.A., MC, 4, 117, 125, 138–9
Standard Beaverette, 6
Steadman, Annabel (née Church), 203
Stirling bomber, 51, 65
Stirling, Lieutenant Colonel D.A., 5, 7, 9
Stokes Bay, 26–7

Straeton, 130
Straussler, Nicholas, 18
Stuart 'Honey' Tank (M5), 69–71, 94, 113, 118, 123
Supermarine Spitfire, 59, 154
Supreme Headquarters Allied Expeditionary Force (SHAEF), 47, 178
Surey, Trooper F.E., 68
Susteren, 135, 137, 208
Sutherland, Trooper W.H., 158
Sweetapple, Corporal, 53, 81
Sweeting, Captain F., 17
Sword Beach, xi, 38, 48–51, 54, 59, 62, 66, 128, 193, 195, 198, 206
Symons, Trooper C., 168

T-34 tank, 73
Tank Suit, 134, 194
Tank, Trooper C., 66
Tapley, Lance Corporal F., 167–8
Tarmstedt, 178
Taylor, Captain (Royal Artillery), 136–7, 140, 152
Telford, Trooper M.M., 65
Tetley, Captain D.R., 142–3, 166
Teveren, 128
TEWT (Tactical Exercise Without Troops), 86
The Island, 124–5
Thetford, 9
Thomas, General Sir G.I., GCB, KBE, DSO, MC & BAR, 101, 161
Thomas, Major R.M.C., 100
Thury-Harcourt, 109
Tidworth, 10, 199
Tommy Cookers, 24
Touffréville, 88–9, 91
Tournai, 3–4, 117
Towcester, 7, 9–10
Trident Conference, 32
Tripsrath, 130
Troan, 89
Trooper Aladdin, 9–10
Trout (WN21), 59–60
Trun, 111
Turing, Alan S., OBE, FRS, 35
Turner, WOII (MQMS) T., 92
Twenthe Canal, 169

U-boats, 35
Uedum, 144
Ulestraten, 132, 135
Ultra intercepts, 5, 35, 96, 110
Underhay, Corporal F., 32
Urquhart, Trooper, 77
US Army Air Force (USAAF), 34, 73, 141
US Army Units:
  Divisions:
    82nd Airborne Division, 120
    101st Airborne Division, 50, 120–1
    84th Infantry Division, 180
    102nd Infantry Division, 128
  Battalions:
    3rd Battalion, 506th Parachute Infantry Regiment, 49
    70th Tank Battalion, 206
    741st Tank Battalion, 27, 59, 206
    743rd Tank Battalion, 27, 206
  Other formations:
    3rd Army, 110
    9th Army, 141
    US VII Corps, 111
    US XV Corps, 111
Utah Beach, 38, 48–9, 206
Utterath, 130
Uttley, Lieutenant P.B.R., 83, 169, 172

V1 flying bomb, 135
Valentine Tank, 12, 18–19, 24, 27, 29
Valkenswaard, 121
Varssveld, 169
Veert, 155
Vernon, 133
Vickers Mk VI light tank, 2–3
Vickery, Squadron Sergeant Major A.C., 11, 186
Victoria Cross (VC), 43
Victory Parade, 187–8, 192, 198
Vienenburg, 185
Villers-Bocage, 95
Vire, 96
von Kluge, Generalfeldmarschall G.A.F., 109–10
von Luck, Major H., 92
von Rundstedt, Generalfeldmarschall K.R.G., 36, 110

Waal River, 122, 125
Waldenrath, 130
Waldfeucht, 136–40, 144
Walker, Captain J.A.O., 152
Walle, 174
Warcop, 17
Wardlaw, Captain J.I.H., 77, 106
Watson, Captain H.S.R., 182
Watt, Lieutenant A.G., 125
Weeze, 149–50, 154–5, 159
Wehrmacht, 3–5, 13, 35, 38, 63, 73, 78, 81–2, 87, 127, 133, 177, 179
Welchman, William Gordon, OBE, 35
Wesel, 155, 158, 162
Weser River, 174, 180
Westheer, 36
Weston, Corporal A., 139
Weurt, 125
Whittaker, Trooper N., 65
Wickham Market, xi, 18, 22–4, 28
Wilcox, Trooper R.B., 143
Wildeshausen, 174
Wileman, Trooper (Slim), 58
Wilson, Lance Sergeant W., MM, 195
Wilton, Trooper G., 207
Window, 50
Winssen, 127
Wohlde, 174
Wolfenbüttel, 188, 199
Women's Voluntary Service (WVS), 15
Wood, Trooper F., 160
Woodcock, Lance Corporal R., 91
Wormald, Major D.B., DSO, MC & BAR, 4–5, 16, 56, 59, 67, 71–2, 75, 84, 88–90, 101, 103–104, 107, 117, 123, 125, 132, 136–7, 143–4, 146–7, 152–3, 155, 158, 166, 170, 176–6, 177
Wotton-under-Edge, 7
Wyler, 141–2

Y shoulder patch (5th Infantry Division), 185
Yalta Conference, 180
Yeomans, Sergeant J.W., 146
Young Man in a Tank, 12
Young, Major P., DSO, MC & 2 BARS, 72
Ypres–Comines Canal, 5

Zyfflich, 142

Dear Reader,

We hope you have enjoyed this book, but why not share your views on social media? You can also follow our pages to see more about our other products: facebook.com/penandswordbooks or follow us on Twitter @penswordbooks

You can also view our products at www.pen-and-sword.co.uk (UK and ROW) or www.penandswordbooks.com (North America).

To keep up to date with our latest releases and online catalogues, please sign up to our newsletter at: www.pen-and-sword.co.uk/newsletter

If you would like a printed catalogue with our latest books, then please email: enquiries@pen-and-sword.co.uk or telephone: 01226 734555 (UK and ROW) or email: Uspen-and-sword@casematepublishers.com or telephone: (610) 853-9131 (North America).

We respect your privacy and we will only use personal information to send you information about our products.

Thank you!